Social Change in an Industrial Town

Social Change in an Industrial Town

Patterns of Progress in Warren, Pennsylvania,
from Civil War to World War I

Michael P. Weber

The Pennsylvania State University Press
University Park and London

Library of Congress Cataloging in Publication Data

Weber, Michael P
  Social change in an industrial town.

  Includes bibliographical references.

  1. Warren, Pa.—Social conditions. 2. Warren, Pa.—Economic conditions. 3. Urbanization—Warren, Pa. 4. Occupational mobility—Warren, Pa. I. Title.

HN80.W22W4   309.1'748'67   75-16341
ISBN 0-271-01201-3

Copyright © 1976   The Pennsylvania State University

Designed by Andrew Vargo

Printed in the United States of America

Portions of Chapter 5 reprinted from
The Ethnic Experience in Pennsylvania, John Bodnar, editor,
Bucknell University Press, Lewisburg, Pa., 1973.

FOR PATRICIA,
LISA, AND HEIDI

Contents

Tables

Acknowledgments

During the preparation and writing of a book one becomes indebted to a number of people who willingly give their time, advice, and encouragement. This study is no exception. Whatever merits it possesses are due in large part to the kind cooperation and assistance of these people. A number of contemporary Warren residents provided access to valuable historical data. Dr. David Rice, Warren County Commissioner, made it possible for me to examine all official records pertaining to Warren during the 1870-1910 period. Ernest Miller generously granted access to his remarkable collection of data relating to the early history of oil production in Warren. Robert Freedman and Daniel Doherty, Sr., provided data from the Warren Public Library and the Warren Savings Bank. The staffs of the Warren Public Library and the Warren County Historical Society cheerfully assisted me in the search for data.

I am grateful to Diane Grego, Kaye Dudas, and Patricia Weber, who typed various portions of the manuscript and often corrected my grammatical and spelling idiosyncrasies. I also owe a special debt of gratitude to Gerald Weber, who contributed numerous hours in both preparing the data for computer analysis and performing many computations.

A number of colleagues and scholars offered useful advice, information, support, and encouragement. Walter S. Glazer and Michael H. Frisch read parts of the early manuscript and offered valuable suggestions. Stephan Thernstrom and Laurence Glasco generously sent me data from their own work which proved invaluable. My colleagues Anthony Penna, Edwin Fenton, and Roland Smith of Carnegie-Mellon University made important editorial comments. Ludwig Schaefer enabled me to secure financial assistance from the Sarah Mellon Scaife Foundation, and Peter N. Stearns provided scholarly support and encouragement.

I owe a great debt to Joel A. Tarr. He introduced me to the exciting field of American urban history and willingly provided guidance through several versions of this study. His penetrating questions and intellectual challenges have left a lasting mark on both this work and its author.

Finally, I owe the greatest debt to my family, to whom this book is dedicated. Lisa and Heidi provided love and often laughter during the years this book was in preparation. My wife, Patricia, suffered through my low periods and shared my moments of exhilaration. She rejoiced with me when things went well and tolerated my grumbling when they did not. She also provided love, warmth, and stimulation throughout the years of this study.

Michael P. Weber

1
Introduction

The middle of the nineteenth century to the outbreak of the First World War was an era of great industrialization throughout the United States. Accompanied by the development of massive urban centers, industrial growth produced a major transformation in the established American social order. New forms of transportation and communication linked small towns and large industrial centers, creating an interdependent nation. Mass production, with its specialized tasks, its reliance on large capital accumulations, and its expanding technology, resulted in a greater dependence of people upon each other to satisfy their needs. Eager to participate in the new economic growth, millions of people from Europe and rural America journeyed to such cities as Boston, Philadelphia, Chicago, and Pittsburgh in search of jobs and a better way of life. In 1880 approximately 15 million persons, 29.5 percent of the total United States population, lived in areas classified by the Census Bureau as urban. By 1910 the number of urban residents grew to nearly 43 million persons, or 46.3 percent of the nation's population.

Large urban centers experienced the greatest growth in population during this thirty-year period. In 1880, one out of every eight persons in the nation, approximately 6 million people, lived in twenty American cities of 100,000 or more. By 1910, fifty cities contained more than 100,000 persons. Combined, these cities held more than 20 million persons, 22.1 percent of the nation's population.

While large urban centers experienced the greatest social transformation, a similar but less spectacular change transpired in hundreds of smaller cities throughout the nation. Between 1880 and 1910 more than 1,000 cities emerged which ranged in size from 2,500 to 25,000 persons. By 1910 these cities contained 15.3 percent of the nation's total population. Table 1-1 illustrates the growth rate of America's smaller cities.

From 1880 to 1910, the number of small cities (2,500 to 25,000 persons) in the nation more than doubled. The combined population

TABLE 1-1

Urban Growth of Small-Sized Cities, 1880-1910 (2,500-25,000 persons)

	1880	1890	1900	1910
Number of cities	1,022	1,941	1,730	2,173
Total population	6,134,847	8,685,929	11,032,794	14,079,567
Percentage of U.S. population	12.2	13.8	14.5	15.3

of these cities increased by two and a third times, growing from approximately 6.1 million in 1880 to more than 14 million in 1910. At the close of the first decade of the twentieth century 15.3 percent of the nation's population lived in cities of this size while 22.1 percent of the total population resided in the nation's fifty largest cities.

Urban growth in these small cities resulted from a variety of factors. The discovery of natural resources, inventions, technological and economic developments, and improved means of transportation all contributed to the urbanization of late-nineteenth-century America. Gold, silver, and copper strikes in the West produced a number of new cities. Similarly, the discovery of coal deposits in Pennsylvania, West Virginia, and Kentucky and oil drilling in Pennsylvania and New York provided the impetus for urbanization of many small cities in the eastern United States. Other small cities grew because of specialized technological and economic developments. Manufacturing of such products as furniture in Jamestown, New York, and paper in Holyoke, Massachusetts, contributed to the growth of new urban communities. Still others developed through the completion of the urban network of railroads. Champaign and LaSalle, Illinois, and Hannibal, Missouri, for instance, owe their rapid expansion to the completion of railroad lines through the Midwest and the central plains. In the East the railroad influenced the urban expansion of a number of small and moderate-sized cities along the New York Central, Pennsylvania, Erie, and Southern rail lines. Other cities, of course, developed through a combination of factors—natural resources, manufacturing developments, and transportation—and all were a part of the national pattern of urban growth.

American historians disagree on whether these small cities developed social patterns similar to those of the nation's largest urban centers. Recent studies of America's smaller nineteenth-century communities suggest that the process of urbanization affected large and small cities differently. Herbert G. Gutman, in his analysis of "The Workers' Search for Power" during the Gilded Age, contends that the direct economic relationships in large cities and in small towns and outlying regions were similar, but the social structures differed profoundly. Private enterprise was central to the economy of both the small industrial town and the large metropolitan city, but functioned in a different social environment. . . . In a time of rapid economic and social transformation, when industrial capitalism was relatively new, parts of an ideology alien to industrialism retained a powerful hold on many who lived outside large cities.[1]

The social structure of such cities, according to Gutman, "unavoidably widened the distance between social and economic classes."

Robert H. Wiebe, however, offers a contrary point of view. He suggests that although both large and small late-nineteenth-century cities presented different surface appearances, their social patterns were in reality quite similar:

From a distance, the towns exemplified a levelled democracy, sustaining neither an aristocracy of name nor an aristocracy of occupation. Almost anyone with incentive, it seemed, could acquire the skills of a profession. Lawyers and doctors, ministers and teachers, either trained themselves or, like the town's craftsmen, apprenticed themselves briefly with masters. But beneath that flat surface, each community was divided by innumerable fine graduations. Distinctions that would have eluded an outsider. . . . At the top stood the few who not only had a greater wealth than their neighbors but controlled access to it as well. . . . In the same fashion, variations in religion, accent, and skin coloring distinguished individuals, groups and even entire communities from one another. . . .

Even in the cities, life often retained much of the town's flavor. . . . In all, it [America] was a nation of loosely connected islands, similar in kind, whose restless natives often moved only to settle down again as part of another island.[2]

Wiebe also asserts that both large and small cities responded to the challenges of urbanization and industrialization in a like fashion.[3]

Stephan Thernstrom, in his analysis of working-class mobility in Newburyport, Massachusetts, contends that the greatest variations in social patterns are more likely to be found in small towns than in great cities. As late as 1900, Thernstrom suggests,

The United States still contained quiet villages and market towns in which the factory and the immigrant were unknown . . . there were American towns in this period which remained relatively static and traditional. . . . The point is that this [Newburyport] was a community undergoing a process of transformation that eventually affected all American cities and towns to one or another degree, and that it is likely that there were important uniformities in the social consequences of urbanization and industrialization in each of these communities.

Thernstrom's hypothesis suggests a need for additional comparative analysis of changing social structure in communities of all sizes. During the last few years, however, historians using quantitative data have become embroiled in a controversy over the value of unique methodology versus the importance of engaging in comparative analysis in their studies. Those within each group claim that their research, frequently involving small urban communities, provides insight into the patterns of the larger American society. Despite the increasingly frequent use of quantitative methods, the similarity of subjects studied, and the use of similar data sources, we have made little progress toward direct comparability. For example, we have not yet answered questions about the "normal" patterns of mobility of nineteenth-century workers. Moreover, we know nothing of the experiences of workers in the Middle Atlantic states or the Midwest. In what ways were they similar to or different from workers in New England or other parts of the United States? What relationships existed between the changing community structure and the process of mobility? Did industrialization and urban growth foster common experiences or did regional differences lead to differing career patterns? Finally, we need to know whether a community's rate of economic growth contributed to the social opportunities of workers residing within that community.

This study deals with the changing social position of manual workers in a small Pennsylvania community from 1870 through 1910. Warren, Pennsylvania, was in some ways unique, as was urban development in other small cities of the late nineteenth century. In other important respects, however, the social patterns and experiences of workers in nineteenth-century Warren paralleled those found in other cities of the era. Conscious efforts have been made to employ techniques that would permit extensive comparisons with other cities and towns which underwent similar urban transformation.[5] Thus, rather than generate new or unique methods, I adopted techniques similar to those employed by other researchers. This choice fostered comparisons of differing mobility patterns as well as analysis of the influence of community size, social structure, and rate of economic growth on the prevailing labor conditions and the level of social opportunity within various nineteenth-century communities. This study of Warren and the comparisons with other large and small cities may provide further insight into the experience of workers in nineteenth-century urban America.

2 Social, Economic, and Historical Setting of the Community

Warren, Pennsylvania, lies in the northwest corner of the state approximately 65 miles east of the city of Erie and 135 miles north of Pittsburgh. Here the Conewango Creek intersects the Allegheny River at a right angle. The two streams cut through the rich green foothills of the Allegheny Mountains, providing an ideal site for a settlement. During the first half of the nineteenth century dense maple, cherry, and pine forests lined these valleys, leading to the development of an extensive lumbering industry. The community's southern boundary—the winding Allegheny River—provided a natural transportation route to Pittsburgh, 192 river miles away.

In 1794 and 1795 the Holland Land Company purchased for speculation large tracts of land in western Pennsylvania and New York. Following an initial survey in 1795, the company erected a surveyor's warehouse, the first permanent building in Warren County.[1] Disputes between the Holland Land Company and lumbermen over land titles retarded development of the town for the next two decades. By 1813 only five permanent homes existed in the settlement. At the close of the War of 1812, however, a number of people migrated to Warren from New England and New York, providing the population base for a small community.[2] In 1819 the Pennsylvania State Legislature made Warren the county seat. Henceforth, since all chief county officers maintained offices in Warren, county political and governmental power resided here. Warren's central position in county affairs has continued into the twentieth century.

By 1832 the community had a population of 358 and began to take on characteristics of a permanent settlement. On 3 April 1832 Warren was incorporated as a borough and held its first elections the next month. During the succeeding years the number of permanent homes increased rapidly and a small business district began to grow along the banks of the Allegheny River. A wide avenue, Water Street (now Pennsylvania Avenue), ran roughly parallel to the bank of the Allegheny River and then at a right angle up the Conewango Creek to the borough limits. This street became the main thoroughfare for the community. Later, following construction of a bridge across the Conewango, the extension of Water Street through the eastern sector of town provided new areas for growth in the 1890s. Back from the river, High Street (now Fourth Avenue) ran in a straight line perpendicular to the bank of the Conewango to the western limit of the borough. Market Street, the town's other major avenue, extended from the northern boundary directly to the Allegheny River. At the intersection of Water and Market streets a large square reserved for public use became the focal point of many community activities.

From 1810 to the mid-1840s the lumbering industry dominated the economy of the community. During the era when lumbering was at its height, loggers floated lumber to Warren from the upper Allegheny and the Conewango. At Warren the lumber from both streams was tied together and formed a huge raft of logs known as the "Allegheny Fleet." Each spring these streams for miles were almost covered with floating rafts.[3] Warren thus became a convenient break-in-bulk point where loggers tended their "fleets" while awaiting the annual spring rise in the Allegheny River. The timber was then sent down the Allegheny River to Pittsburgh and points south. By the 1830s "Warren . . . had become a great lumber center and the leading financial institution was the Lumberman's Bank organized in 1834 with a paid capital of $100,000."[4]

The timber business in the county reached its peak between 1836 and 1840. Then hard times, a depression in prices, and a bank suspension crippled the lumber industry. Before timber prices rose again the supply diminished as loggers stripped the land immediately adjacent to the river banks. Dragging the lumber a considerable distance to the river proved difficult and costly; hence the natural advantage of river transportation declined. The county lumber industry never completely recovered. While lumbering continued to hold a significant place in the economy of the area—of 212 business establishments in the county in 1860, 147 were lumber mills—it never again achieved dominance.[5]

Following the decline of the lumber industry, agriculture became the main economic activity of the community. The presence of rich soil, however, could not overcome other natural obstacles. Burdened with heavy snows, late and early frosts, and rough terrain, agriculture, although significant, never assumed the economic importance of the lumbering industry. With the establishment of a Farmers' Exchange Market in 1843, Warren became a center for trade and a source of supplies for the agricultural hinterland.[6] The *Warren Mail*, attesting to the community's role as a central market place, proclaimed: "During the rafting season the greatest activity prevails here, but owing to the farming land adjoining and extending for miles around, it is seldom that the town presents anything but an animated appearance for the farmers and their families regularly get all their necessary supplies here."[7]

During the three decades after 1840, however, in spite of the agricultural activities, Warren's economy grew slowly.[8] A number of minor manufacturing enterprises—tanning, planing mills, furniture and machine shops—established during this period failed to survive. Of thirty-one men in business in 1840, only six continued in the same business in 1860.[9]

Following the decline of lumbering in the 1840s, break-of-bulk activities lost their importance in the economic structure of the community. From the 1840s through 1875 Warren's economy diversified, but the town experienced only limited growth. Leather tanneries became important in the 1840s and 1850s. In 1851 a foundry, which later became the chief employer in the borough, began operations. A sash and door factory was built in the 1860s. In December 1850 the Western Division of the Sunbury and Erie Railroad opened the first rail line from Erie to Warren amid a gala celebration. As one editor stated, "For Warren the era of the river has ended only to be replaced by the era of the railroad."[10] The railroad, which ran a daily passenger train and a freight train on alternate days, stimulated some economic activity and increased the importance of the borough. In 1866 the Warren and Franklin Railroad completed rail lines to Pittsburgh and reported some 65,000 passengers during the first five months of operation.[11]

A number of other changes signified the moderate growth between 1860 and 1870. Residential homes increased from 308 to 365.[12] Two newspapers, one Republican (The *Warren Mail*) and one Democrat (The *Warren Ledger*), competed vigorously. Several new establishments opened their doors along the main business streets. However, the mild population growth from 1,738 in 1860 to 2,014 in 1870, mostly native-born Americans, illustrated the limited extent of the community's growth.[13] The community was not stagnant, but clearly no major business boom occurred before 1870.

On Thursday, 17 February 1870, a major fire broke out in the business section of town. The town's firefighting equipment proved inadequate, and the inferno quickly spread from one frame building to another. By nightfall twenty-six buildings and residences, mostly uninsured, were damaged or destroyed.[14] Two city blocks suffered total destruction. The national financial depression of 1873-1874 further contributed to the deteriorating economic outlook of the borough. As the editor of the *Ledger* pointed out, "The products of the county have been comparatively worthless during the past two years and the problem is how the businessmen have borne the pressure."[15] By 1875, because of the gradual depletion of its most important known natural resource—lumber—and fire and depression, the community's future seemed bleak. However, the discovery of a far more important and valuable natural resource—petroleum— provided the impetus for economic recovery.

From 1875 through 1910 the economy of Warren centered around the extraction and refining of oil. The discovery of this resource contributed significantly to the urbanization and industrialization of the borough. A detailed examination of the social and economic life in Warren before its industrialization will aid one's understanding of urbanization during the last quarter of the nineteenth century. The discovery of Warren's first oil well in March 1875 conveniently dis- sects the 1870-1880 decade, and analysis of the 1870 social order reveals much about the nature of the preindustrial community. Un- like many American cities, Warren in 1870 had not yet experienced any major industrial growth. Of the town's seventy-one business establishments only twenty employed more than four persons, with only four having over fifteen employees. The largest firm, the Struthers Iron Works, employed less than fifty men. Independent tradesmen employing one or two persons conducted most of the town's commerce.

At the time of the 1870 census 2,014 persons, organized into 392 families, lived in Warren. Family structure ranged from one adult living alone to a husband and wife and several children. In general, any living unit listed by the census enumerator as a separate facility is considered a family. Approximately 60 percent (365 persons) of the adult male population was married with 3.1 children living at home.[16] The range of children per family extended from zero to eleven.

Many homes in the community, particularly those of manual work- ers, housed at least one adult boarder. One hundred sixty-five unmar- ried adult males boarded in local homes in 1870. Nearly 65 percent of these men were native-born, while the remaining 35 percent (58 men) were of foreign birth. Not surprisingly, young men comprised the great majority of boarders. The 1870 age breakdown of adult male boarders was as follows: age 18-19, 12 men; 20-29, 97 men; 30-39, 31 men; 40-49, 12 men; 50-59, 5 men; and over 59 years of age, 8 men. Of these men 97 lived in the homes of blue-collar workers.[17] The room

and board money paid by these boarders no doubt made home ownership possible for many laboring families.

In 1870, approximately 30 percent of the total population of the
borough (609 persons) constituted the labor force of males over 18
years of age. Female labor, aside from domestic workers and a small
number of seamstresses, remained almost nonexistent in Warren
throughout the nineteenth century. The data derived from the 1870
manuscript census also suggest a limited amount of child labor in
Warren during the same era. Extensive school enrollment throughout
the period strengthens this conclusion, although irregular attendance
and a high dropout rate suggest part-time employment of some of the
community's youth. An examination of the composition of the male
labor force over the age of 18 will therefore provide the greatest
insight into the social and economic structure of both preindustrial
and postindustrial Warren.

The Warren work force in 1870 was scattered throughout a number
of occupational groups with little concentration in any particular
category. Table 2-1 displays the distribution of workers engaged in
fourteen occupations.

At the time of the 1870 census the distribution of Warren's labor

TABLE 2-1

Distribution of the Warren Work Force by Selected Occupational Groups, 1870

Occupational Category	Number of Workers	Percentage of Total Labor Force
Construction	88	14.5
Metal workers	84	13.8
Unskilled	75	12.3
Professional	62	10.2
Wood products	58	9.5
Retired, not employed	54	8.9
Services	40	6.6
Food and tobacco products	33	5.4
Leather products	27	4.3
Transportation	19	3.1
Clerical workers	18	2.9
Banking, insurance, finance, land speculation	12	2.0
Miscellaneous	39	6.2
Totals	609	99.7*

*Total does not equal 100 percent due to rounding.

force exemplified the pattern present in many small towns throughout the nation. As illustrated in Table 2-1, no occupational group in the community exceeded 15 percent of the total labor force. Moreover, six small construction firms, employing a total of forty-one men, and two competing iron works, employing sixty-six men, contributed even further to the decentralization of the labor force. The remaining construction and metal workers—carpenters, brickmasons, blacksmiths, and tinsmiths—worked in one-, two-, or three-man shops producing locally consumed goods. Similarly, whereas some workers listed under the rubric "wood products" worked in logging camps scattered throughout Warren County, others produced barrels, furniture, cabinets, and carriages. Producers of food and tobacco goods included several bakers, restaurant owners, butchers, three candy makers, and thirteen independent cigar makers. Those working in leather production included eighteen men employed by a local tannery as well as nine skilled leather craftsmen.[18] The seventy-five unskilled workers labored at a variety of tasks depending upon the availability of work. Thus a rather independent, highly decentralized pattern of labor characterized the 1870 Warren work force. Most men worked in small shops or alone. Moreover, little occupational specialization existed in the community.

Similarly, with the exception of the native-born workers, no particular ethnic group dominated the Warren labor force. In 1870, 397 of the 609 persons employed in Warren were native-born Americans. The remaining 212 persons came primarily from France, Germany, Ireland, and England. As Table 2-2 indicates, the majority of the immigrant population in 1870 originated in northern Europe.

TABLE 2-2

Nativity of Work Force, 1870

Birthplace	Number of Manual Laborers	Number of Nonmanual Laborers	Total Number of Workers	Percentage of Total Work Force
U.S.A.	197	200	397	65
France	38	18	56	9
Germany	31	19	50	8
Ireland	41	5	46	8
England	16	2	18	2
Denmark	13	2	15	2
Other	21	6	27	4
Totals	357	252	609	98*

*Total does not equal 100 percent due to rounding.

Of the total work force listed in the 1870 manuscript census, 58 percent engaged in manual labor whereas 252, or 42 percent, may be classified as white-collar or professional personnel.[19] Only 52, or 20 percent, of the 252 nonmanual workers were foreign-born.[20] Most immigrants in Warren in 1870, with the exception of the Irish, were skilled workers or craftsmen. French and German immigrants usually became tailors, bootmakers, gunsmiths, or other self-employed craftsmen. In addition, a large number of laborers from France, Germany, and England worked as carpenters and machinists. Most immigrants who came to the community possessing skills found a relatively open occupational structure within the skilled universe. The Irish, conversely, supplied almost one-third of all unskilled labor even though they constituted only 8 percent of the work force.[21]

Unskilled labor in Warren, as elsewhere, found erratic rather than steady employment, often drifting from job to job throughout the year. The logging industry, though declining in Warren, required the seasonal services of a number of unskilled laborers to load and haul cut timber to railroad lines. Similarly, construction of roads, erection of public and private buildings, and the tanning industry provided jobs for those lacking marketable skills.

Wages of unskilled workers were approximately 60 percent of those of skilled workers. The Pennsylvania Secretary of Internal Affairs reported wages of skilled workers in Warren in the 1870s at $1.91 per day while unskilled laborers earned $1.22 per day.[22] The low wage rate combined with the sporadic nature of employment meant that this group lived on the brink of poverty and often required assistance to survive the long northern winters.

Lack of home ownership provided further evidence of the weak economic position of the unskilled in 1870. Only 20 percent of the unskilled owned real property as compared with 40 percent of semi-skilled and skilled laborers. Of those holding nonmanual positions, 57 percent owned property in 1870.[23]

Patterns of residence, however, suggest the absence of a highly stratified society. In 1870 patterns of residential segregation based upon one's ethnic background began to appear but were not clearly defined. The majority of the population continued to live along the town's main business arteries. Residential and commercial establishments often shared the same building and the town's better homes were erected on the choice downtown locations. Moreover, blue-collar workers of all levels often lived in close proximity to white-collar and professional workers. Wealth and poverty coexisted, at least residentially if not socially. The Irish again provided the exception to this heterogeneous residential arrangement. While no discernible patterns of ethnic segregation existed for French, German, or British immigrants in 1870, thirty-nine of the forty-six Irish immigrants lived in the western sector of town.[24] By 1870 the west side, which housed the major industrial plants and the railroad depot, began to acquire the characteristics of an area in transition. Editorials frequently complained of "unsavory characters" seen in this section of town. Minor crimes apparently increased as the west-end citizens continually petitioned the borough council for "a police force of four or more men to protect citizens from hoods and vandals."[25]

TABLE 2-3

Estate Holdings and Savings Accounts by Nativity, 1870

Birthplace	Percentage Holding Estate over $500	Percentage Holding Savings Accounts
U.S.A.	40	41
France	67	57
Germany	34	38
Ireland	4	8

The lack of occupational and residential status of the Irish immigrant in the 1870 Warren community was matched by a poor record of savings. As Table 2-3 indicates, no other ethnic group deviated so significantly from the average estate holdings or number of savings accounts when compared with native-born citizens. The high percentage of holdings by French immigrants reflected their status as skilled craftsmen and proprietor-workers in the Warren community. Fully two-thirds of the French-born workers held estates exceeding $500 and 57 percent maintained savings accounts in the Citizens Savings Bank.[26] German-born citizens also succeeded in accumulating savings and property. One-third of all adult male German workers held property exceeding $500 in 1870. In addition, 38 percent managed to accumulate some savings in the town's bank. However, only 4 percent of the Irish-born citizens in the borough held estates valued at over $500 and fewer than 10 percent maintained savings accounts.

If one combines both the real and personal wealth of all adult males in the community, a somewhat different pattern of wealth distribution appears. In 1870 just over 6 percent of the adult male population held wealth in excess of $10,000. Another 30 percent reported holdings of between $1,001 and $10,000, while 64 percent held property valued at $1,000 or less. Moreover, the top 6 percent of the population held 62 percent of the community's reported wealth.[27] Thus although a substantial number of workers held both property and savings, the extent of their holdings remained modest.

The position of the Irish-born citizens in preindustrial Warren suggests a differentiated social pattern. However, the position of other ethnic groups in Warren in 1870 also deserves attention. German, British, French, and Danish immigrants, primarily skilled craftsmen, participated freely in community affairs. Eight immigrants served on the Warren Borough Council from 1870 to 1880. All came from the above four groups.[28] In addition, almost one-third of these four immigrant groups held positions in nonmanual occupations. With the exception of the predominately unskilled Irish, other immigrants found acceptance in preindustrial Warren.

In addition to occupation, residence, and wealth, religion and education also played a major role in the lives of Warren's citizens. The church and the school were primary sources of stability in preindustrial Warren. Religion in 1870 provided one mechanism for social control. Six churches—Baptist, Methodist-Episcopalian, German-Methodist, Presbyterian, Lutheran, and Roman Catholic—provided spiritual and often social guidance for members of the community. The religious denominations maintained harmonious relations with each other, but an analysis of church membership and economic status in 1870 reveals clear-cut status lines between various churches. At the top, containing almost all the economically and politically influential members of the community, stood the Presbyterian, Methodist-Episcopalian, and Baptist churches. These three churches not only inhabited the most splendid buildings in the community but through their members strongly influenced the town. The ministers of these churches were counted among the elite of the community. They spoke not only from the pulpit but often through the local press on matters ranging from local morals to national labor disputes.[29] Mindful of their important role in the community, the leaders of these three churches often publicly supported various political candidates. In addition, they accepted the responsibility of caring for the town's poor by organizing or at least supporting various relief and charitable associations.[30]

Standing clearly apart from these three churches in status were the German-Methodist, Lutheran, and Roman Catholic churches. Located generally in the industrial districts or the poorer sections of Warren, these three exercised less influence than the three status churches. With primarily a laboring and immigrant membership, they reflected the class structure of the community. Their ministers rarely exercised a voice in the town's affairs and, like the members of these churches, they held little status within the community. The Roman Catholic church, in particular, with a primarily Irish congregation, had little influence in Warren. Moreover, as the following comment by the county superintendent of schools illustrates, some discrimination occurred occasionally against the Roman Catholics. In 1875 he declared:

> The Catholics are growing very strong at this time. . . and as soon as the parochial school is fully established commences the attack on the public school . . . now there is just the trouble. We don't object to Catholicism because it is Catholicism, but because it is wrong and its fruits are bad. We have had Catholic pupils and Catholic teachers and in both we have found the same restraint and lack of development—that superstitious something which seems to bind his intellect.[31]

The editor of the *Warren Mail*, the local teachers' organization, and letters to the editor endorsed the superintendent's statement. However, not all held these views. The Democratic *Warren Ledger*, in contrast, not only disagreed with the superintendent but actually demanded his resignation.[32] No action resulted, but the town's Roman Catholic population was clearly reminded of its low status in the community.

The second major agency providing stability in the community, the school, often functioned as a vehicle of social control. Maintaining the largest organization in Warren, the school directors exercised probably more power and influence than any other group of men in the community. As might be expected, the directors were also men of influence in other spheres of community life. Fourteen men, all born in the United States, served as school directors between 1870 and 1879. Four of the men engaged in either the legal or banking professions and the remaining ten were merchants or manufacturers. The per capita estate holdings of these fourteen exceeded $26,000 in 1870.[33] Six of the directors also served on the Warren Borough Council during the same decade.

The citizens of the community valued education. In 1870, 402 of 535, or 75 percent of all children aged 6 to 16, attended school, although this may be an inflated figure since the census-taker made no distinction between part-time and full-time attendance.[34] The school directors, while primarily concerned with finances, also selected all books and emphasized training in the prevailing social and moral attitudes. Both the school directors and press often admonished teachers and administrators about truant, swearing, or cigar-smoking boys. The directors also exercised control over proposed courses of study.

In 1874 the school directors adopted a new course of study which set the educational pattern for the next decade. Upon completion of the first five years of school all students remaining in school followed four years of either academic or classical training.[35] The only course approaching anything of a practical nature—bookkeeping—was limited to a one-year study for those pursuing the academic course. The school superintendent perhaps best expressed the attitude of the community leaders by calling attention to the influence which the academic department exerted upon the rest of the school:

> Though comparatively few enter it [the academic department], it presents every child in the school an open door to a liberal education. The privileges of the academic department stand from day to day before the eyes of 500 children and before the minds of as many parents. Who would be willing to put a low estimate upon such an influence acting upon such impressionable material?[36]

Few children completed either the academic or classical course of study. Indeed, as late as 1880 only thirteen students graduated from the secondary school.[37] Citizens of Warren apparently considered five or six years of school adequate for most of the borough's youth in the 1870s. The typical educational pattern consisted of five years of formal training—grammar, history, reading, and so on—followed by approximately five additional years of learning a trade or skill. Industrialization, as we shall see, changed this pattern significantly.

Here then was a community which exhibited a considerable amount of unity and organization. Occupation, particularly within the manual classifications, and residence location remained open and available to most workers in the borough. Perhaps because the town lacked occupational specialization, newcomers possessing work skills frequently assumed a position in the existing social and economic structures. With the exception of the Irish, the town readily accepted and assimilated most immigrants.

The status arrangement was clear and the major public and private organizations supported that arrangement. The school and the religious agencies generally followed the same pattern. This hierarchical pattern resulted in a minimum of social or economic disorganization in preindustrial Warren.[38] The existence of several relief organizations to assist the poor also indicated a sense of responsibility toward the less fortunate. In addition, both local newspapers frequently noted the fact of neighbors assisting others in the building of homes. Community functions and public building projects were heavily supported by voluntary labor and cash contributions. Moreover, the disastrous fire of 1870 resulted in offers of aid to businessmen and homeowners affected. These events, as well as frequent company outings for employees and grand holiday festivals for all citizens, demonstrated a sense of community in preindustrial Warren.[39]

3 Economic Growth

On 30 August 1859, Colonel Edwin Drake successfully drilled the world's first producing oil well. The site—Titusville, Pennsylvania— lay just a few miles from the Warren County line and approximately twenty-five miles from the town of Warren. Drilling of other wells began immediately, and "oil fever" quickly spread across the county line into southern Warren County.[1] Although oil was not discovered in the vicinity of Warren for another sixteen years, the oil rush had an almost immediate effect on the community. Prospectors shipped oil in barrels and floated it down the Allegheny River. At Oil City in Venango County and at Warren, men transferred the barrels to boats and steamers for shipment downriver. In 1865 more than a thousand barges and thirty steamers engaged in oil traffic on the Allegheny River, most of them originating from these two "ports."[2] Unfortunately, no records exist showing the exact amount of oil emanating from Warren. However, since most oil production at this time occurred south of Warren, the major shipments probably originated from Oil City.[3]

On 14 March 1875, David Beaty, a wealthy oilman drilling for gas on his newly acquired estate, made the first significant oil strike in the immediate vicinity of Warren.[4] Beaty, realizing that a new boom would have an adverse effect on oil prices, closed his well site to all visitors.[5] A special dispatch to the *Titusville Herald* illustrates the wisdom, although futility, of this attempt:

> Friday's dispatch to the *Herald* was substantially correct. The Beaty well started pumping on Friday at 6:00 P.M. Mr. Beaty claims it pumped at the rate of 100 barrels per day, other authorities place it at 200 barrels a day. . . . There have been many applications for leases in the vicinity. . . many prominent oil men are heading for Warren from all parts and in consequence travel is rapidly increasing on the Dunkirk, Warren and Pittsburgh Railroads.[6]

Shortly after the drilling of the Beaty well, another prominent oilman, John Bell, struck the second successful well in the same vicinity, just across the Conewango Creek. By June 1875 this well pumped 200 barrels per day.[7] The *Warren Ledger* boasted, "Warren is the headquarters of a new oil field, rich in yield and richer in quality than most of the territory south of us."[8] However, several more promising oil fields opened in northwestern Pennsylvania simultaneously, and operators who followed the oil fields of the various counties went to Bradford or Butler. Hence the Warren development, in spite of claims by the press, received little attention and the field was left to local speculators.

In March and April of 1876 James Roy drilled two more successful wells in the vicinity of the Beaty well. A large number of men arrived in town from Oil City and Pittsburgh looking for locations to put down other wells. The *Warren Mail* reported:

> The last and best strike has started the oil fever in this section. Several rigs are going up soon and other parts of our territory will be tested without delay. Sales and leases of land are taking place every day and we expect to see a brisk business in oil and oil lands this coming season. . . . The derricks and shantys are plastered [with oil] as well as the workmen and the smell of oil is strong enough for the most sanguine.[9]

In May 1876 there were at least fifteen derricks in the Warren oil field and developers installed a pipeline running from the producing wells across the Conewango Creek to a hastily erected railroad loading dock.[10] Both local newspapers added an "oil news" column as a regular feature and reported the erection of new rigs and the arrival of new prospectors in town. Demand for land rapidly increased as prospectors attempted to purchase potential oil-bearing sites. Owners leased much of the available land to these prospectors rather than sell; nevertheless, sales and prices of land continued to climb rapidly. The *Warren Mail* reported the sale of an unused twenty-acre portion of one farm for "more than $8,000."[11]

Although no accurate information exists indicating the number of persons who migrated to the community in search of oil, the extent of immigration in the late 1870s must have been considerable. One source estimated as many as 500 oilmen in town during the summer of 1876.[12] In May the *Warren Ledger* exclaimed, "There are numerous strangers in Warren about these days on the lookout for leases. Some of the most successful operators are here. . . . The land all about Warren is being leased, but certain sections have the preference. . . ."[13] Interest in the community's new source of wealth continued throughout the summer. Some local men, particularly those with skills in construction or knowledge of machinery, left their jobs to speculate in the oil fields. In addition, speculators continued to flock to the town, giving Warren the appearance of a west coast gold mining town. In midsummer the *Warren Mail* reported, "The excitement in regard to oil matters has been very intense . . . and seems to be increasing. The town is crowded with strangers who are mainly experienced oilmen and considerable land is being leased and sold. From the toll bridge can now be seen eighteen derricks which look like an oil region."[14]

With the opportunity to strike oil via backyard drilling, the borough's citizens were tempted to exploit all available land. The Warren Borough Council, however, in spite of obvious financial opportunities, passed an ordinance prohibiting the "putting down of oil wells within the limits of the Borough."[15] Both newspapers applauded this decision. The *Warren Mail*, perhaps fearful of the effects of the oil boom on the community, provided the following counsel:

> In the mad race for wealth we can surely afford to set aside some little portion of God's footstool. . . . We live in a charming town. To surrender it to the speculator and oil producer would be to ruin it utterly as a desirable place of residence; and superadd the constant frightful chance of being swept from existence in a single day or night's conflagration. There are some among us, doubtless, who would trample down the dearest rights and privileges of their neighbors. There are some who would regard a forest of derricks in our midst as an ornament rather than a disfigurement. . . . But these thank heaven are in a hopeless minority. The town council have taken a just and decided stand on this question.[16]

As a result of the action by the borough council, the Warren oil field was restricted to the area across the Conewango Creek—the borough limits—for several miles. By the end of the summer, speculators held leases on every farm along the creek within ten miles of the Beaty well. Farmers granting oil leases asked for large leasing fees and a 50 percent royalty on all oil found.[17] By September the editors of the *Warren Mail*, in contrast to their earlier counsel, were unable to contain their enthusiasm:

> Great is oil and desirable is its profits. Who can fathom its mysteries or foretell its coming or going? . . . How the barren hillside blossoms with greenbacks like the leaves of June! Look across the Conewango where we used to go for pious meditation or a lonely drive. Two months have made marvelous changes. Keen, shrewd

operators jostle each other at every turn and the "bulls" and the "bears" of Wall Street have worthy imitators. You can count from 50 to 100 new rigs and more going up. Loads of coal, loads of timber, loads of boards, loads of old rigs, loads of pipe and loads of tiles are constantly crossing. Three or four hundred men are busy as bees. Nearly every house in town is a boarding house. The toll bridge which in the spring could not pay its repairs is now taking from $90 to $100 a week. Hotels are crowded. Beer saloons have flowing wells with no falling off. In short, business is lively and one can hardly keep pace with the progress of operators.[18]

By year's end several hundred rigs obliterated the northern skyline; in some cases there were a number of rigs per acre. Although gushers were few, most wells produced regularly. By May 1877 oil production in the area reached 2,000 barrels per day at a market price of $42.19 per barrel.[19]

Due to overdrilling, which cut the pressure necessary to force oil to the surface, oil production began to decline by late 1877. In addition, increased competition from the Standard Oil Company of New Jersey began to have an adverse effect on oil prices. In January 1878 the Star Oil Company—a Standard subsidiary—opened a depot in Warren and began underselling locally owned crude oil.[20] Unable to meet this competition, a group of oilmen formed an organization and in an advertisement on 23 April 1878 warned oilmen, "It is in your interest, producers, to discharge your rig-builders, hang up your drills . . . until such times as developments will pay. It will not pay at present prices though you may hope so. In the end you will find you will have lost money. Matters have not yet become desperate but they soon will."[21] Oil producers either heeded this warning or the low price and declining production failed to attract new drillers, for by mid-1878 daily production in the district fell to a few hundred barrels.

The recession in oil production continued until July 1880, when a new strike was made at a small village six miles east of Warren. Oilmen once again flocked to the Warren district ready to buy or lease land. In July a 165-acre farm in this area sold for $10,000; by August rapidly inflated prices brought $12,000 for a 20-acre farm, and another 15-acre farm returned $9,000 to its owner.[22] Hotels reported the first full houses in two years, and oil well suppliers made hasty trips to various cities to purchase materials for resale. Struthers Iron Works, soon to become the major employer in the community, produced and erected a 17,000-barrel storage tank near the railroad depot. The United Pipe Line Company extended its pipeline to the new district and pumped 4,000 barrels by August 1880. The modest boom continued through 1882 with an average daily production of 260 barrels.[23]

Warren men played an important role in the oil speculation, but the evidence suggests that few oilmen resided in the community for any length of time. Of the ninety-five speculators listed in the *Warren Mail* through 1877, only forty appeared in either the 1870 or 1880 manuscript census. Furthermore, only seventeen oilmen appeared in both censuses, indicating that much of the oil money earned in the Warren oil district before 1880 did not remain in the community.[24]

Residents of the borough also benefited by supplying goods and services to the new strike. The spectacular oil strike at Cherry Grove, a few miles east of Warren, illustrated the role of the borough as a producer of goods and services for speculators at the nearby oil fields. From March 1882 to May 1883 oilmen pumped as many as 40,000 barrels in a single day. Before the area ran dry, 319 successful wells produced oil in an area several miles square.[25] During this period several Warren firms manufactured oil well equipment which was sold by a number of the borough's retailers. Lumber for oil rigs, supplied by local loggers, produced a mild revival in the lumbering industry. Warren men provided labor for laying both pipeline and track for a narrow gauge railroad to the oil site. The Struthers Iron Works began production of railroad tank cars. Oil speculators filled the rooms of the town's five hotels. Local retail merchants undoubtedly also benefited in increased sales. Unfortunately for the town, the massive oil strike at Cherry Grove, like others of the area, maintained its flow for only a few months. Production by mid-1883 dwindled to a few barrels per day, and the village soon disappeared. Oil production in the Warren area stabilized at several hundred barrels per day as the boom period ended.

But while oil production stabilized, the community consolidated its industry and enjoyed a high degree of prosperity. Oil and oil-related industries dominated the economic growth of the borough. In 1877 a group of Warren oilmen joined forces to establish the first successful oil refinery, the Conewango Oil Company.[26] Although the Standard Oil Company gained control of this refinery within less than a year, other independent companies quickly formed. By 1890 five local refineries produced oil valued in excess of $2,000,000 annually.[27] In addition, a group of independent oilmen formed an Oil Stock Exchange with its main office in Warren. The *Warren Ledger* estimated as early as 1885 that between 150,000 and 200,000 barrels of oil were bought and sold daily in the Warren exchange.[28]

During the years from 1890 to 1910 the growth of the refining industry completely eclipsed oil speculation as the major activity of oilmen. As Table 3-1 indicates, in 1900 seven independent oil refineries produced 846,000 barrels of refined oil and employed 169 men. Ten years later two more refining firms began production. By 1910 the refineries produced in excess of 1,500,000 barrels of oil annually. Land valuations on acreage owned by the refineries increased significantly (the amount of land remained essentially the same), indicating again the effect of the oil industry on land value. Based on a six-day work week, the 327 men employed in 1910 earned an average of $5,800 weekly, or a daily per worker income of almost $3.00.[29]

TABLE 3-1

Oil Refining Growth, 1900-1910

Company	Production Capacity (thousands of barrels)		Land Valuation (thousands of dollars)		Number of Employees	
	1900	1910	1900	1910	1900	1910
Briggs, Ellis and Company	162	300	$ 16	$ 23	47	73
Conewango Refining Company	55	130	7	9	11	27
Cornplanter Refining Company	144	300	18	30	26	85
Crew-Levick Company	180	216	28	46	27	42
Seneca Oil Works	120	120	14	26	13	16
Superior Oil Works	—	96	—	14	—	12
United Refining Company	—	120	—	17	—	20
Warren Refining Company	120	120	8	22	31	35
Wiliburine Oil Works	65	110	26	48	15	17
Totals	846	1,512	$117	$238	170	327

A special 1905 *Manufacturers' Report* of the United States Bureau of the Census reveals the importance of the oil industry to the Borough of Warren. Warren was the only municipality in Pennsylvania in which the value of petroleum products exceeded all other products combined. In 1905 the value of petroleum products was over $3,000,000, or 50.8 percent of the total manufacturing production for the borough.[30] Foundry and machine shop products, valued at $1,220,165, followed petroleum products in importance.[31]

TABLE 3-2

Percentage Distribution of Business Firms in Operation by Major Industry Groups, 1870-1910

Industry*	1870	1880	1890	1900	1910
Construction	10.0%	13.9%	8.8%	8.1%	6.6%
Manufacturing	40.0	33.3	41.2	38.4	35.8
Commercial trade	10.0	16.7	22.1	18.6	17.0
Finance	10.0	8.3	4.4	4.7	6.6
Personal services	20.0	16.7	11.8	16.3	20.8
Lumbering	10.0	5.6	4.4	3.5	2.8
Petroleum	—	5.5	7.3	10.4	10.4
Total percentage	100.0	100.0	100.0	100.0	100.0
Total number of firms	20	36	68	86	106

*Table includes only those business firms which employed a minimum of four persons.

Concurrent with the growth of the oil industry, development of both oil-related and nonrelated businesses proceeded at a rapid pace. The total number of business enterprises employing four or more men rose from 20 in 1870 to 106 in 1910. Table 3-2 represents the changes in the industrial composition of the Warren business structure. As measured by the total number of businesses employing four or more persons, the Warren economy experienced its greatest growth—increasing by nearly 90 percent—in the 1880 to 1890 decade. Each succeeding decade through 1910 also exhibited considerable change in the distribution of businesses although not as great as the decade immediately following the discovery of oil.

Before the oil strikes, manufacturing—mostly small machine shops—constituted 40 percent of the business firms in Warren. Throughout each decade manufacturing and construction illustrate greater stability than all other industrial groups. The proportion of manufacturing and construction enterprises declined slightly from a total of 50 percent in 1870 to 42.2 percent in 1910. This loss resulted not because of any decline in the importance of these activities but because of changes in the size of the average manufacturing establishment. As the community's growth began to stabilize, industries becoming more financially secure began to expand. The decline in the proportion of firms engaged in lumbering, however, is indicative of the general decline in the importance of lumbering throughout the county. During each succeeding decade both the number of men engaged in logging and the number of planing mills declined.[32]

While the proportion of the three major industrial groups—manufacturing, construction, and lumbering—declined, both the commercial trade and petroleum industries increased significantly. The petroleum industry captured the largest new proportion of the economy, increasing from 0.0 percent in 1870 to 10.4 percent in 1910. In addition, as noted, Table 3-2 includes only firms employing four or more persons, thereby excluding most independent oil drillers. This, of course, adds to the already significant figures discussed above. The number of firms in commercial trade increased from 10.0 to 17.0 percent during the same period, although there was a decline from a peak of 22.1 percent in 1890.[33] With the exception of lumbering, no major industrial category experienced any decline in the absolute number of enterprises during the 1870-1910 period.

The establishment and development of the oil industry also led to the organization of new oil-related enterprises and contributed to the urbanization of Warren. The largest and by far the most significant of all these companies, the Struthers Iron Works, was organized in 1851. In 1875 the forty men employed by this firm produced tanning machinery and engaged in general repairing of machine tools and metal implements. Five years later the firm produced almost exclusively oil drilling equipment, pumps, rig-irons, and, later, barrels and tank cars. The principal market for these products originated in the oil fields north of Warren and Bradford. The firm then employed some 100 men drawing an annual payroll of $50,000, or a yearly per worker income of $500.[34] Since this figure includes foremen and other nonmanual workers, it should not be considered representative of the average salary for laboring personnel, who received considerably less. Fifteen years later, in 1895, this same Struthers Iron Works employed 250-300 men and occupied five acres of land.[35]

In addition to the iron works, other businesses developed to fill the needs of the oil industry. During the three decades following the discovery of oil, thirty-one petroleum-related enterprises began activity in Warren. Eight of these new businesses, utilizing various oil by-products, manufactured such products as sulfuric acid, oil carbons, and grease. Seven companies produced natural gas, a direct result of drilling operations in the area. In addition to the Struthers Iron Works, three other machine shops produced oil drilling tools which were marketed by four new retail stores dealing in oil well supplies. Three of the larger new companies, which employed several hundred men by 1910, manufactured various types of oil containers ranging from barrels to railroad tank cars. Two torpedo manufacturing firms, prohibited within borough limits, opened their doors in 1882 and 1887 just across the boundaries to supply torpedoes to oil well drillers. Finally, three firms producing oil pipelines opened during the two decades following the original oil strike.[36] The Beaty discovery in 1875 had clearly resulted in a high rate of economic expansion in Warren. By 1910, 1,898 men or 57 percent of all working men engaged in some type of oil or oil-related industry.[37]

More difficult to measure but equally important is the effect of the oil boom on nonrelated enterprises. The increase in banks from two in 1870 to six in 1910, of hotels from two in 1870 to fourteen in 1910, and of contractors and builders from six to twenty-seven was directly related to the growth of the oil industry. The majority of the principal officers in the town's financial institutions held prominent positions in the petroleum industry, while a large number of oilmen held deposits or accounts in the local lending institutions.[38] The only bank spanning the 1870-1910 period, the Warren Savings Bank, illustrates the financial growth experienced by the town's lending institutions.

TABLE 3-3

Financial Growth of the Warren Savings Bank, 1870-1910

Year	Net Profit	Deposits in Savings Accounts	Amount of Interest Paid Depositors
1870	$ —	$ 86,528	$ 1,712
1880	8,178	328,496	9,107
1890	50,585	1,252,504	21,095
1900	49,273	1,805,027	37,164
1910	65,605	2,941,981	81,527

The increase of savings account deposits in the Warren Savings Bank each decade suggests a sustained rise in the amount of money available for investment.[39] The greatest increase in the percentage of deposits held by this bank occurred in the two decades between 1870 and 1890. Money was needed for home mortgages, industrial expansion, and capital investment, and five new banks opened during the 1880-1910 period. By 1910 Warren's six banks held deposits valued at over $7,000,000 and had capital resources in excess of $10,000,000.[40] In all likelihood, much of the capital available for investment in the Warren banks was derived from oil revenues.

Two other areas of economic activity, hotels and housing construction, also provide evidence of the growth of the community. Hotels not only increased in number but also in size and provided accommodations at the turn of the century for more than 500 visitors; the majority of registrants at Warren hotels listed their primary occupation as oilman, oil producer, or oil driller.[41] Indicative of the importance of oil production for the hotel business was the sharp decrease in vacancies whenever large oil strikes occurred in the Warren area.

Construction activity also appears related to the petroleum industry. As the community grew after the discovery of oil, the demand for new housing increased. Warren newspapers constantly mentioned a shortage of adequate permanent housing and in 1884 suggested the possibility of Warren businessmen building tenement houses to eliminate the existing scarcity.[42] The building boom continued, and in 1890 the *Warren Ledger* observed:

> The outlook for a busy summer in Warren is very probable to say the least. A large number of houses are to be erected in this city. The Home and Trust Fund Association has applications for nearly all their available funds that will go into building. . . . There is not a vacant house in the city and the demand increases every day. Rents have advanced a trifle this spring and are as high now as they should be. The oil business was never better and many fortunes have been made during the last two or three years.[43]

The press reported 125 new homes erected in 1904, more than 150 erected in 1905, and a similar amount in 1906. One newspaper estimated that in the summer of 1904 more than $500,000 had been spent "in the building of business blocks, homes, expenditures for trolly lines, etc."[44] The number of residential homes alone grew from 553 in 1880 to 2,670 in 1910, and the total assessed valuation of real estate in the borough increased from $199,000 to more than $4,000,000.[45]

By 1910 Warren had completed its transformation from a placid rural village to a dynamic progressive industrial community. In addition to petroleum-related enterprises, six furniture factories, a box manufacturer, two flour mills, several foundries, a cigar factory, a bottling works, and various other businesses had commenced operations. Table 3-4 illustrates both the importance of the oil industry and the extent of diversification in Warren by 1910. Oil refineries alone employed 327 men and accounted for slightly more than one-third of the community's business. If oil by-products—acid, grease, and so on—and the value of extracted crude oil are added to the above, the petroleum industry produced an annual volume of $3,600,000, or slightly more than 50 percent of all production in Warren.[46] In addition, five firms employing more than 1,100 men produced materials used essentially in either the extraction or refining of oil.

TABLE 3-4

Major Warren Industries, 1910

Company	Major Product	Acreage	Employees	Volume of Business
Allegheny Foundry	Oil tank cars	3	75	$250,000
Conewango Furniture	Furniture	2	60	150,000
F. A. Steber Company	Cigars	2	125	185,000
Gisholt Mfg. Co.	Boring mills	2	100	300,000
Hammond Iron	Refining equipment	4	250	500,000
Jacobson Machine	Gas engine	3	200	500,000
Phoenix Furniture	Furniture	2	50	100,000
Struthers-Wells	Petroleum equipment	5	500	800,000
Warren Table Works	Furniture	3	200	400,000
Warren Veneer	Paneled wood	2	75	225,000
Briggs-Ellis and Co.	Refined oil	9	73	519,000*
Conewango Refining	Refined oil	6	27	224,000
Cornplanter Refining	Refined oil	6	85	519,000
Crew-Levick Co.	Refined oil	16	42	373,680
Seneca Oil Works	Refined oil	4	16	207,600
Superior Oil Works	Refined oil	6	12	166,080
United Refining	Refined oil	11	20	207,600
Warren Refining	Refined oil	7	35	207,600
Wiliburine Oil	Refined oil	20	17	190,160

*Computed by multiplying production capacity (Table 3-1) by $1.73, the average 1910 value per barrel of oil.

A number of other changes signified the growth and progress of Warren as an urban area. In 1876 the town fathers dedicated a new $100,000 courthouse, and in the 1880s the city constructed a town hall and several firehouses. In 1883, through the generosity of a leading citizen who donated $80,000, construction of a new library began.[47] Street lights in the town's main business district and natural gas for fuel and lighting were installed in the 1880s. Electricity for private consumption came in 1890, and constructir of paved streets began the following year. By the turn of the century, electric streetcar service provided transportation from most residential areas to Warren's main business districts. By 1910 two daily and two weekly newspapers were published on a regular basis.

TABLE 3-5

Population Growth in Warren, 1830-1970

Year	Population	Absolute Increase or Decrease Over Previous Census	Percentage Increase Over Previous Census
1970	12,998	−1,507	
1960	14,505	− 344	
1950	14,849	− 42	
1940	14,891	28	00.2
1930	14,863	591	04.1
1920	14,272	3,192	28.8
1910	11,080	3,037	38.2
1900	8,043	3,711	85.6
1890	4,332	1,522	54.1
1880	2,810	796	39.5
1870	2,014	276	15.9
1860	1,738	725	71.6
1850	1,013	276	37.4
1840	737	379	106.0
1832*	358	—	—

*Warren incorporated as a borough this year.

The population growth of the community, indicated by Table 3-5, roughly paralleled the expansion of both the petroleum industry and the general industrial groups. In 1840 Warren's population totaled only 737. During the next thirty years the population increased by only 1,277 persons. From 1880—following the establishment of the oil industry—through 1900, Warren's population grew by 184 percent while the number of business firms employing more than four persons increased by 139 percent. No other twenty-year period in the borough's history shows as great an increase in either business or population. Following the 1900 census, Warren's population grew at a rapidly declining rate until growth completely ceased in 1940. Within a period of thirty years—1880 to 1910— a stagnant village of 2,800 had become a booming city of more than 11,000. The *Warren Ledger* boasted, "Warren is the nucleus of all surrounding places and they all pay tribute to her. Warren has become a town of importance within twenty years and is the center of a large and growing population. . . . We have only begun to grow and show our strength. The time will come when an immense population will fill this valley."[48]

Warren, then, was a community which underwent major transformation in four decades. By 1910 the economic and social institutions of 1870 were unrecognizable.[49] Industrialization created an urban community, but what changes occurred in the lives of the citizens of that community? Did industrialization and urbanization produce new opportunities for Warren's residents? Were manual workers able to achieve economic security through occupational mobility? Did the changing social structure provide avenues enabling men of talent to earn positions of leadership within the community? America's open class system presumably promised success to individuals willing to work. Was it merely an unfulfilled promise or a reality enjoyed by many?

4 Patterns of Progress: Occupational Mobility of Manual Workers

Recent studies of social mobility in nineteenth-century American cities have produced important new insights into the occupational patterns of the nation's manual workers.[1] Employing quantifiable data, these studies accurately describe the mobility patterns of the nation's inarticulate majority.

The most recent research suggests that a significant number of manual workers in nineteenth-century American cities experienced at least modest occupational mobility. In his pioneering analysis of unskilled laborers in Newburyport, Massachusetts, Stephan Thernstrom demonstrated that however limited the attainments of these men, "the ordinary workmen of Newburyport . . . could view America as a land of opportunity despite the fact that the class realities which governed their life chances confined most of them to the working class."[2] Other studies tend to reinforce Thernstrom's conclusions about the degree of opportunity present in nineteenth-century America. Manual workers in Poughkeepsie, New York, between 1850 and 1880, in Boston, Massachusetts, both before and after the Civil War, in Norristown, Pennsylvania, from 1910 to 1950, in Birmingham, Alabama, from 1880 to 1914, and in Atlanta, Georgia, from 1870 to 1896, all enjoyed modest advances within the working-class strata.[3] Few workers in any of these cities, conversely, experienced mobility into the ranks of management or became wealthy entrepreneurs.

These studies reveal much that is new and significant about the mobility patterns of nineteenth-century manual workers. Each scholar, however, has tempered his conclusions with justifiable caution. We need to know a great deal about nineteenth-century cities, both large and small, before we can develop any sound generalizations. This study, an analysis of all adult male workers in a particular community at the height of its industrial and urban growth, is part of that endeavor.

The cases of the following four men illustrate the mobility patterns experienced by most nineteenth-century American laborers. In 1880

Charles H. Smith, son of an English immigrant, secured his first job working as an unskilled errand and stock boy for a local merchandiser. He apparently rented a flat as he owned no real estate; the 1880 tax records valued his real and personal property at less than $100. Ten years later, although he still owned no real property, Smith was a clerk in a hardware store and held an estate valued at $800. He continued his ascent throughout the next decade, acquiring not only a partnership in the hardware and oil well supply store but also his own home. In 1900, assessor's valuation lists indicated that Smith held an estate valued at $3,200. During the first decade of the twentieth century, he achieved the height of his success. Shortly after the turn of the century he purchased his partner's share of the hardware store. Not content with extending his stock of oil supplies, Smith ventured into land speculation, purchasing a large tract of land in Warren's burgeoning east side. Subsequent land sales and purchases of rental housing increased his wealth throughout the decade. By 1910 Charles Smith, hardware store proprietor and land speculator, owned seven houses and held real and personal estate valued in excess of $70,000.[4]

Like Charles Smith, Frank Witz's father migrated to the United States from France about the time of the Civil War. Finding his way to Warren, the elder Witz secured employment on the section gangs of the Erie to Warren railroad. His son, Frank, began working at about the time of the oil discovery in Warren. The 1880 manuscript census lists him simply unskilled. By 1890 he held a position as mail carrier for the borough and had saved enough money to purchase his first house, valued at $600. At the turn of the century Witz went into business for himself, renting a small grocery store. During the next decade Witz's modest success continued and by 1910 he owned a store as well as his home. The assessor's valuation lists set the combined value of the house and store at $1,700.[5] The success of Frank Witz, although not as spectacular as that of Charles Smith, nevertheless illustrates the presence of occupational opportunity in nineteenth-century Warren.

Tom Glasby, an Irish immigrant, and Edward Blunt from England began their careers as unskilled laborers in 1870 and 1880 respectively. Unlike Smith and Witz, however, neither of these two men found occupational or social success in Warren. Tom Glasby lived in Warren from 1870 through 1900. During that thirty-year period he failed to rise above the level of unskilled worker. His singular economic success in life consisted of the purchase of a house valued in 1890 at $500. By 1900 Glasby lost the house. At the turn of the century the value of his combined real and personal estate did not exceed $100. Similar to Glasby, Edward Blunt worked at various jobs, all of them unskilled, from 1880 through 1900. His estate reached its maximum value of $250 in 1900. Like so many other unskilled workers, Blunt never enjoyed the security of home ownership and left town in 1900.[6]

How typical were these four men? It is a simple task to search the history of any community to discover the presence of a few Charles Smiths or Frank Witzes. Almost all nineteenth-century communities possessed men who experienced similar success. Their presence attests to at least some degree of economic mobility in American society. However, to say that a few men could achieve mobility despite backgrounds of poverty fails to provide convincing evidence of an open system in which one's willingness to work hard insured success. Neither can one measure mobility in a society by examining the lives of the wealthy who happened to originate from poverty backgrounds. Rather the lives of the hundreds of men who began their careers as manual workers must be analyzed. What portion of these men achieved spectacular success similar to that of Smith or the more modest mobility of Frank Witz? Conversely, how many unknown men's lives paralleled those of Edward Blunt and Thomas Glasby? The answers to these questions lie in a more detailed examination of social mobility.

The term social mobility, as used here, refers to the way in which an individual changes his social position. The process of this change may follow several different lines. Some individuals may move up the social scale within the course of their lives. Others may fail to experience any mobility. Their sons may enjoy much greater success. By measuring both intragenerational and intergenerational mobility of workers within a community, one is able to not only reconstruct the careers of individuals but also study the changing social position from father to son. In this study of nineteenth-century Warren, both kinds of mobility measures were utilized.

Both intragenerational and intergenerational mobility require data on individuals and their sons over a span of thirty or forty or more years. High rates of outward migration, however, frequently reduced the size of each occupational universe, and in a number of instances an additional measurement of mobility has been included. Certain groups of individuals have been traced over a single decade to measure the extent of mobility within the decade. All adult males who lived in the community in 1870, for example, were traced to the 1880 census data to determine the mobility within that decade. Similarly, all individuals who resided in the community in 1880 were again traced to the 1890 city directory and so on. In a community undergoing rapid social and economic change, this type of measurement enables one to isolate and compare the extent of opportunity from decade to decade. By including the above three types of measurement —intragenerational, intergenerational, and decade mobility—one is able to examine the career mobility of fathers and sons as well as compare rates of mobility within various decades.

Historians studying social mobility frequently utilize two and often three determinants of social position. The lack of appropriate data prevents the use of the sociological concepts of status and prestige in a study of historical nature. An analysis of changing social position requires the combining of traditional historical data with quantifiable evidence. Social mobility in nineteenth-century Warren, as elsewhere, was a function of three major factors: occupational mobility, home ownership, and the acquisition of other forms of wealth.

An unskilled worker who acquired a skilled occupation no longer resided at the bottom of the class structure. Similarly, a person who accumulated enough money to purchase his own business gained social status. Occupational mobility also often provided an opportunity to acquire other important means necessary to achieve social status. An individual who has experienced occupational mobility may also achieve property mobility through the purchase of a home. Of course, individuals frequently achieved property mobility without prior occupational advancement. One type of mobility did not necessarily determine another. The third and often less visible determinant of mobility concerns the accumulation of real and personal wealth. A man who improved his occupational position, acquired several houses, and accumulated large savings demonstrates a clear example of social mobility. The cases of hundreds of men who experienced limited mobility in one or two of the above areas remain less obvious. For the purpose of simplicity the phenomenon of occupational mobility will be discussed first, followed by an examination of property mobility and wealth accumulation in nineteenth-century Warren.

The term occupational mobility implies that one may organize the existing occupations into a hierarchy ranging jobs from low status to those carrying a marked degree of status. Unfortunately, no agreeable method exists to organize the thousands of nineteenth-century occupations—some now extinct—into a definitive hierarchy. Does a silversmith hold greater status than a bootmaker or a carpenter? Therefore, broader, more general occupational classifications must be utilized. The occupational classification scheme followed throughout this book organizes workers into four broad groups: three manual classifications—the unskilled, the semiskilled, and the skilled worker—and the nonmanual.[7] A move from any one of these classifications to another in the course of four decades constitutes occupational mobility.

Various degrees of social distance separated each of the above four groups from decade to decade. Unskilled workers, on the whole, generally engaged in part-time, transient occupations rather than steady work. Conversely, the position of the semiskilled worker usually provided at least a modicum of security against unemployment. The semiskilled worker performed a certain type of work as compared to the unskilled worker whose job lacked any specific function. Above the semiskilled in the occupational hierarchy stood the skilled worker. The social distance observed here presents a sharper distinction than that separating the bottom two groups. The skilled worker possessed expertise at his craft, usually acquired after years of training; he held, as the term implies, a skill.

A large number of workers performed various tasks which fall under the rubric nonmanual. These men worked at a variety of highly diversified occupations such as clerks, proprietors, or professional personnel, and, to a degree, they constituted a separate class hierarchy. The social distance, however, between individuals within the nonmanual classification appears much smaller than the distance between the three manual groupings. Individuals classified as nonmanual enjoyed more job stability, higher rates of geographical persistence, and greater economic security than manual workers. The ordinary white-collar worker in nineteenth-century America received at least twice the annual wage of most manual laborers.[8] Any blue-collar worker bridging the gulf separating manual and nonmanual workers experienced a major change in occupational status, and all white-collar workers have been combined into the single classification—nonmanual. Although there are limitations in this classification scheme, it nevertheless provides a sufficient vehicle to examine occupational mobility in nineteenth-century Warren.

Before determining the rate of occupational mobility one final determinant variable must be examined. The overall occupational structure of the community determines, to a large degree, the amount of mobility one may expect to find there. A town with a very small ratio of nonmanual workers obviously presents little opportunity for advancement of manual laborers. Conversely, in an area composed of large numbers of nonmanual workers and comparatively few manual laborers, one might expect a considerably higher rate of occupational mobility.

Warren's occupational pattern during the second half of the

nineteenth century varied somewhat from decade to decade. Generally, however, the town had a large number of white-collar workers. The proportion of unskilled workers ranged between 11 and 20 percent of the adult labor force, whereas the semiskilled constituted an almost even 10 percent in all decades. While the number of skilled workers declined significantly from 36 percent of the total work force in 1870 to 25 percent from 1890 through 1910, skilled workers constituted roughly one-half of the manual laborers in all decades. In addition, nonmanual workers and skilled laborers combined made up approximately 70 percent of the work force in each decade from 1870 through 1910.[9] The large number of nonmanual and skilled laborers in the work force suggests the possibility of occupational mobility in nineteenth-century Warren. Of course, the availability of sufficient positions does not provide any guarantee of the occurrence of occupational mobility, nor will the incidence of such mobility necessarily be high. Nevertheless, one may proceed with the assumption that, given a relatively open society, occupational mobility might frequently occur.

The use of census materials and other similar data restricts the study of social mobility to an examination of the careers of individuals remaining in the community for more than one decade. Thus an analysis of geographic mobility must precede any examination of social mobility. Table 4-1 displays the differing persistence rates for foreign- and native-born adult males between 1870 and 1910.

TABLE 4-1

Rate of Persistence* Among the Native-Born and Foreign-Born

Decade	Native-Born Adult Males (%)	Foreign-Born Adult Males (%)
1870-1880	36	31
1880-1890	39	30
1890-1900	40	35
1900-1910	46	45

*The rate of persistence of a group for a particular decade is defined as that proportion of the group recorded on the census at the start of the decade that is still present at the end of the decade. Thus 31 percent of all foreign-born adult males of 1870 still lived in Warren in 1880; 30 percent of all foreign-born adult males residing in the community in 1880 continued to reside there in 1890, and so on.

Comparison of rates of persistence in Warren from 1870 through 1910 shows a mean difference of 5 percent between the native-born and the foreign-born population. As Table 4-1 demonstrates, both native-born residents and immigrants consistently left Warren more frequently than they stayed. During the first two decades of industrialization, slightly more than one-third of all United States-born workers remained in the community for a full decade, as did a similar, although slightly smaller, proportion of immigrant workers.[10] During the last two decades of this study, rates of persistence increased for both groups and approached 50 percent in 1910. In addition, the difference in persistence rates between native-born workers and immigrants had largely disappeared by 1910.[11] By the first decade of the twentieth century, as the rate of industrial and population growth leveled off, community stability increased markedly.

Throughout the period of industrialization, rates of persistence among specific groups of immigrants varied widely. During the period of rapid growth after 1880 the French and Danish immigrants, later joined by the Swedish, remained as frequently as native-born workers. The English, Irish, and German immigrants, in contrast, showed the greatest turnover of any nationality with not much more than one-third remaining in any single decade.[12]

In nineteenth-century Warren the level of skill, specific occupation, and age rather than place of birth appeared to affect one's propensity to become a permanent member of the community. Analysis of the persistence of the five major skill groups residing in the community from 1870 through 1910 (Table 4-2) reveals several important facts.

TABLE 4-2

Rate of Persistence Among Selected Levels of Skill

Decade	Unskilled, Semiskilled (%)	Skilled (%)	Clerk (%)	Proprietor (%)	Professional (%)
1870-1880	26	26	17	72	40
1880-1890	39	39	46	78	43
1890-1900	41	43	44	52	51
1900-1910	48	49	46	63	56

Proprietors, who were usually property owners, demonstrated the greatest staying power of any group during the period of growth. Even throughout the period of business consolidation (1890-1910) more than one-half of the proprietors remained in the borough. By contrast, all other groups left the community, even during its period of greatest growth, more frequently than they stayed. Rising persistence rates in each group, however, suggest that industrialization apparently in-

creased the possibility that one might settle. Skilled as well as unskilled workers found conditions more favorable to settlement in a
period of economic expansion. Nonmanual workers had an even
higher persistence rate and, as Table 4-3 illustrates, their rate exceeded that of manual workers in every decade.

TABLE 4-3

Rate of Persistence Among Manual and Nonmanual Workers

Decade	Manual (%)	Nonmanual (%)
1870-1880	26	36
1880-1890	38	54
1890-1900	42	45
1900-1910	48	50

The increasing rate of persistence displayed in Table 4-3 suggests at
least one tentative conclusion. Periods of economic expansion in-
duced a greater number of manual workers to remain in Warren each
decade although nonmanual workers enjoyed greater stability than
manual workers in times of economic growth as well as in periods of
recession. Considering the large turnover—74 percent—prior to industrialization, the increased persistence rates indicate that industrial growth greatly increased the manual worker's ability or desire to
become a permanent member of the community.

A more detailed analysis of intragenerational geographical mobility of four groups of workers reveals a somewhat higher rate of persistence that occasionally exceeded 50 percent. As Table 4-4 indicates,
persistence rates for each of the four occupational groups increased
throughout Warren's industrial era. Furthermore, with the exception
of the unskilled workers in the 1870 and 1880 groups, stability increased markedly for any group remaining in the community longer
than a full decade.

During the first decade following their arrival in the community,
unskilled laborers in each census group through 1890 left Warren at a
rate ranging between 60 and 80 percent. Similarly, semiskilled and
skilled workers during the same period left Warren as frequently as
the unskilled, with persistence rates exceeding 40 percent only once
in thirty years. In contrast to the manual workers, 54 percent of the
white-collar workers in the 1880 group remained in the community in
1890, and 45 percent of the 1890 census group still resided in Warren
one decade later. Apparently, large numbers of manual workers
floated in and out of Warren each decade, never achieving enough

TABLE 4-4

Rate of Persistence of Four Groups of Workers

Level of Skill	1880 (%)	1890 (%)	1900 (%)	1910 (%)	Original Number in Group
		1870 Census Group*			
Unskilled	23	25	60	33	75
Semiskilled	28	81	53	11	67
Skilled	26	62	66	65	215
Nonmanual	36	65	50	39	252
		1880 Census Group			
Unskilled		43	47	40	115
Semiskilled		35	66	48	91
Skilled		39	54	42	205
Nonmanual		54	56	48	300
		1890 Census Group			
Unskilled			36	52	75
Semiskilled			48	56	81
Skilled			43	57	191
Nonmanual			45	53	396
		1900 Census Group			
Unskilled				49	382
Semiskilled				48	147
Skilled				49	422
Nonmanual				50	648

*The rate of persistence of a census group for a particular decade is defined as that portion of the group recorded on the census at the start of the decade that is still present at the end of the decade. Thus 23 percent of the unskilled laborers of 1870 still lived in Warren in 1880; 25 percent of the men in this group as of 1880 still lived in Warren in 1890, and so on. This table differs from Table 4-1 in that each census group does not include men listed in any previous decade.

social or economic benefits to induce them to stay. Death undoubtedly accounted for a small portion of those not listed in succeeding decades. However, nothing indicates that the mortality rate—ranging from 7 to 10 percent of the total population per year—among manual workers significantly exceeded that of nonmanual workers.[13]

Consistently higher rates of out-migration by Warren's manual workers during their first decade of residence indicates that the major mobility pattern they followed was geographical. Manual workers at all skill levels left Warren much more frequently than they stayed. The main speaker at the town's centennial celebration perhaps underscored the reason for this exodus, stating: "Warren has its poor, and a small degraded element; but its atmosphere is wholesome and elevating. Those who cannot rise into better conditions do not find it congenial and soon leave."[14]

Those workers remaining in the borough beyond the first decade exhibited a much greater degree of stability. Persistence rates for all three groups of manual workers remaining in Warren for more than one decade frequently reached 50 and even 60 percent. No marked differences in persistence existed between the three groups of manual workers during their first decade of residency. With few exceptions, however, both semiskilled and skilled workers achieved a much higher rate of persistence in succeeding decades than the unskilled. This increasing rate of geographical stability suggests that these individuals found the community somewhat more hospitable and saw greater opportunities for advancement.

The ages of those migrating out of the community, however, suggest the presence of another factor influencing rates of geographic mobility. The overwhelming majority of those leaving Warren within a single decade of residence were young men between the ages of 18 and 39. Moreover, between 30 and 45 percent of the most transient members of the Warren work force left the community before their thirtieth birthday. Table 4-5 displays the ages of all emigrants from four census groups, 1870-1900.

The age data on outward migrants confirm the hypothesis suggested by this and other studies of a floating population moving in and out of the nineteenth-century cities. A large proportion of these floaters, however, were relatively young men in the process of seeking a suitable career. It is likely, as Table 4-5 demonstrates, that as they aged they became geographically less mobile.

Nearly 70 percent of the men in the 1870 census group left Warren by 1880. More than two-thirds of these men were less than 40 years old. Moreover, nearly 42 percent left before reaching the age of 30. By 1890 the rate of overall outward migration declined to one-third of the remaining group. Between 1880 and 1890 all men in the 1870 group reached the age of 30. Men in their thirties now constituted the largest proportion of emigrants from the community. The high rates shown for men over 59 years of age result primarily from death rather than geographic mobility. During the next decade, 1890-1900, the majority of outward migrants came from the age 40-49 group. However, with each succeeding decade a smaller proportion of those remaining from the 1870 census group left the community. This suggests that as the population grew older residents became increasingly less mobile.

Data from each of the other three census groups confirm this rela-

TABLE 4-5

Emigration of Four Census Groups by Age

Age*	Emigrated by 1880 (%)	Emigrated by 1890 (%)	Emigrated by 1900 (%)	Emigrated by 1910 (%)	Remained in 1910 (%)
		1870 Census Group			
18-29	41.42	07.81	—	—	—
30-39	24.02	28.12	01.92	02.56	—
40-49	15.93	18.75	32.96	20.51	—
50-59	08.33	14.06	11.53	35.90	13.79
Over 59	10.29	31.25	53.61	41.03	86.21
Total N in sample	408	64	52	39	29
		1880 Census Group			
18-29		43.67	08.73	—	—
30-39		28.17	26.19	03.95	—
40-49		12.66	18.25	39.47	07.04
50-59		09.30	19.05	17.10	47.89
Over 59		06.20	27.78	39.47	45.07
Total N in sample		387	126	76	71
		1890 Census Group			
18-29			30.39	06.15	—
30-39			25.49	29.23	03.94
40-49			16.34	35.38	30.92
50-59			15.43	20.00	34.87
Over 59			12.42	09.23	30.26
Total N in sample			306	130	152
		1900 Census Group			
18-29				44.91	05.29
30-39				26.94	41.09
40-49				18.86	27.02
50-59				06.58	19.22
Over 59				02.69	07.38
Total N in sample				668	718

*The rate of emigration of a census group by age is defined as that portion of the total emigrants within a particular age group. Thus, of the 408 men listed in the 1870 census who left Warren between 1870 and 1880, whose ages are known, 41.42 percent (169 men) were between the ages of 18 and 29. Data on the ages of men at death were unavailable. It is assumed that most of the men listed as over 59 who failed to appear in subsequent data sources died.

tionship between age and geographic mobility. Nearly 44 percent of the 1880 group, 30 percent of the 1890 group, and 45 percent of the 1900 group leaving Warren within one decade were less than 30 years old. Those in their thirties constituted another one-fourth of the workers from each census group who lived in Warren for less than ten years. Similarly, as each group grew older the age of outward migrants increased but the rate of emigration decreased markedly.

Several factors appear to affect mobility patterns in nineteenth-century Warren. Economic factors, as suggested earlier, likely influenced persistence in the community. As Warren's prosperity increased throughout the late nineteenth century a greater proportion of workers, both manual and nonmanual, remained in the community. Second, a large number of young workers floated in and out of the community each decade, greatly increasing the transient nature of the community. Persistence rates by skill level (see Table 4-2) indicate that most of these men held low-level blue-collar jobs during their short stay in the community. Finally, following the first wave of outward migration of young workers, stability of each census group increased dramatically. Thus the frequently posited "floating industrial proletariat," at least in Warren, consisted of young men. Older men continued to leave the community with each succeeding decade but in much smaller proportions.

The importance of the above data concerning persistence rates is twofold. First, one must conclude that no matter what degree of opportunity actually existed in the Warren social system large numbers of workers, particularly the young, frequently left the community in search of success elsewhere. The second factor concerning rates of persistence of manual workers concerns the problem of investigating social mobility among those who remain. As previously mentioned, workers residing in Warren two or more decades apparently found some favorable factors encouraging them to remain in the community. These same factors tended to enhance the workers' opportunities for occupational mobility. Consequently the built-in bias of this study, analyzing social mobility patterns of the more stable minority among the manual workers in nineteenth-century Warren, favors findings of positive occupational mobility.

Table 4-6 illustrates the general occupational mobility patterns of Warren's manual laborers from decade to decade, 1870 through 1910.

Comparison of general mobility rates by decade for all manual workers reveals several interesting characteristics. Both unskilled and semiskilled workers, with some exceptions, moved in the occupational hierarchy more frequently than skilled laborers. Combining

TABLE 4-6

Occupational Status Attained by Decade

Decade	Original Number in Group	Rate of Persistence (%)	Level of Skill Un-changed (%)	Upward Mobility (%)	Downward Mobility (%)
		Unskilled Workers*			
1870-1880	75	23	70	30	—
1880-1890	151	42	52	48	—
1890-1900	116	53	71	29	—
1900-1910	482	50	62	38	—
		Semiskilled Workers			
1870-1880	67	28	37	47	16
1880-1890	116	40	52	33	15
1890-1900	125	64	44	31	25
1900-1910	191	60	48	22	30
		Skilled Workers			
1870-1880	215	26	66	23	10
1880-1890	248	48	48	24	28
1890-1900	272	59	65	17	18
1900-1910	526	57	69	16	15

*Each group includes those individuals shown in previous decades.

mobility, as Table 4-6 does, into single steps of upward or downward mobility, however, conceals several important distinctions. Semiskilled and unskilled workers could move up two or three occupational classifications while skilled workers could move only into the nonmanual classification. It was perhaps easier to move from an unskilled to a skilled position. However, as later mobility tables will show, all three groups moved up one position in the occupational scale with similar frequency.

Although the mobility rate of the unskilled and semiskilled groups was somewhat erratic, the earlier decades, paralleling the major period of Warren's growth, proved more favorable for occupational advancement than the last two decades. Thirty percent of the unskilled workers of 1870 still residing in Warren in the next decade no longer held unskilled positions. The succeeding decade proved even more favorable, with 48 percent of the unskilled laborers advancing to a higher skill group. The years 1880 to 1890 was Warren's greatest decade of economic growth, suggesting a strong positive relationship between economic expansion and occupational mobility. The least amount of mobility for unskilled workers occurred in the 1890-1900 decade when only 29 percent advanced beyond that position. By this time many of the opportunities provided by the oil fields declined, thus closing an important avenue of mobility. The high percentage of upward mobility, particularly for the unskilled, indicates that Warren did indeed confirm a measure of truth in the "American success story."

Rates of downward mobility, however, for the semiskilled workers, demonstrate the absence of occupational security for that particular skill group. While upward mobility of semiskilled workers ranged between 47 percent from 1870 to 1880 and 22 percent from 1900 to 1910, those falling into the unskilled group exceeded those advancing in the first decade of the twentieth century. Many of those failing to maintain jobs of a semiskilled nature had perhaps originated in the unskilled group. Achieving brief success by moving into a semiskilled position, they often fell back into their lower position within the next decade.

Skilled workers exhibited the greatest degree of both geographic and occupational stability throughout the period of this study. With the exception of the 1880-1890 decade, when a fairly large number of skilled workers abandoned their occupations to "wildcat" in the oil fields (classified as semiskilled), an almost even 65 percent of all skilled workers maintained that position in each succeeding decade. The gulf separating manual workers from white-collar jobs proved formidable although not insurmountable. During the first two decades of this study, encompassing the era of economic expansion, approximately one-fourth of all skilled workers left that position for nonmanual jobs. During the last two decades of this study, however, as the community began to consolidate its gains, opportunities in the white-collar world decreased. It became increasingly difficult, although not impossible, for skilled workers to bridge the gap separating manual from nonmanual workers. While skilled workers remained in the borough at a much greater rate at the turn of the century than in previous decades, less than 20 percent were able to attain a nonmanual position. Indeed, as in almost all previous decades, unskilled and semiskilled workers experienced greater upward mobility than skilled workers in the final two decades of this study.

The preceding examination of the general trend of mobility conceals several important elements of social mobility within the community. Manual laborers lived and worked in Warren for varying periods of time. One might therefore expect those with the longest periods of residence to experience greater upward mobility than short-term residents. In addition, occupational mobility, as used in this study, ranges from a single forward step in the existing hierarchy to a more spectacular leap from the ranks of the unskilled to that of white-collar worker. Did the average unskilled or semiskilled worker simply move into the ranks of the skilled workers? The following three tables, examining the degree of intragenerational mobility occurring within each census group, trace individuals throughout their careers in the community and illustrate both the extent of upward mobility and the advantages of longevity within the community.

Table 4-7 reveals the career patterns of the hundreds of unskilled

TABLE 4-7

Intragenerational Occupational Mobility, 1870-1910: Occupational Status Attained by Unskilled Workers

Year	Unskilled (%)	Semiskilled (%)	Skilled (%)	Nonmanual (%)	Rate of Persistence (%)	Number in Group
			1870 Census Group			
1870	100	—	—	—	—	75
1880	70	6	6	18	23	17
1890	80	20	—	—	25	5
1900	67	33	—	—	60	3
1910	100	—	—	—	33	1
			1880 Census Group			
1880	100	—	—	—	—	115
1890	55	10	16	18	43	49
1900	39	9	26	26	47	23
1910	33	11	22	33	40	9
			1890 Census Group			
1890	100	—	—	—	—	75
1900	66	15	15	4	36	27
1910	57	7	14	21	52	14
			1900 Census Group			
1900	100	—	—	—	—	382
1910	67	9	14	10	49	187

*Differences may be noted between the percentages shown here and those presented in Table 4-5. This table includes only those workers first recorded in any particular census year. Thus, workers from a previous census group are not included with a later group. The reader is reminded that in some instances the limited absolute numbers from which percentages were derived cause occupational shifts by a relatively few men to appear as a rather large change in percentage.

workers residing in Warren between 1870 and 1910. As previously discussed, less than half of the unskilled workers residing in the borough in any one decade remained there ten years later. With the exception of the 1880 census group, only a minority of those remaining within the community achieved a higher status occupation. Of the original seventy-five unskilled workers residing in Warren in 1870, fifty-eight, or 77 percent, left the community by 1880. Of those who remained, a full 70 percent continued as unskilled laborers in the succeeding decade. However, during the decade spanning the oil boom years—1880 to 1890—18 percent of those experiencing upward mobility moved into a nonmanual position, while 12 percent achieved semiskilled or skilled occupations. During the next three decades the few remaining members of the 1870 census group of unskilled workers attained neither skilled nor white-collar positions. In 1890 only 20 percent of the workers remaining from the 1870 group held semiskilled occupations, while 33 percent attained that classification by 1900.

Occupational opportunities for the 115 unskilled workers first appearing in the 1880 census improved markedly compared with the 1870 census group. In fact, the 1880 group, which joined the Warren work force concurrently with the oil boom, experienced greater occupational mobility than any other group of unskilled workers. In addition, both the rate and the extent of upward mobility for unskilled workers in the 1880 census group increased with each decade they remained in Warren. Within ten years 45 percent of these men achieved some measure of mobility. During the next two decades 61 percent and 67 percent respectively of the unskilled workers remaining in the community had risen on the occupational scale. The percentage of men from this group joining the ranks of skilled and nonmanual workers increased with each succeeding decade. By 1890, 16 percent of the 1880 unskilled laboring group held some type of skilled occupation and 18 percent attained a nonmanual position. Ten years later 61 percent of the 1880 unskilled workers advanced to a higher level of occupation. More importantly, 26 percent of these men moved beyond the ranks of semiskilled work into the ranks of the skilled, and another 26 percent attained a nonmanual position. During the following decade the remaining laborers from 1880 continued to enjoy significant mobility. By 1910 only 33 percent of the remaining unskilled workers from the 1880 group still held unskilled jobs. A similar number—33 percent—were white-collar workers while another 22 percent achieved the rank of skilled laborer. The 1880 group arrived in Warren at the onset of the era of economic growth. These unskilled workers clearly enjoyed dramatic mobility throughout the three succeeding decades. The men in this group who remained in Warren frequently advanced into skilled and nonmanual occupations, demonstrating the presence of considerable opportunity for occupational mobility.

The unskilled workers in the 1890 and 1900 census groups arrived in Warren near the end of the period of economic growth. They experienced less mobility than the 1880 group, although a significant degree of improvement continued.[15] After residing within the community for one decade, two-thirds of the 1890 group still worked at unskilled jobs. Ten years later, in 1910, 57 percent of the remaining men continued to hold unskilled positions. Of the men in the 1890 group who advanced into higher skill classifications, 19 percent became either skilled laborers or white-collar workers by 1900 and 35 percent achieved these positions by 1910. Moreover, almost one-fourth of the 1900 census group moved up at least two skill classifications during a single decade. With the exception of the 1870 census group of unskilled workers, one may conclude that unskilled workers in Warren enjoyed a high rate of mobility during the town's period of industrial growth.

However, before reaching any final conclusions regarding mobility in Warren, work patterns of several other groups of the town's laborers must be analyzed. Industrialization and the degree of economic opportunity also affected the lives of the semiskilled and skilled workers in Warren. Occupational mobility of these two groups is of particular significance in a study of social mobility because, unlike the unskilled workers, they had status to lose. High rates of downward mobility by the skilled and particularly the semiskilled workers would suggest a mere shifting of occupational roles among manual workers. Conversely, occupational advances by the two upper work groups, equaling the upward mobility demonstrated by the unskilled, suggest the presence of considerable economic opportunity.

Table 4-8 reveals rates of both increasing and decreasing mobility of four groups of semiskilled workers who lived in Warren from 1870 through 1910. Persistence rates generally improved for each succeeding group of semiskilled workers residing in Warren. Rates also continued to increase for any group remaining in the community beyond one decade. In fact, well over one-half of the semiskilled workers able to remain in Warren for one full decade still lived there in succeeding decades. For those workers who did not leave the community within their first ten years of residency, longevity was the rule rather than an exception.

TABLE 4-8

Intragenerational Occupational Mobility, 1870-1910: Occupational Status Attained by Semiskilled Workers

Year	Unskilled (%)	Semiskilled (%)	Skilled (%)	Nonmanual (%)	Rate of Persistence (%)	Number in Group
			1870 Census Group			
1870	—	100	—	—	—	67
1880	16	37	16	31	28	19
1890	12	35	6	47	81	17
1900	—	22	—	78	53	9
1910	—	—	100	—	11	1
			1880 Census Group			
1880	—	100	—	—	—	91
1890	10	43	24	22	35	32
1900	9	35	30	26	66	27
1910	—	31	54	15	48	13
			1890 Census Group			
1890	—	100	—	—	—	81
1900	10	61	7	22	48	39
1910	9	36	14	41	56	22
			1900 Census Group			
1900	—	100	—	—	—	147
1910	7	77	6	10	48	71

Frequent upward mobility for semiskilled workers in Warren again demonstrates the presence of considerable economic opportunity for those workers remaining in Warren from the 1870 census group. Nearly one-third attained a nonmanual position within ten years. In addition, 16 percent moved up one position into the skilled classification. By 1890 fully 53 percent of the men in this group advanced into the ranks of either the skilled or the white-collar worker. Occupational progress continued throughout the next decade as seven of the nine semiskilled men from the 1870 group still in town worked at some type of nonmanual occupation.

Semiskilled workers from the 1880 census group also experienced frequent upward mobility. Of the thirty-two men in this group who still resided in Warren in 1890, 46 percent held better occupations than in the previous decade. By 1900 the percentage of men from the 1880 group who moved up the occupational ladder increased to 56 percent, including a full 26 percent holding nonmanual positions.

Throughout the first decade of the twentieth century, although the number of men from this group holding nonmanual occupations slipped to 15 percent, more than one-half maintained a job within the skilled classification. Similar to the unskilled laborers who joined the Warren work force in 1880, semiskilled workers from the same census year enjoyed significant upward mobility. More than one-half of the men from either group moved up at least one occupational position and nearly one-fourth obtained a white-collar occupation.

Upward mobility for the 1890 census group of semiskilled workers declined somewhat from the previous decades although the rate continued to be impressive. At the turn of the century nearly 30 percent of the remaining 1890 semiskilled laborers were able to leave this classification for a better occupation. By 1910 the percentage improving their occupational status climbed to more than one-half, with 41 percent achieving some type of nonmanual work. The men entering the work force as semiskilled workers in 1900, however, failed to enjoy the high rate of occupational mobility. Only eleven men or 16 percent of the remaining semiskilled workers in this group were able to move into better occupations. As previously indicated, Warren's rate of industrial growth began to decline at the turn of the century. Both the unskilled and the semiskilled workers joining the work force in 1900 apparently felt the effect of declining growth; occupational mobility for both groups declined in the first decade of the twentieth century.

Unlike the unskilled worker, the semiskilled laborer was subject to the effects of downward mobility. As indicated in Table 4-8, approximately 10 percent of all semiskilled workers fell into the ranks of the unskilled during their first two decades of residency. However, no members of the first two census groups of semiskilled workers—1870-1880—were classified as unskilled by the time they reached the third decade of residence in the community. Some of these men no doubt left Warren; others found it possible to reverse their downward movement and regained work in a semiskilled or higher classification. Clearly, downward mobility for men beginning their careers as semiskilled workers in Warren occurred infrequently. And when compared with the number of men attaining higher positions, the rate of downward mobility appears insignificant. The occupational patterns of the semiskilled workers who remained in the community longer than one decade attest to the presence of considerable economic opportunity. Particularly for those joining the Warren work force in 1870 or 1880, the industrialization and urbanization of Warren provided sufficient opportunities for occupational mobility.

TABLE 4-9

Intragenerational Occupational Mobility, 1870-1910: Occupational Status Attained by Skilled Workers

Year	Unskilled (%)	Semiskilled (%)	Skilled (%)	Nonmanual (%)	Rate of Persistence (%)	Number in Group
			1870 Census Group			
1870	—	—	100	—	—	215
1880	5	5	66	23	26	56
1890	—	11	54	34	62	35
1900	—	17	52	30	66	23
1910	—	13	60	27	65	15
			1880 Census Group			
1880	—	—	100	—	—	205
1890	4	4	63	28	39	79
1900	4	7	60	28	54	43
1910	6	—	50	44	42	18
			1890 Census Group			
1890	—	—	100	—	—	191
1900	2	4	77	17	43	82
1910	—	—	70	30	57	47
			1900 Census Group			
1900	—	—	100	—	—	422
1910	4	3	77	16	49	205

Analysis of the occupational patterns of skilled laborers in Warren between 1870 and 1910 provides the final test of occupational mobility in the community during its era of industrial growth. Unlike the unskilled and semiskilled workers, the work tasks of these men indicated a specific type of craftsmanship. Often they owned property and frequently held proprietorship of small one- or two-man shops. Consequently, they tended to be less mobile, both geographically and occupationally, than the other two groups of manual workers.

As indicated in Table 4-9, the propensity to remain within Warren was frequently greater for skilled workers than that previously discussed for unskilled laborers. Skilled craftsmen, like the other two groups of manual workers, left Warren more often than they remained during their first decade of residency within the community. However, persistence rates increased markedly for all skilled workers able to remain in the community beyond ten years. Well over one-half of these men continued to live in Warren during each succeeding decade.

More importantly, skilled workers experienced the greatest occupational stability of any group of manual workers. Of the hundreds of skilled workers living in Warren between 1870 and 1910, between 50 and 77 percent continued to hold skilled positions in any succeeding decade. The 1870 and 1880 census groups proved the most fluid in this respect, often moving up or down the occupational ladder. Of the original 215 skilled craftsmen in the 1870 census group, 56 men or 26 percent still lived in Warren in 1880. Fully two-thirds of this group continued in some type of skilled labor. By 1890 this had declined to 54 percent and reached a low of 52 percent in 1900. Some of the men leaving the skilled group moved down, particularly into the semi-skilled classification. Many skilled laborers, especially those with a knowledge of machine tools, left their craft to "wildcat" in the oil fields between 1880 and 1900.

The largest percentage of 1870 skilled workers experiencing mobility found it possible to move upward into a nonmanual position. Of the skilled workers still in the community in 1880, 23 percent obtained nonmanual employment. Between 1880 and 1890, the most dynamic period in Warren's history, 34 percent of the 1870 census group attained a white-collar occupation. Although economic opportunity declined somewhat during the last two decades of Warren's industrialization, 30 percent of the 1870 group of skilled workers maintained nonmanual positions in 1900 and 27 percent continued in that classification in 1910. Skilled craftsmen joining the Warren work force in 1880 experienced approximately the same amount of upward mobility as the 1870 group of skilled workers. By 1890, twenty-two skilled workers or 28 percent of those remaining in Warren from 1880 left their occupations for a nonmanual position. The same percentage held white-collar jobs in 1900 and by 1910 fully 44 percent maintained nonmanual positions.

Those joining the Warren work force in either 1890 or 1900 found it increasingly difficult to move up the occupational ladder, again suggesting the importance of economic growth on occupational opportunity. From 1875 to 1890 the community experienced its greatest era of economic growth. During the last two decades of this study economic growth continued to increase but at a declining rate. Only 17 percent of the 1890 census group and 16 percent of the 1900 group were upwardly mobile during their first decade in the community. Interestingly, the rate of upward mobility for the 1890 census group of skilled workers increased to 30 percent by 1910. In fact, mobility rates for all groups of skilled workers, except those joining the work force in 1900, exceeded 27 percent in 1910. This again illustrates the strong relationship between residential longevity and occupational mobility. The factors encouraging manual workers to remain in the community also apparently contributed to the positive economic mobility of these same laborers.

The preceding analysis of the career patterns of Warren's manual workers in the 1870-1910 period suggests the following conclusions:

1. The composition of the laboring class in Warren remained unstable throughout the era of industrialization. Manual laborers from all three skilled groups moved in and out of the community, but only a minority remained. This factor, of course, directly affected the composition of the work force and mobility rates since the less successful were the most likely to leave the community.

2. Rates of persistence for all groups of Warren's manual workers generally improved in each succeeding decade through 1910. Thus, as the community experienced its industrial urban growth, larger numbers of workers were able to find sufficient employment to encourage them to remain in the community. As Warren's industrial growth leveled off at the turn of the century, nearly 50 percent of all manual workers found it possible to remain in the community longer than one decade.

3. Workers who left the community were likely to be young and unskilled or semiskilled. In all four census groups, workers under 30 years of age constituted the largest group of outward migrants. Moreover, low-level blue-collar workers left Warren more frequently than did workers in the two highest skill groups.

4. Ability to persist in the community carried with it marked advantages. Occupational mobility for those remaining in Warren always exceeded mobility of one-decade residents. Occupational mobility of third-decade residents also generally exceeded mobility of those remaining in the community for only two decades. Of course, the relationship between horizontal and vertical mobility may be the reverse. Occupationally mobile individuals may be more likely to remain in the community.

5. Manual workers employed in Warren in 1870 and 1880 enjoyed somewhat greater mobility opportunity than those joining the work force in 1890 or 1900, excepting the 1870 unskilled workers. Generally one-half of all groups of manual workers joining the work force in 1870 or 1880 experienced some type of occupational mobility. On the other hand, between two-thirds and three-fourths of all manual workers joining the work force in 1890 or 1900 remained in the same skill

classification. One is tempted to conclude that this shrinkage of occupational mobility resulted from a decline in economic opportunities available to manual workers. However, large numbers of Irish, Swedes, and Italians migrated into Warren between 1890 and 1910 (see Table 8-1). Possibly these immigrants enjoyed fewer economic opportunities than their native-born counterparts during the last two decades of this study. A detailed analysis of immigrants and their sons follows in Chapter 5. For the moment, therefore, the stated reasons regarding declining occupational mobility for the 1890 and 1900 census group must remain tentative.

6. The impressive upward mobility of all groups of manual workers in Warren during the town's era of industrialization indicates the presence of considerable economic opportunity. Although only a minority of workers in the three skill groups attained a higher level occupation, a large percentage of those moved up two or even three occupational classifications.[16] Mobility into nonmanual positions occurred frequently, demonstrating the distinct possibility that workers could bridge the gap separating manual and nonmanual workers.

Comparison with another nineteenth-century community possessing similar characteristics—Newburyport, Massachusetts— illustrates the extent of this mobility and the effect of industrialization upon unskilled workers. Like Warren, the population of Newburyport grew rapidly during its era of industrialization. Inhabited by 7,161 residents in 1840, the town expanded to nearly 13,000 at midcentury.[17] In addition, industrial growth, telescoped into a ten-year period in Newburyport, centered around one particular industry: textiles. Similarly, both the Warren and Newburyport populations included a small but important proportion of immigrants. During the years of Stephan Thernstrom's study (1850-1880), between 15 and 18 percent of the Newburyport residents were foreign born.[18] Warren contained a similar, although slightly larger proportion—19 to 23 percent—of immigrant residents from 1870 to 1910.[19] Finally, nonmanual workers and skilled craftsmen constituted roughly two-thirds of the respective work forces of each community.[20] As previously discussed, the shape of the community's occupational structure determines the range of mobility one might expect within a community. Both Warren and Newburyport contained a sufficient number of higher level occupations to justify expectations of upward mobility for unskilled workers.

At least one major difference exists between this study and Thernstrom's examination of social mobility in nineteenth-century Newburyport. The great economic and social changes in the city of

Newburyport occurred between 1840 and 1850. Population growth, industrial expansion, building construction, and retail business nearly doubled during this single dynamic decade.[21] At midcentury, however, Newburyport completed its era of expansion and the community's growth reached a stable plateau. From 1850 through 1880— the period of Thernstrom's study—little economic or social growth occurred in Newburyport. Warren, however, experienced its greatest growth during the decades spanning this study. Therefore, a comparison of the occupational patterns of unskilled workers in the two communities illustrates the effects of industrialization upon economic mobility.

Comparison of persistence rates of unskilled workers in the two communities reveals strikingly similar patterns of geographical mobility. Thernstrom reports that "Less than half of the unskilled laborers listed in the city on the census of 1850, 1860 or 1870 remained there for as much as a decade."[22] Warren's day laborers also left the community at a rate exceeding 50 percent during their first decade of residency. However, persistence rates for Newburyport's three groups of unskilled workers remained fairly stable throughout the period from 1850 to 1880. Two-thirds of the unskilled laborers residing in Newburyport in 1850 had left the community by 1860. The 1860 census group left Newburyport at the same rate, while only 59 percent of the 1870 group left the community within a decade.[23] Table 4-4 reveals much more erratic persistence rates for Warren's unskilled workers. Fully 77 percent of the 1870 census group left Warren within one decade. However, by 1910 almost one-half—49 percent—of the 1900 census group remained within the community. The increasing rates of persistence for the unskilled in Warren suggest that as industrialization in the town progressed sufficient opportunities arose to encourage larger numbers to remain.

Rates of occupational mobility for Warren and Newburyport also indicate the presence of greater opportunity for unskilled workers in the Pennsylvania town. The number of men in both towns maintaining an unskilled status, with few exceptions, ranges between 55 and 70 percent. However, the unskilled workers in Warren experienced a much greater range of mobility. Thernstrom concludes by stating:

> In none of the groups of laborers did as much as a quarter of the men succeed in obtaining either *skilled or non-manual* positions in the period studied. From 75 to 85 percent of them remained near the bottom of the social ladder in the low-skill, low-pay occupational universe. The great majority continued to work as day laborers; most of those who did change occupations became semi-skilled

workmen, performing simple manual tasks at slightly higher wages and with somewhat more regular employment than they had previously enjoyed.[24]

Unskilled laborers in Warren enjoyed much greater success. Once again, excepting the 1870 census group, Warren's unskilled workers became skilled craftsmen and nonmanual workers with marked regularity. Between one-third and one-half of all unskilled laborers of the 1880 census group managed to achieve white-collar status. During their first decade of residency, the 1890 census group experienced the smallest rate of mobility—19 percent—into the upper two skill groups. Yet this minimum amount of mobility in Warren approached the maximum rate in Newburyport. Only 24 percent of any group of Newburyport workers ever achieved white-collar status, with the rate dropping as low as 5 percent for several work groups.[25] Comparison of the mobility rates of unskilled workers in the two communities reveals striking contrasts. Almost without exception, Warren's unskilled workers enjoyed greater upward mobility than the laborers of Newburyport. Clearly, Warren during its era of industrial expansion represents a more fluid community than the Newburyport society following its major period of growth. For the unskilled workers in Warren considerable economic opportunity existed providing some basis for the belief that workers could ascend the occupational ladder.

Some unskilled workers in Warren obtained nonmanual occupations, but only a small minority actually succeeded. Both the semiskilled and skilled workers in Warren demonstrated greater mobility into middle-class positions than did the unskilled. The position that one held at the start of his employment in the community clearly influenced his chances for mobility into the nonmanual classification.

Stephan Thernstrom, in his analysis of social mobility of nineteenth-century Newburyport workers, examined the career patterns of the unskilled workers. The previous comparison of Warren and Newburyport workers revealed that day laborers in Warren experienced greater occupational mobility than the unskilled workers of Newburyport. Of particular interest, however, is the failure of the Newburyport workers to achieve white-collar occupations. Thernstrom concludes: "The common workman who remained in Newburyport in these years [1850-1880] had only a slight chance of rising into a middle class occupation. . . . The climb into a nonmanual occupation was not impossible for the unskilled workman, but it was achieved by only a tiny minority."[26] The occupational mobility of both the semiskilled and the skilled workers in Newburyport would have, in all likelihood, improved upon the dismal record set by the unskilled workers of Newburyport.[27]

The impressive success of Warren workers in attaining nonmanual positions is tempered by the small number achieving proprietorship in anything other than one-man craft shops.

TABLE 4-10

Proprietorships Attained by Manual Workers, 1870-1910

Original Level of Skill	Number of Proprietorships Attained			
	1880	1890	1900	1910
Unskilled	1	3	2	2
Semiskilled	1	3	3	2
Skilled	2	7	5	7
Total of all manual workers	4	13	10	11

Table 4-10 enumerates the total number of manual workers who became proprietors of businesses employing more than two men during the 1870-1910 period. A comparison of the above data with the mobility rates of manual workers reveals that few of those men became proprietors. Of the 44 nonmanual positions attained by unskilled workers from 1870-1910, only 8 men became affluent enough to purchase their own businesses. During the same period, semiskilled workers attained a total of 62 nonmanual positions; only 9 of these became proprietors.[28] Skilled workers fared no better, achieving only 21 proprietorships out of a total of 137 nonmanual positions attained from 1870 through 1910. Obviously, the great majority of Warren's manual laborers attaining white-collar work joined the growing ranks of foremen, service employees, self-employed craftsmen, and clerical workers.[29] A few manual workers in Warren became proprietors, but the chances of this happening were remote.

Thus we may conclude that a fluid occupational structure and considerable economic opportunity accompanied the industrialization and urbanization of Warren. Large numbers of workers migrated in and out of the community each decade, but those who remained often advanced into higher level occupations. Clearly, few workers experienced the spectacular mobility enjoyed by the heroes in the novels of Horatio Alger, but middle-class occupations became a distinct possibility. For the workers of Warren, the promise of mobility was a reality enjoyed by many.

5 Immigrants, Indigents, and Labor Problems

Migration of immigrants both in and out of Warren between 1870 and 1910 played a significant role in the changing labor scene. In preindustrial Warren, immigrants constituted 35 percent of the adult labor force. By 1890 the proportion of foreign workers reached its apex at 42 percent, followed by a steady decline to 34 percent in 1900 and 27 percent in 1910 (see Table 8-1). Throughout Warren's era of industrialization, the composition of the labor force presented a diverse ethnic pattern.[1] The foreign-born workers in 1870 were mainly the English, Irish, German, and French. By 1910 the Swedes, Italians, Danes, and migrants from eighteen other nations added to the original diversity of the town's labor force. Most of these men entered the community as manual laborers and, with few exceptions, remained blue-collar workers throughout their careers, with 75 percent of all immigrants performing manual work in 1870, 1880, and 1900. Only in 1890 did the percentage of immigrants doing manual labor fall below 75 percent, with 63 percent engaged in blue-collar work. In comparison, 48 percent or more of all United States-born adult males wore white collars to work in each decade from 1870 through 1910.[2] In addition to performing mostly manual labor, foreign-born workers also did the majority of unskilled work in the community. More than one-half of the men classified as unskilled in any decade of this study came from the ranks of the foreign-born.

Fortunately for the European migrants, the industrial and urban expansion of Warren created needs for semiskilled and skilled workmen. Comparison of the first occupations held by immigrants with those held by native-born citizens reveals considerable opportunities for foreign-born workmen possessing marketable skills.

Table 5-1 reveals the relationship between the initial occupations of workers and ethnicity. In each census group from 1870 through 1910 the proportion of immigrants joining the work force as unskilled laborers remained three or more times as great as the proportion of native-born day laborers. Foreign-born workers experienced even

TABLE 5-1

Percentage of Native-Born and Foreign-Born Workers in Each Skill Group at the Start of Career

Skill Classification	1870*	1880	1890	1900
Unskilled†	12%	16%	10%	23%
U.S.-born‡	7	10	5	14
Foreign-born	22	29	16	44
Semi-skilled	11	13	11	9
U.S.-born	12	9	8	10
Foreign-born	9	20	15	8
Skilled	36	29	26	26
U.S.-born	31	24	20	25
Foreign-born	44	39	33	30
Nonmanual	41	42	53	42
U.S.-born	50	57	67	51
Foreign-born	25	12	36	18
Total number each decade				
U.S.-born	397	470	413	1,081
Foreign-born	212	241	330	518
Total	609	711	743	1,599

*Workers in this category had already begun their careers.

†Indicates percentage of the total work force in each skill group.

‡Indicates percentage of origin working in each skill.

greater occupational difficulties in 1900. A large number of Italian and Swedish immigrants migrated into the community concurrent with the decline of Warren's industrial growth, forcing many of these men (44 percent) into unskilled positions.

Immigrants arriving in Warren possessing skills, however, suffered only mild disadvantages when compared with native-born Americans. Before the industrialization of the community, the proportion of immigrants attaining semiskilled work nearly equaled the percentage of United States-born laborers who began their careers in this skill group. During the next two decade intervals immigrants joining the work force managed to obtain an even larger proportion of the semi-skilled occupations. In 1880 and 1890 foreign-born men were nearly twice as likely to begin work in semiskilled occupations as were native-born men. By 1900 the opportunities for immigrants to attain these minimal-skill positions declined. By that time only 8 percent of all immigrants had achieved semiskilled positions, compared with 10 percent of all United States-born workers. This shrinkage in opportunity again appears related to both the stabilization of the economy and the large influx of foreign-born workers. During the latter part of the nineteenth century, as the community rapidly expanded, immigrants experienced considerable opportunities, although never as great as that enjoyed by native-born workers. However, as industrial and urban expansion began to decline, the disadvantages of lacking specific skills and of being foreign-born became particularly acute.

Skilled workers also felt the effects of the changing industrialization within the community. From 1870 through 1910 a large number of immigrants entering Warren began their careers as skilled craftsmen. In 1870, 44 percent of all foreign-born workers held some type of skilled position. During the next three decades the percentage of foreign-born workers joining the work force as skilled craftsmen, although declining somewhat, remained significant. In each of the last three decades of the nineteenth century, immigrants entering the work force obtained skilled occupations more frequently than native-born workers. Nearly four of every ten immigrant workers in 1880 began as skilled craftsmen whereas only 24 percent of all United States-born workers attained similar positions. One decade later, as the total percentage of skilled workers in the labor force declined, one-third of all foreign-born workers began their careers as skilled craftsmen. Only 20 percent of the native-born workers joining the work force in the same decade became skilled workers. Finally, three in ten of all foreign-born workmen joining the work force in 1900 captured skilled positions while one of every four United States-born workmen attained similar occupations. This evidence clearly indicates the presence of considerable occupational opportunity for those moving into Warren during the late nineteenth century.

Occupational opportunity, however, did not extend into the area of the white-collar worker. The initial disadvantage (Table 5-1) of immigrants in the quest for middle-class occupations becomes immediately apparent. In 1870 one-fourth of all immigrants held white-collar jobs while one-half of all United States-born men worked with their heads rather than their hands. By 1880 the percentage of native-born Americans beginning work wearing white collars reached 57 percent, although only 12 percent of all new immigrants attained such a position. During the succeeding decade two of every three United States-born workers initially started their careers in nonmanual positions while one in three of all immigrants began work as white-collar workers. The disadvantage of one's birth widened during the next decade as nonmanual opportunities for all workers declined. Only 18 percent of the immigrants starting work in 1900 could secure a non-manual occupation while one-half of all native-born Americans held white-collar jobs.[3]

Although we know little of the actual skills possessed by immigrants starting work in the lower two job classifications (some of these men may have been craftsmen forced to accept jobs demanding lesser skills), it seems apparent that skilled newcomers to the community had little difficulty securing skilled occupations. But when compared with native-born Americans, immigrants arriving in Warren were at a distinct disadvantage in both the bottom and top skill groups. Clearly, foreign-born workers did the majority of the unskilled work in the community. Conversely, with the exception of the immigrants arriving in Warren at the height of industrialization—1880 to 1890—few found it possible to secure nonmanual occupations in their initial endeavor in the work force.

If immigrants experienced a disadvantage in securing an occupation, one might expect that as they became familiar with American customs and language they would experience mobility similar to their American-born counterparts. A comparison of the occupational mobility of these two groups, however, reveals that the initial disadvantage experienced by immigrant workers continued throughout their careers.

As indicated in Chapter 4 (Table 4-1), rates of persistence of all workers improved in each succeeding decade of this study. Foreign-born workers left Warren at only a slightly greater rate than native-born Americans from 1870 through 1910. A minority of both immigrants and native-born Americans remained in Warren for more than a single decade; thus the data suggest little relationship between persistence and ethnicity. Table 5-2 reveals a much stronger relationship between one's birth and occupational mobility.

Although the numbers from which the percentages in Table 5-2 are derived remained small throughout the industrial era, the lack of mobility of foreign-born unskilled workers is dramatic. Native-born unskilled laborers from every census group experienced upward mobility in each decade. Of the forty-seven unskilled immigrants residing in Warren in 1870 only thirteen continued to live there one decade later. Two of these day laborers managed to obtain nonmanual positions by 1880. None of the others achieved even limited mobility into the semiskilled classification.

Mobility of the 1880 census group of unskilled laborers presents a more accurate pattern of the relationship between ethnicity and occupational opportunity. Seventy of the 115 unskilled workers joining

TABLE 5-2

Ethnic Differences in Intragenerational Occupational Mobility, 1870-1910:
Occupational Status Attained by Unskilled Workers

Year	Unskilled (%)		Semiskilled (%)		Skilled (%)		Nonmanual (%)		Number in Group	
	N.B.*	F.B.†	N.B.	F.B.	N.B.	F.B.	N.B.	F.B.	N.B.	F.B.
1870 Census Group										
1870	100	100	—	—	—	—	—	—	28	47
1880	25	85	25	—	25	—	25	15	4	13
1890	—	100	100	—	—	—	—	—	1	4
1900	—	100	100	—	—	—	—	—	1	2
1910	100	—	—	—	—	—	—	—	1	0
1880 Census Group										
1880	100	100	—	—	—	—	—	—	45	70
1890	32	79	16	4	32	—	20	17	25	24
1900	16	64	16	—	25	27	42	9	12	11
1910	—	60	—	20	25	20	75	—	4	5
1890 Census Group										
1890	100	100	—	—	—	—	—	—	22	53
1900	33	83	33	6	22	11	11	—	9	18
1910	25	70	—	10	25	10	50	10	4	10
1900 Census Group										
1900	100	100	—	—	—	—	—	—	153	229
1910	50	80	15	4	20	9	15	7	80	107

*NB indicates native-born Americans.   †FB indicates foreign-born.

the work force in 1880 were immigrants. One decade later only 34 percent of these men remained while 55 percent of the native-born Americans persisted. The rate of occupational mobility clearly demonstrates the disadvantages of foreign birth. Fully 79 percent of all immigrants remained unskilled by 1890 while only 32 percent of the native Americans achieved no mobility at all. Moreover, 52 percent of all United States-born menial laborers advanced at least two skill classifications as opposed to only 20 percent of the foreign-born laborers. In addition, none in the immigrant group managed to attain a skilled position during this decade. By 1900 immigrants from the 1880 census group improved upon this record, but only slightly. Nearly two-thirds of all foreign-born workers remained unskilled after twenty years in the community. Conversely, only 16 percent of the native-born Americans remained day laborers during the same period. Furthermore, 42 percent of all United States-born unskilled workers managed to attain the security of a white-collar position as compared with only 9 percent of the immigrant group. During the first decade of the twentieth century only five of the original seventy immigrant workers from the 1880 group still lived in Warren. Three of these men remained in the low-skill, low-pay classification while all American-born workers escaped this occupational group. The lack of occupational opportunity for 1880 immigrants is particularly striking, considering that these men arrived in Warren at the onset of industrialization. From 1880 through 1900 jobs remained plentiful and labor was constantly in demand. In the earlier analysis of all unskilled workers combined, the upward mobility of the 1880 group exceeded all other census groups. Occupational opportunity for workers in the 1880 census group occurred frequently for all but immigrants.

Occupational advancements by unskilled immigrants joining the work force in 1890 or 1900 present a similar pattern. Only 17 percent of the immigrants arriving in Warren in 1890 without skills could move even one step up the occupational ladder, and by 1900 none achieved white-collar status. In contrast, two-thirds of all native-born Americans starting work in the same low classification attained a better occupation, although only 11 percent of the group attained a nonmanual position, suggesting a shrinking of opportunities for all workers by 1900. Only a few unskilled workers joining the labor force in 1890 remained in Warren by 1910. Of this limited number, however, 70 percent of the immigrants still held unskilled occupations as compared with 25 percent of the American-born workers.

During the first decade of the twentieth century, as Warren's industrial growth stabilized, 229 immigrant workers and their families, mainly from Sweden and Italy, arrived in the borough. By 1910, 107 of these men still lived in the community. The disadvantages of foreign birth continued to exist, however, and 80 percent of all immigrants from the 1900 group remained concentrated in the lower skill classification. One-half of the native-born day laborers from this group failed to achieve upward mobility during the same (1900 to 1910) period.[4]

The impressive mobility of Warren's day laborers, noted in Chapter 4, did not extend to foreign-born workers who lacked skills. While a few immigrants achieved skilled or nonmanual positions, most found it impossible to move up even one small step into the ranks of the semiskilled. Stephan Thernstrom, in his study of unskilled workers in Newburyport, noted similar disadvantages for the unskilled immigrants in that New England city. Nearly three-fourths of the 1850 census group of unskilled immigrants in Newburyport failed to move up one skill classification by 1860. In addition, less than 20 percent of the 1860 and 1870 census groups experienced even limited mobility. Thernstrom concludes that immigrant workers in Newburyport also enjoyed less success than native-born men in climbing out of the ranks of the unskilled.[5]

Of course, not all immigrants arriving in Warren during the 1870-1910 period began their working careers as unskilled laborers. An impressively large number of immigrants arriving in Warren each decade possessed skills and initially entered the labor force in the three higher skill classifications (see Table 5-1). A significant number joined the labor force as semiskilled workers. Similarly, foreign-born workers were successful in obtaining work as skilled laborers in the late nineteenth century. A comparison of the mobility experienced by native-born and foreign-born semiskilled and skilled workers reveals that one's place of birth continued to influence his chances for success. The relationship between ethnicity and occupational mobility of semiskilled workers appears in Table 5-3.

TABLE 5-3

Ethnic Differences in Intragenerational Occupational Mobility, 1870-1910: Occupational Status Attained by Semiskilled Workers

Year	Unskilled (%) NB	FB	Semiskilled (%) NB	FB	Skilled (%) NB	FB	Nonmanual (%) NB	FB	Number in Group NB	FB
				1870 Census Group						
1870	—	—	100	100	—	—	—	—	47	20
1880	9	25	18	63	18	12	55	—	11	8
1890	9	16	45	16	9	—	36	66	11	6
1900	—	—	33	—	—	—	67	100	6	3
1910	—	—	—	—	—	100	—	—	—	1
				1880 Census Group						
1880	—	—	100	100	—	—	—	—	44	47
1890	11	7	39	50	22	29	28	14	18	14
1900	6	8	27	50	27	33	40	8	15	12
1910	—	—	—	57	83	28	17	14	6	7
				1890 Census Group						
1890	—	—	100	100	—	—	—	—	32	49
1900	11	10	55	62	11	5	22	23	18	21
1910	—	18	36	36	18	9	45	36	11	11
				1900 Census Group						
1900	—	—	100	100	—	—	—	—	107	40
1910	4	18	83	56	3	13	9	12	55	16

All workers initially joining the labor force as semiskilled enjoyed greater mobility than unskilled laborers. Consequently, immigrants who found it possible to secure semiskilled occupations enjoyed better prospects for mobility than their unskilled counterparts. However, when compared with native-born semiskilled workers the disadvantage of foreign birth again becomes clear.

Semiskilled workers constituted the smallest portion of the labor force throughout the 1870-1910 period. Therefore, small shifts in the occupations of these workers result in a more erratic occupational pattern. However, with few exceptions, the relationship between one's birth and economic advancement remained consistent. Nearly three-fourths of the semiskilled workers residing in Warren in 1870 left the community by 1880. Of the few who remained, 73 percent of those born in America advanced to a higher skill classification, whereas only 12 percent of the immigrant group attained skilled positions and none were able to achieve white-collar work. Interestingly, during the next decade native Americans and immigrants from this census group reversed positions. United States-born workers previously experiencing mobility into skilled and nonmanual positions failed to maintain these newly acquired positions while two-thirds of the remaining foreign-born workers joined the white-collar group. Semiskilled laborers from the 1870 census group continued to leave the community and by 1900 the small number remaining renders any further conclusions meaningless.

The succeeding three census groups—1880, 1890, and 1900—of foreign-born semiskilled workers fared no better than those from 1870. Even length of residence failed to improve one's chances for occupational mobility. Well over one-half of all foreign-born semiskilled workers from these three groups remained in that classification or fell to unskilled throughout the entire length of their work careers in Warren. Conversely, native-born workers from each of these groups frequently improved their positions, particularly after one decade or more in the community. Fully one-half of the 1880 census group born in America advanced at least one position by 1890. One decade later 67 percent of the workers from this group had experienced some mobility. In addition, 40 percent were able to bridge the gap into the ranks of the nonmanual workers. By 1910 only six of the original American-born workers from the 1880 census group still resided in the community, but none of them remained in the ranks of the semiskilled.

Both American-born and foreign-born semiskilled workers from the 1890 and 1900 groups experienced less mobility than either of the two previous census groups. Only 33 percent of the 1890 group of native-born semiskilled laborers and 28 percent of the immigrants moved up the occupational ladder. During the succeeding decade nearly two out of every three native-born workers remaining from the 1890 group left that classification for a better job, with 45 percent attaining nonmanual occupations. In addition, the disadvantage of foreign-birth decreased as nearly one-half of the immigrants remaining from the 1890 group became either skilled or nonmanual workers. Finally, foreign-born semiskilled laborers joining the labor force in 1900 apparently suffered no disadvantages as their mobility exceeded that of the native-born workers. However, the increased disparity in rates of persistence distorts the pattern. Six of every ten American-born semiskilled workers joining the labor force in 1900 continued to live in Warren at the close of the decade, but only four of every ten immigrant workers persisted a full decade. If the least successful most frequently left the community, it seems reasonable to conclude that the higher mobility of immigrants in the 1900 group displayed in Table 5-3 is somewhat misleading. Nevertheless, the negative relationship between occupational mobility and foreign birth largely disappeared by 1910. Both immigrants and native-born semiskilled workers from the 1900 group experienced limited mobility. The shrinkage of economic opportunity rather than ethnicity became the most significant factor affecting mobility of semiskilled workers in the period 1900-1910.

As previously noted, immigrants arriving in Warren, particularly between 1870 and 1890, more often began work in the skilled classification than in any other group. Immigrants beginning work in this classification held greater occupational security, and one might reasonably expect a less negative relationship between one's birth and occupational mobility. Table 5-4 illustrates that while native-born skilled workers continued to enjoy greater upward mobility than foreign-born craftsmen, the degree of inequality is not as striking as that experienced by the unskilled and semiskilled immigrants. Conversely, skilled immigrants, particularly from the 1870 and 1880 census groups, fell from that classification with greater frequency than their native-born counterparts.

In 1870 Warren's 212 skilled workers constituted slightly over one-third of the total labor force. Within one decade only one-fourth of these craftsmen—divided nearly equally between foreign-born and native-born—continued to reside in Warren. Upward mobility of both foreign-born and native-born skilled workers from this group yields interesting but inconclusive evidence regarding the relationship be-

TABLE 5-4

Ethnic Differences in Intragenerational Occupational Mobility, 1870-1910:
Occupational Status Attained by Skilled Workers

Year	Unskilled (%)		Semiskilled (%)		Skilled (%)		Nonmanual (%)		Number in Group	
	NB	FB	NB	FB	NB	FB	NB	FB	NB	FB
				1870 Census Group						
1870	—	—	—	—	100	100	—	—	122	93
1880	7	4	3	7	73	59	17	29	29	27
1890	—	—	11	12	50	59	39	29	18	17
1900	—	—	8	27	67	36	25	36	12	11
1910	—	—	—	29	62	57	38	14	8	7
				1880 Census Group						
1880	—	—	—	—	100	100	—	—	111	94
1890	4	6	4	3	56	72	35	19	43	36
1900	—	10	—	16	58	63	42	10	24	19
1910	—	12	—	—	50	50	50	38	10	8
				1890 Census Group						
1890	—	—	—	—	100	100	—	—	83	108
1900	3	2	—	6	74	79	23	13	34	48
1910	—	—	—	—	68	71	32	29	14	28
				1900 Census Group						
1900	—	—	—	—	100	100	—	—	268	154
1910	4	6	1	4	81	72	14	18	134	71

tween ethnic background and occupational opportunity. During the decade spanning the onset of industrialization in Warren (1870-1880) 29 percent of the foreign-born workers from this group managed to attain a middle-class occupation. At the same time only 17 percent of the native-born workers moved into a nonmanual position. During the next decade the percentage of immigrant skilled workers from the 1870 group attaining nonmanual occupations remained constant at 29 percent, while the proportion of native sons achieving white-collar work rose to 39 percent. This erratic pattern continued through the next two decades, as a larger percentage of foreign-born workers attained white-collar positions in 1900 and American-born craftsmen achieved a greater percentage of nonmanual positions in 1910. At least for the 1870 group of skilled laborers, the relationship between one's place of birth and occupational mobility remains unclear.

A total of 205 skilled workers joined the Warren work force during the decade prior to 1880. The 104 foreign-born workers among this group labored under greater handicaps than the skilled immigrants from the 1870 group. The members of the 1880 census group had little chance to become established in the community before the industrial boom began. Consequently, the relationship between one's place of birth and occupational mobility appears much stronger than with the 1870 group. By 1890, 35 percent of the remaining American-born skilled workers from the 1880 group had attained some type of non-manual position. At the same time only 19 percent of the remaining immigrants joined the ranks of the white-collar worker. During the succeeding decade—1890-1900—almost one-half of all the skilled workers from the 1880 census group left Warren, yet the gap between immigrants and native sons continued to widen. Only one-tenth of the immigrants from this group held nonmanual positions by 1900 while two-fifths of the native-born laborers no longer worked with their hands. The disadvantages of foreign birth continued to exist through the first decade of the twentieth century although the gap narrowed considerably. By this time the few remaining foreign-born workers from the 1880 group were older and more securely settled. Fully 38 percent of them managed to achieve a middle-class occupation by 1910 while one-half of the native sons from 1880 attained a similar position. The skilled workers first listed in the 1880 census arrived in Warren at a most fortuitous time. Some industrial expansion occurred in every succeeding decade through 1910. The occupational mobility experienced by native-born skilled workers from this group provides evidence of considerable economic opportunity. Yet only a few foreign-born skilled workers could bridge the gap into the nonmanual work world.

Foreign-born skilled workers joining the labor force in 1890 fared no better than the 1880 group, although native-born Americans also experienced limited mobility. By 1900 only 23 percent of the native sons and 13 percent of the foreign-born skilled workers from 1890 had attained nonmanual occupations. One decade later 32 percent of the remaining native-born skilled workers and 29 percent of the immigrants from this group still in Warren held white-collar occupations. Native-born workers apparently still held some advantage in 1900, but by 1910 the distinction between skilled workers born in America and those born in Europe ceased to exist. Mobility of skilled workers joining Warren's labor force in 1900 also reflects this shrinkage of opportunity for all workers but increasing equality of opportunity for foreign-born workers. While nearly one-half of all the men in this group remained in the community for the full decade, only 16 percent enjoyed mobility into the nonmanual classification. This decline of opportunities in the nonmanual occupations occurred because of stabilization of the economy rather than from the change in ethnic composition of the skilled labor force in Warren. Only in this decade—1900-1910—did the number of native-born craftsmen entering the labor force exceed the number of foreign-born skilled workers. Immigrants, however, experienced a slightly higher rate of upward mobility than skilled workers from the 1900 group born in America. For skilled craftsmen joining the labor force at the turn of the century, the relationship between ethnicity and occupational mobility was negligible.

Rates of downward mobility (Table 5-4) for skilled workers also reflect the relationship between one's place of birth and occupational security. The percentage of immigrant skilled workers moving down the occupational ladder exceeded the downward percentage of native-born Americans in every decade of this study. Immigrants from the 1870 and 1880 census groups experienced greater downward mobility than the later arrivals to the community. During the last two decades of this study more than one-fourth of the remaining skilled immigrants from the 1870 census group slipped to semiskilled occupations. In addition, 26 percent of the 1880 group of immigrant craftsmen fell from the skilled classification by 1900. No more than 11 percent of the native-born skilled workers ever experienced loss of occupational status. Furthermore, both the 1890 and 1900 skilled immigrants experienced some downward mobility but the disparity between native sons and foreign-born craftsmen largely disappeared.

The comparison of the career patterns of both native-born American workers and foreign-born laborers suggests the following conclusions:

1. Immigrants arriving in the community most often joined the labor force as manual laborers. However, while immigrants performed most of the unskilled work in Warren, a large number of foreign-born workers secured skilled work throughout the 1870-1910 period.

2. American-born workers most often joined the labor force as white-collar workers while only a minority of the foreign-born ever found employment in nonmanual positions.

3. The initial economic opportunity of immigrants most closely reflected the overall economic conditions of the community. During the period of greatest economic expansion in Warren—1880-1890— immigrants had little difficulty securing work in the higher skill classifications. However, when the economic growth of the community declined—around 1900—a much larger percentage of immigrants

was forced to accept unskilled occupations.

4. Unskilled immigrants were almost totally immobile throughout their careers in Warren while a majority of native-born Americans beginning work in the lowest classification advanced to higher positions in each succeeding decade. The prospect of an immigrant beginning work as an unskilled worker and rising to a nonmanual position was remote.

5. Semiskilled and skilled immigrants fared better than unskilled foreign-born workers but continued to experience limited mobility when compared with native sons beginning their careers from the same groups. The remarkable upward mobility of manual laborers discussed in Chapter 4 occurred largely within the ranks of American-born.

6. During the period of economic expansion in Warren, occupational mobility existed mainly for the native sons. However, when the expansion declined, primarily during the last decade of this study, the gap between native-born Americans and immigrants decreased. Thus the advantages of economic growth in Warren applied mainly, but not exclusively, to those workers born on American soil.

If immigrants experienced serious disadvantages in the process of mobility, what became of their sons born in America? Did the fact of foreign-born parents constitute a similar handicap for first-generation Americans in Warren? The compilers of Warren's city directories failed to include offspring in their compilations; therefore, an examination of career patterns of all immigrants' sons cannot be attempted. Fortunately, both the 1870 and 1880 manuscript censuses for Warren not only listed all immigrants' children but included their place of birth as well. A systematic analysis of the mobility patterns of the 1880 group (the small size of the 1870 group precludes any valid observations) should at least suggest the type of relationship between foreign-born parentage and occupational mobility.

American-born manual laborers of foreign-born parents demonstrated only a slightly greater propensity to remain in Warren than immigrants from the same era. Only one-third of the immigrants joining the manual laboring force in 1880 continued to live in Warren in 1890. During the same period of time 41 percent of all native-born sons of immigrants holding manual occupations remained in Warren. Throughout each succeeding decade persistence rates for each group varied somewhat but the relationship between immigrants and sons of immigrants, with some exceptions, remained similar. Occupational mobility, however, varied greatly. Although the number of immigrants' sons is smaller in all cases, the impressive upward mobility they experienced indicates that they enjoyed greater opportunity than did immigrants. Within two decades none of the sons of immigrants still residing in the community who began their careers as day laborers continued in this low-skill, low-pay classification. Furthermore, although only three men remained from this group by 1910, all of them had attained a white-collar occupation. In contrast to this dramatic mobility, nearly two-thirds of the immigrants from this group continued to work at unskilled jobs in 1900 and 60 percent remained day laborers in 1910.

TABLE 5-5

Occupational Mobility of 1880 Immigrants and Sons of Immigrants

	Unskilled (%)		Semiskilled (%)		Skilled (%)		Nonmanual (%)		Original Number in Group	
Year	FB*	NBFP†	FB	NBFP	FB	NBFP	FB	NBFP	FB	NBFP
				Unskilled Workers						
1880	100	100	—	—	—	—	—	—	70	18
1890	79	50	4	12	—	12	17	25	24	8
1900	64	—	—	—	27	60	9	40	11	5
1910	60	—	20	—	20	—	—	100	5	3
				Semiskilled Workers						
1880	—	—	100	100	—	—	—	—	47	17
1890	7	—	50	33	29	17	14	50	14	6
1900	8	—	50	—	33	50	8	50	12	2
1910	—	—	57	—	28	50	14	50	7	2
				Skilled Workers						
1880	—	—	—	—	100	100	—	—	94	34
1890	6	—	3	—	72	50	19	50	36	14
1900	10	—	16	—	63	62	10	38	19	8
1910	12	—	—	—	50	67	38	33	8	3

*FB indicates foreign-born †NBFP indicates native-born with foreign-born parents.

Sons of immigrants beginning work as semiskilled or skilled workers enjoyed greater upward mobility than immigrants starting work in the same classifications. By 1890 two-thirds of the immigrants' sons still living in Warren left the semiskilled classification for a higher occupation group. In addition, one-half of the group managed to secure nonmanual positions, whereas only 43 percent of the immigrants starting work as semiskilled workers moved up during the same decade. More significantly, only 14 percent of the immigrant group achieved mobility into the white-collar world. During the next decade most of the immigrants' sons left the community (only two remained), rendering further comparison of the semiskilled group meaningless.

Native-born American sons of immigrants beginning work in 1880 as skilled workers also exhibited greater upward mobility than immigrants from this group. Fully 50 percent of them bridged the gap into the white-collar world within one decade, compared with only 19 percent of their foreign-born counterparts. By the end of the century the percentage of immigrants' sons starting as skilled workers but moving into the nonmanual classification fell to 38 percent. However, during the same decade, the proportion of immigrant skilled workers attaining nonmanual positions fell to 10 percent. Furthermore, none of the sons of immigrants ever experienced any downward mobility, while 9 percent of the immigrants fell from the skilled labor group in 1890, 26 percent fell in 1900, and 12 percent worked at unskilled occupations in 1910.

Immigrants experienced limited mobility throughout Warren's period of industrial expansion. Their sons, however (at least those in the 1880 group), found considerable opportunity for occupational mobility. Immigrants starting work as unskilled laborers generally remained unskilled throughout their lives. The sons of immigrants quickly left the unskilled classification for better paying and more secure occupations. Furthermore, foreign-born manual workers rarely attained middle-class nonmanual occupations, whereas the sons of immigrants frequently enjoyed this type of occupational success. In fact, little distinction exists between the mobility rates of all native-born manual workers and the mobility of American-born sons of immigrants. In late nineteenth-century Warren both groups frequently achieved impressive success.[6]

Of course, not all immigrant groups experienced the same degree of opportunity in nineteenth-century Warren. But when one divides each ethnic group into specific skill classifications, the numbers remaining after outward migration become too small to yield generalizations. In at least a few aspects, however, we may ascertain the relationship between specific nativity and occupational opportunity. Analysis of the initial occupations attained by specific ethnic groups (Table 5-6) indicates that certain groups performed primarily skilled and nonmanual work while others were relegated to the less desirable unskilled tasks.

Throughout the last three decades of the nineteenth century, Germans migrating to Warren enjoyed greater possibilities of success

TABLE 5-6

Initial Occupation of All Workers by Nativity

Birthplace	1870*				1880			
	Unsk.	Semisk.	Sk.	Nonman.	Unsk.	Semisk.	Sk.	Nonman.
U.S.	28	47	122	200	45	44	111	270
Canada	1	2	4	1	4	6	6	2
England	2	—	14	2	5	12	14	—
Ireland	24	2	15	5	29	4	7	2
Germany	4	4	23	19	3	7	30	11
Sweden	1	—	2	—	5	6	8	5
Denmark	3	3	7	2	6	3	13	2
France	11	7	20	18	11	9	12	8
Italy	—	—	—	—	—	—	—	—
Other	1	2	8	5	7	—	4	—
Total	75	67	215	252	115	91	205	300

*The 1870-group held these occupations at the initiation of this study; thus, the indicated occupation may not have been the first task performed by members of this group.

than any other group of foreign-born workers. Four of every five German-born workers attained either skilled or nonmanual occupations upon first joining the Warren labor force. The rapid industrialization of Warren created a demand for trained workers, particularly in machine and tool making, and the townsfolk willingly accommodated workers from Germany. As early as 1852 the growth of the German-born population of Warren warranted the building of a German-Methodist church, and by 1870 the press regularly reported on the activities of two German-American lodges.[7] A large number of German children attended school, reflecting the financial security of the German-born population—they could afford to pay for books and a modest tuition—as well as the favored position of German immigrants in the community. Beginning in 1874, following a petition by German citizens, the school board hired a full-time teacher to instruct the school's 130 German students in the language of their parents.[8] No other ethnic group in the town's history received such favored treatment.

The French and British also found considerable occupational opportunity in nineteenth-century Warren. Ancestors of both groups were among the early settlers of the community. "It seems quite appropriate that natives of France," wrote the town's local historian in 1887, "should at last become occupants and owners, in part at least, of a region which was first explored and honored by Frenchmen. They are good and honored citizens and when Americanized compare favorably with those who came before them."[9] Nearly 68 percent of the French residents in Warren in 1870 held jobs in the two higher skill groups. One-half of those joining the labor force during the next decade also succeeded in attaining either skilled or nonmanual occupations. The French residents during these two decades demonstrated a greater rate of persistence than Warren's German population, with nearly 40 percent of the 1870 group of French residents continuing to live in the community in 1880 and one-half of the 1880 group remaining in 1890. The German migrants, in spite of their initial occupational success, left Warren at a more rapid rate. Only 30 percent of the 1870 group of German workers still lived in Warren by 1880, and less than one-fourth of the 1880 group remained as long as one full decade.[10] Persistence rates of the 1890 and 1900 German residents increased significantly but never exceeded that of Warren's French residents.

Warren's British residents apparently possessed some skills and had little difficulty in securing craft work. Three of every four English workers in preindustrial Warren held skilled occupations. One decade later 45 percent of the newly arrived English workers secured skilled positions and only 16 percent had to accept unskilled work. During the first full decade, coinciding with Warren's industrialization, the English immigrant fared even better. Fully 45 percent attained nonmanual occupations upon their initial entry into Warren's labor force, and another one-fourth acquired skilled positions.

Of the major immigrant groups through 1890, only the Irish reflect any negative relationship between initial occupation and place of birth. Over one-half of the Irish residing in Warren in 1870 worked at low paying and often temporary unskilled labor. This group held one-third of all the unskilled occupations while constituting only 8 percent of the total population. Even the Irish, however, enjoyed some economic opportunity—nearly one-third of the men in the 1870 group worked at skilled occupations and a few held white-collar positions. But during the decade between 1870 and 1880 opportunity for the Irish worker decreased (industrial growth had just begun) as only 30 percent of the newly arrived adult males from Ireland could attain work above the unskilled classification. Warren's economy continued to grow through 1890, however, and the Irish, although still performing a large share of the unskilled labor, gained a significant number of skilled and nonmanual occupations. Sixty-five Irish workers joined the labor force during Warren's major decade of expansion. Almost one-half of them managed to find employment in either the skilled or nonmanual occupations, attesting to the relationship between an expanding economy and occupational opportunity.

Two other ethnic groups—the Swedes and the Italians—although later arrivals to the community, played an important role in the economic development of the borough. Swedish immigrants migrated to several villages around Warren as early as 1850 and, although only a few of the Scandinavian families actually lived within the borough's boundaries in 1870, they were apparently considered an asset to the community. As early as 1880 the *Warren Mail* proclaimed:

> The Swedish inhabitants [of the county] have recently built a fine church. It is built in modern style and is a standing monument to the industry and thrift of this intelligent, economical and persevering class of the adopted citizens of our county. The disinterested looker on must . . . be led to the conclusion that the settling of this people in our midst was to our country a godsend. In short, they bid fair at no distant day to become a power for good in our county.[11]

The first significant number of Swedish immigrant families arrived in the borough during the height of the town's industrial growth. The success of the 1890 group of Swedes in attaining initial higher level occupations indicates the hospitable attitude toward the foreign-born. Over one-quarter of this most recent group of immigrants to Warren attained white-collar jobs upon joining the labor force. In addition, one-third of the 1890 group of Scandinavian workers attained skilled occupations upon initial entry into Warren's work force.

By the mid-1890s, as the flow of immigration from southern Europe began to affect Warren, the town's accommodating attitude toward the foreign-born began to change. The Chicago Pullman Strike of July 1894 created considerable controversy and some anti-immigrant feelings within the community. In a series of sermons the pastor of the Presbyterian church condemned the strike and concluded "it had led some capitalists to import foreign laborers from the lowest classes and thus . . . force the American workmen to accept a lower wage."[12]

One month later, in August 1894, Warren experienced its own labor difficulties when the molders employed by the Struthers Iron Works refused to accept a 20 percent cut in wages and struck.[13] The management quickly imported a number of Irish workers from Buffalo, New York, to replace the striking workers. Violence occurred and several men were injured as townsmen retaliated by refusing to permit the nonunion employees to enter the Iron Works. Both local newspapers condemned the violence but agreed that the company was largely at fault for hiring the "Irish scabs" into the community.[14] The strike continued for several weeks and anti-immigrant sentiment began to crystallize. Letters to the editor reflecting this attitude appeared regularly throughout the month. Finally, on 8 August, the editors of the *Warren Mail* reversed their previously hospitable attitude toward immigrants. A front-page editorial entitled "Restrict Immigration" proclaimed:

> The public sentiment in favor of a more rigorous restriction on immigration is gaining strength constantly in all parts of the country. Keep out the agitators, keep out mob leaders, keep out the idle, the vicious, the restless, the turbulent, the disorderly. America has long been the wash-pot of Europe. Restrict immigration. That is the urgent demand of truly patriotic Americans in this age and generation.[15]

The initial occupations attained by immigrants arriving in Warren after 1895 (Table 5-6) reflect both the decline in economic expansion and the new attitude toward the foreign-born. Forty-four percent of all immigrants joining the Warren labor force in 1900 accepted jobs as unskilled laborers. In addition, the decline in occupational opportunity affected nearly every ethnic group, including those who previously had enjoyed initial advantages in the community. Almost one-half of the newly arrived German and French groups began working in the lowest two skill groups in 1900. The English and the Irish fared no better, with 58 percent of each group beginning work as unskilled or semiskilled laborers. However, the greatest burden fell upon the two most recent ethnic additions to the community—the Swedes and the Italians. Over one-half of the Swedes joining the work force in 1900 had to accept work as unskilled laborers, compared to 20 percent who did so in 1890. In addition, only 18 percent of all foreign-born workers secured positions as white-collar workers in 1900, while 51 percent of the native-born Americans began their careers in middle-class occupations.[16]

All groups of foreign-born workers arriving in Warren at the turn of the century experienced greater disadvantages than their earlier counterparts, with the Italians arousing the greatest antagonisms. In a scathing article entitled "No Dago's Wanted," the editors of the *Weekly Democrat* criticized a local leather company for advertising for fifteen Italian families to come to Warren for work: "Just think of it, fifteen Italian families for Warren. Does anyone believe that Warren wants those families here? If they do they had better get an expression from a few people as I have done. . . . We can tell the Penn Leather Company that we don't want any dago's in Warren and if that is the class of people they contemplate bringing here we don't care for the industry."[17] Anti-Italian articles—disparaging Italians' "shiftless ways" or their proclivity to violence—continued in the press with marked frequency through the first decade of the twentieth century. Twenty-seven Italian-born males joined the Warren labor force in 1900; none became white-collar workers and only three secured occupations as skilled laborers. One decade later nearly one-half of these men still lived in the community, but only one Italian worker had moved up even one step on the occupational ladder.

For the immigrants who entered Warren during the height of industrialization, the community provided impressive economic opportunity in the skilled trades. Only the Irish had difficulty in securing occupations above the level of the unskilled. Conversely, with the exception of the economically dynamic 1880s, middle-class non-manual occupations were almost exclusively reserved for the native-born American worker. Immigrants also failed to share in the impressive occupational mobility enjoyed by the native-born manual laborers. For most immigrants remaining in the community, the initial occupation they secured upon arrival became their life's work. In addition, immigrants arriving in Warren after 1890 experienced particular difficulties. The town's rapid economic expansion declined around the turn of the century. Furthermore, anti-immigrant attitudes created a less than hospitable environment for newly arrived ethnic groups. Economic opportunity declined for all groups but particularly affected the newest ethnic groups in the community, the Swedes and the Italians.

The reasons for the striking disparity in occupational opportunity between immigrants and native sons remain unclear. Immigrants arriving in Warren possessing skills, particularly during the period of economic growth from 1875 to 1890, apparently had little difficulty securing a good position in the local occupational structure. They were then frozen in their initial occupation. Native sons from the same census groups and occupational classifications experienced impressive upward mobility, indicating the presence of new job openings.

At first glance one might suggest that the differing persistence rates between immigrants and native-born Americans operated selectively to produce higher rates of occupational mobility for the native-born. If immigrants were geographically less mobile than native sons, a larger proportion of the unsuccessful immigrants remaining in the community would tend to produce lower occupational mobility rates for the foreign-born. This, however, was not the case in nineteenth-century Warren. Persistence of native sons slightly exceeded that of immigrants in every decade from 1870 through 1910 (see Table 4-1). Thus the greater outmigration of immigrants would tend to bias the occupational mobility of those who remained upward since the most successful were the most likely to remain.

Nativist attitudes in the community, particularly after 1890, no doubt prevented some immigrant workers from achieving upward occupational mobility. Much of the anti-immigrant feeling in Warren was directed against the Irish and Italians. Workers from these two groups frequently began their careers in the lowest two occupational groups and rarely advanced into the ranks of the skilled or white-collar workers. German, French, Danish, and English immigrants seem to have been accepted in the community and often succeeded in securing higher level jobs upon their arrival. These latter groups, however, remained in their initial occupation almost as often as their counterparts from Ireland, Sweden, and Italy.

Thus although discrimination may have been an important factor in limiting the occupational mobility of immigrants, other conditions, such as cultural differences between immigrant and native-born workers, may have operated to limit the mobility of immigrants.[18] Moreover, the impressive success of immigrants' sons provides suggestive, although limited, evidence supporting this hypothesis. Sons of immigrants, born in America, may have become "Americanized" enough to overcome the cultural difficulties experienced by their fathers.[19]

Immigrant workers in Warren, however, clearly did not develop any strong sense of class solidarity. The high rate of outward migration, particularly among the unskilled, prevented a continuity of residence within the community. The transient members of this group obviously could not act with unity to correct common grievances.[20] In addition, unemployed laborers—those most likely to express discontent—were treated severely in nineteenth-century Warren. Local law decreed that vagrants be arrested, forced to work on a chain gang for two days, and then evicted from the community.[21] Furthermore, local citizens occasionally took matters into their own hands; the *Warren Ledger* reported, "Fifteen tramps were confined in the calaboose for refusing to work. A mob of unknown citizens overpowered the guard, took the tramps out and administered thirty-nine lashes, well laid on each and told them to 'git.' They 'got' and not a tramp is seen in town today and no more is expected this season."[22]

The impressive success experienced by immigrants in attaining skilled work upon arriving in the community also hindered the development of a proletarian conscience. Warren's highly diversified economy and ethnic composition created varying opportunities for workers in different occupations and at several skill levels. A common base of interests did not exist. Labor organization for the purpose of increasing wages and improving working conditions aroused no more than temporary interest and never involved more than one craft. Even craft unionism had a difficult time surviving in a community of small shops and factories. Only one trade union—the Cigarmakers' Union—had a continuous existence; and it was not listed in the directories until 1890.[23] Moreover, although immigrants experienced limited mobility, some unskilled workers did advance up the occupational ladder. Workmen tended to generalize from the familiar experiences within their own community. For most manual laborers of Warren, frequent occupational mobility gave credence to their belief in America as a land of opportunity.[24] The social structure and ideology of small communities, as labor historian Herbert Gutman has suggested, operated to reduce the labor-management antagonisms which existed in the large urban centers. This too would tend to hinder the development of a proletarian conscience. Citing several examples, Gutman notes:

> The social structure in these small towns and the ideology of many of their residents, who were neither workers nor employers, shaped the behavior of employers who reached outside local environments to win industrial disputes. . . . Workers [in small industrial towns] made up a large proportion of the electorate and often participated actively in local politics, they influenced local and regional affairs more than wage earners in the larger cities. . . . In other instances, town officials and other officeholders who were not wage earners sympathized with the problems and difficulties of local workers or displayed an unusual degree of objectivity during local industrial disputes.
>
> Many local newspapers criticized the industrial entrepreneur, and editorials defended *local* workers and demanded redress for their grievances.[25]

As the Struthers Iron Works strike of 1894 illustrates, these factors also operated to a degree in Warren.

The Chamber of Commerce, however, best illustrated the attitude of manual workers in Warren when it declared:

> Labor is reasonably well paid and therefore is contented and prosperous. Laboring men are industrious, frugal and intelligent. They realize that regular employment at fair wages affords the greatest measure of prosperity and hence, *Warren is absolutely free from labor disputes either as to wages, conditions of employment or other surroundings* which in other localities interfere with the business of the employer and the wage earning of the employee.[26]

6 Property Mobility

Occupation is not the sole determinant of social mobility in a community. The accumulation of property or money also constitutes a measurement of one's social standing. Movement from the property-less to the property-holding class frequently enhances one's position in society. Similarly, individuals who accumulate wealth, both real and personal, gain standing within the community. The preceding assessment of the career patterns of manual workers in Warren from 1870 to 1910 revealed that native-born Americans enjoyed considerable occupational mobility. Foreign-born manual workers frequently succeeded in securing higher level occupations but rarely moved very far up the occupational ladder. The following analysis examines property mobility to determine if it followed a similar pattern.

Home ownership in Warren grew rapidly between 1870 and 1910. Before industrialization 365 homes existed in the community. By 1910, the number of homes grew more than sevenfold, to 2,670, while the population quadrupled.[1] In addition, the assessed valuation of all real estate in the borough increased from $199,425 in 1870 to more than $4,000,000 in 1910.[2] But to what extent did manual workers share in this increase in property? An examination of the property holdings of each classification of workers during the census years from 1870 to 1910 reveals a strikingly consistent pattern. In 1870, before the industrialization of the community, 79 percent of Warren's unskilled workers were landless. During each succeeding decade the proportion of unskilled laborers without property varied no more than 4 percent. In 1880, 75 percent of all unskilled workers living in Warren owned no property and slightly more than four-fifths remained propertyless from 1890 through 1900.[3]

Semiskilled and skilled workers improved upon this record, but only slightly. At no time did even one-half of these two groups own any property. In 1870, 42 percent of the town's sixty-seven semiskilled workers owned at least a parcel of land. Ten years later only 20 percent of all semiskilled workers residing in the borough claimed ownership of any property. By 1890 property ownership among the semiskilled had increased to 30 percent; it reached a maximum of 41 percent in 1900. Similarly, 41 percent of all skilled workers residing in Warren owned property in both 1870 and 1900. During the intervening decades—1880 and 1890—the proportion of skilled property owners fell to 26 percent and 36 percent respectively.[4]

Nonmanual workers consistently controlled most of the property in the community. Prior to the industrialization of the borough nearly six of every ten white-collar workers living in Warren owned their own homes. Ten years later the proportion of home ownership slipped to just under one-half.[5] Housing construction lagged behind the rapid growth of the community and the *Warren Ledger* called for construction of tenant housing to meet the increased demand.[6] By 1890, 59 percent of the white-collar workers owned property, increasing to 62 percent at the beginning of the twentieth century. In addition, an average of one-third of all white-collar workers owned more than one home throughout the 1870-1900 period.[7]

A worker's place of birth also contributed significantly toward his chances of home ownership in late nineteenth-century Warren. Table 6-1 displays the relationship between ownership of real property and one's origin.

Analysis of all property holders in Warren by ethnicity reveals a strikingly uniform pattern. From 1870 through 1900 less than one-half of all the adult workers living in Warren each decade owned property. Furthermore, native-born Americans and immigrants from France and Germany maintained an advantage over other ethnic groups throughout the 1870-1900 period. Nearly 400 native-born adult males lived in Warren in 1870; over one-half of these men (56 percent) owned no property; of the 44 percent who did, nearly one-fourth owned two or more dwellings. In comparison, a greater percentage of immigrant workers from both France and Germany owned property in 1870. Only 29 percent of all French-born workers were propertyless in 1870 while 37 percent owned a single dwelling and an impressive 34 percent owned several homes. Home ownership by German-born workers in 1870 closely paralleled the pattern of native-born adult males. Forty-six percent of all Germans residing in Warren in 1870 reported home ownership and one-fifth held deeds to more than one home.

Three other significant ethnic groups lived in Warren in 1870—the Danes, the English, and the Irish. Of these three groups only the Danes approached the property-holding pattern of the French, Germans, or native-born Americans. Four of every ten Danish-born workers

TABLE 6-1

Percentage of Ethnic Group Holding Property, 1870-1900

Property Holdings	USA	England	Ireland	Germany	Sweden	Denmark	France	Italy
				1870 Group				
No property	56	77	74	54	100	60	29	—
Single ownership	20	18	17	26	—	27	37	—
Multiple ownership	24	5	9	20	—	13	34	—
				1880 Group				
No property	69	72	70	60	100	77	37	—
Single ownership	13	21	26	22	—	13	32	—
Multiple ownership	18	7	4	18	—	10	31	—
				1890 Group				
No property	48	65	74	48	82	46	44	—
Single ownership	28	11	23	39	12	37	31	—
Multiple ownership	24	24	3	13	6	17	25	—
				1900 Group				
No property	53	57	73	51	67	58	40	82
Single ownership	28	33	22	33	28	33	33	18
Multiple ownership	19	10	5	16	5	9	27	—

owned property in 1870 as did approximately one-fourth of the English and Irish immigrants. Few members of the three groups owned more than one home in 1870.

During the ten years between 1870 and 1880, the oil boom occurred and large numbers of single men flocked into Warren. Moreover, construction workers built oil rigs rather than homes; consequently, housing production lagged behind the population increase in 1880. With the exception of the French immigrants, whose rate of persistence in 1870 exceeded all other groups, approximately 70 percent of all adult males owned no property in 1880. The percentage of residents owning several homes also decreased in 1880, although the distribution of multiple home owners among ethnic groups remained similar to 1870. Nearly one-third of the sixty-two French-born workers residing in Warren in 1880 held deeds to several parcels of property, while 18 percent of a similar number of German immigrants reported multiple ownership. In addition, 18 percent of the 553 native-born workers residing in Warren owned two or more dwellings in 1880.

By 1890 the rapid pace of housing construction (325 homes were erected during the decade) enabled a larger proportion of residents to purchase homes, but the supply continued to fall short of the demand. As the editor of the *Warren Ledger* reported, "There is not a vacant house in the city and the demand increases every day. Rents have advanced a trifle this spring and are as high now as they should be."[8] Slightly more than one-half of all adult workers in Warren in 1890 owned their own homes. Moreover, only the Irish failed to increase their proportion of home ownership during the decade from 1880 through 1890. A total of 52 percent of all native-born workers owned their own homes and nearly one-half of that group owned at least two residences. Furthermore, a similar proportion, 44 to 48 percent, of Danish-, French-, and German-born residents enjoyed the security of home ownership in 1890. Irish-born workers, however, and Swedish immigrants—the most recent ethnic group in the community— owned the fewest homes. Only one-fourth of the eighty-seven Irish laborers residing in Warren were able to attain home ownership in 1890, and only three owned more than a single dwelling. Residents born in Sweden fared even worse, as only 18 percent had property holdings in 1890.

Between 1890 and 1900 Warren experienced its greatest population growth as the size of the community increased by 85 percent. Housing construction continued as a major activity in the community with nearly 800 homes erected in the borough during the decade. However, the percentage of adults owning their own homes in 1900 declined somewhat from 1890. Less than one-half, 48 percent of all the adult workers in Warren, owned property in 1900.[9] The distribution of home ownership among the various major ethnic groups remained essentially the same as in earlier decades. French immigrants continued to enjoy the greatest proportion of home ownership. Three-fifths of the French-born workers living in Warren in 1900 owned at least one dwelling and 27 percent held deeds to more than one. As in the previous decade, home ownership by German- and American-born workers remained nearly parallel. Nearly one-half of each group enjoyed the security of home ownership at the turn of the century. Similarly, 16 percent of the German-born laborers and 19 percent of the native-born workers owned more than one home.

Both the English and the Swedes improved upon their previous record of home ownership. By 1900, 43 percent of Warren's English-born residents and one-third of the Swedes joined the propertied class. The Irish and the Danes, in contrast, failed to increase in home ownership during the last decade of the nineteenth century. Nearly three-fourths of the Irish-born residents in Warren continued to rent housing in 1900. The similar pattern of home ownership among the Irish during each decade of this study attests to their lack of status in the community. At no time in the late nineteenth century did more than 30 percent of the Irish-born workers in Warren actually possess the homes in which they lived. In addition, no more than five Irish immigrants in any decade were able to attain more than a single dwelling. However, while home ownership among the Irish remained static during the industrialization of Warren, possession of property among the Danes actually decreased from 54 percent in 1890 to 42 percent in 1900.[10]

This survey of home ownership among the major ethnic groups in Warren suggests several tentative conclusions. The percentage of property owners among the various ethnic groups correlates closely with the occupational opportunity available to each group living in nineteenth-century Warren (see Chapter 5). American-, French-, and German-born workers generally began their careers at higher occupational levels than the other groups residing in Warren. A greater percentage also owned property than did the English-, Irish-, and Swedish-, or Italian-born workers. A larger proportion of both the French and German immigrants owned property than did native-born Americans in each decade of this study. However, a significant proportion of native-born workers in the labor force were sons of second- and third-generation Warren residents living with parents. Hence the ratio of native-born propertyless appears somewhat exaggerated.[11]

Irish-born workers, among the older ethnic groups, and the Swedes and Italians experienced minimal opportunity in both occupational mobility and property holdings. The Irish, in particular, most likely began their careers as unskilled laborers and remained in that low-skill, low-pay classification throughout their lives. In addition, a majority of the Swedes and most of the Italian immigrants worked at unskilled occupations. Similarly, few Italian-, Irish-, or Swedish-born workers attained even the most modest housing in nineteenth-century Warren. However, the high rate of propertyless adults suggests the importance of the relationship between persistence in the community and attainment of one's own home.

Accumulation of property, like occupational mobility, may require a significant length of residence in the community. This analysis of ownership by level of skill and ethnicity provides evidence that few workmen purchased property upon arrival in the community. Tables 6-2 to 6-4 reveal the relationship between persistence in the community and the accumulation of property. The Warren economy grew rapidly between 1870 and 1910; hence it is not surprising that real estate was frequently available to working-class men who remained in Warren for any length of time.

The intragenerational property mobility of unskilled workers in the Warren labor force between 1870 and 1910 appears in Table 6-2. The property mobility of each particular census group correlates closely with the occupational mobility discussed in Chapter 4.

The 1870 census group experienced an erratic pattern of property ownership similar to the occupational mobility of the same group. In 1870 only 21 percent of the day laborers owned any property at all, although nine men (12 percent) owned more than a single parcel of property. During the next ten years most of the men in this group left the community—only 23 percent remained—and the rate of property ownership nearly doubled. In addition, single property owners among this group increased from 9 percent in 1870 to 29 percent in 1880. Throughout the next decade workers from this group continued to leave Warren, and by 1890 only five of the original seventy-five men still resided in the community; only one of these men owned his own home. Property mobility occurred for a tiny minority of unskilled workers in the 1870 Warren work force, but most members remained among the propertyless.

Unskilled workers in the 1880 census group experienced the greatest occupational mobility in nineteenth-century Warren. They also were more successful in attaining property than any other group

TABLE 6-2

Intragenerational Property Mobility: Property Attained by Unskilled Workers

Year	Own No Property (%)	Own One House and Lot (%)	Multiple Property Owners (%)	Rate of Persistence (%)	Number in Group
		1870 Census Group*			
1870	79	9	12	—	75
1880	59	29	12	23	17
1890	80	20	—	25	5
1900	67	33	—	60	3
1910	100	—	—	33	1
		1880 Census Group			
1880	80	16	4	—	115
1890	77	23	—	43	49
1900	52	38	10	47	23
1910	22	66	22	40	9
		1890 Census Group			
1890	89	9	2	—	75
1900	50	44	6	36	27
1910	50	36	14	52	14
		1900 Census Group			
1900	86	12	2	—	382
1910	61	35	4	49	187

*Members of the 1870 group may have joined the labor force before 1870.

of unskilled workers. In 1880, four-fifths of the newest unskilled laborers in the Warren work force rented rather than owned their own homes. During the ensuing decade the proportion of day laborers from the 1880 group owning property increased by only 3 percent. By 1900, however, the remaining members of this group were older and more secure in their occupations. In addition, many of the less successful men in this group left the community, and 61 percent of those remaining no longer worked at unskilled occupations. Nearly one-half of the remaining 1880 unskilled workers owned property in 1900, and four-fifths achieved the status of property owner by 1910.

Unskilled laborers joining the labor force in 1890 and 1900 experienced less occupational mobility than the 1880 group. They also found it more difficult to attain property upon joining the work force. Nevertheless, both the 1890 and 1900 groups of day laborers recorded impressive property mobility. Fully 89 percent of the unskilled laborers joining the labor force in 1890 owned no property. Within one decade the proportion of landless workers among this group declined to 50 percent. However, selective out-migration probably played an important role in this property mobility. Nearly two-thirds of the workers in the 1890 group left town by 1900; many of those leaving Warren probably had failed to attain their own homes. Property ownership likely increased one's propensity to settle. It is possible, of course, that workers may have decided to settle permanently before purchasing a home. Thus a decision to persist might lead to home ownership rather than the reverse. Significantly, more than one-half of the unskilled workers from the 1890 group still living in Warren in 1900 remained through the next decade. While the proportion of property owners remained the same (50 percent), the proportion of multiple property owners increased to 14 percent. Unskilled workers joining the work force in 1900 experienced more limited property mobility than their counterparts from 1880 or 1890. However, within a single decade the proportion of property owners within this group increased by 25 percent.

TABLE 6-3

Intragenerational Property Mobility: Property Attained by Semiskilled Workers

Year	Own No Property (%)	Own One House and Lot (%)	Multiple Property Owners (%)	Rate of Persistence (%)	Number in Group
		1870 Census Group*			
1870	58	30	12	—	67
1880	26	53	21	28	19
1890	35	35	30	81	17
1900	11	22	67	53	9
1910	—	100	—	11	1
		1880 Census Group			
1880	85	9	6	—	91
1890	47	47	4	35	32
1900	22	60	18	66	27
1910	23	61	16	48	13
		1890 Census Group			
1890	78	20	2	—	81
1900	48	36	16	48	39
1910	36	36	28	56	22
		1900 Census Group			
1900	73	20	7	—	147
1910	37	48	15	48	71

*Members of this group may have joined the labor force before 1870.

Semiskilled and skilled workers in the Warren work force between 1870 and 1910 experienced even greater property mobility than the less skilled day laborers during the same period. Men in these groups enjoyed greater occupational security and usually received higher wages for their services. Consequently, they remained in the community in greater numbers and were able to accumulate enough money to purchase their own homes. Table 6-3 demonstrates the relationship between persistence in the community and property mobility for Warren's semiskilled laborers.

Property mobility of four groups of semiskilled laborers also indicates the presence of considerable social mobility in nineteenth-century Warren. Between 65 and 75 percent of the 1870 semiskilled workers remaining in Warren in 1880 and 1890 succeeded in purchasing their own homes. In addition, six of the nine men in this group still in the community in 1900 owned more than one home. This, of course, attests to the strong positive relationship between occupational mobility and attainment of property. Seven of these men joined the ranks of the white-collar workers by 1900. The security and salaries which accompanied this occupational mobility enabled them to acquire the second criterion of social mobility—property—as well.

Members of the succeeding groups of semiskilled workers fared almost as well as the 1870 group, although the proportion of multiple property owners never exceeded 28 percent. More than one-half of the workers in the 1880, 1890, and 1900 census groups attained property after one decade of residence in Warren. Furthermore, nearly 80 percent of the 1880 group and 64 percent of the 1890 group owned their own homes after two decades in the borough. Persistence rates for these men consistently increased, indicating again the positive relationship between property ownership and stability of residence in the community. The property mobility patterns of semiskilled workers provides strong evidence of considerable opportunity for men remaining in the community longer than a decade.

Property mobility of Warren's skilled workers provides the final test of this dimension of social mobility in the industrializing community. The men in this group were generally more stable and affluent than workers in the unskilled and semiskilled classifications. Similarly, men possessing specific skills experienced greater occupational stability than the other groups of manual workers (see Chapter 4). Consequently, a comparison of the property mobility of semiskilled and skilled workers in Warren yields surprising results. Skilled craftsmen living in Warren between 1870 and 1910 frequently succeeded in purchasing their own homes, but the rate of property mobility is strikingly similar to that recorded by semiskilled workers.

Analysis of intragenerational property mobility of Warren's skilled workers again suggests a strong relationship between persistence in the community and the accumulation of property. Thus workers remaining in Warren for longer periods of time were more likely to own their own homes than short-term residents. In addition, property ownership and persistence rates increased in similar, although not direct, proportion each decade, indicating that property mobility directly influenced one's stability of residence.

At the time of the 1870 census, only 41 percent of Warren's skilled craftsmen owned any property. However, within one decade, nearly three-fourths of these men left the community and the proportion of property owners among those remaining increased to 60 percent. During the next decade—1880 to 1890—Warren enjoyed its greatest period of economic growth, and nearly one-third of the 1870 skilled workers still in the community experienced occupational mobility (see Table 4-9). Similarly, skilled workers also enjoyed dramatic property mobility during the same period. Four-fifths of the 1870 craftsmen who remained in the community beyond 1880 owned their own homes. More impressively, between 1880 and 1900 one-fourth of all skilled workers owned more than one home and one-third reported multiple home ownership in 1910.

Skilled craftsmen joining the Warren work force in 1880 and 1890 also experienced considerable property mobility, although not as great as that recorded by the 1870 group. Fully 50 percent or more of the workers in each group reported home ownership after one decade of residence in the borough; after twenty years the proportion of home owners rose to 70 percent in the 1880 group and 62 percent in the 1890 group. Furthermore, 28 percent of the 1880 census group and 19 percent of the 1890 group still in the community after two decades reported owning more than one dwelling.

Skilled workers joining the Warren work force in 1900 failed to achieve either occupational or property mobility. As previously noted, only 16 percent of the men in this group joined the ranks of the white-collar worker by 1910. Similarly, the proportion of property owners among the 1900 group increased by only 7 percent during their first decade of residency in Warren. However, property mobility for all groups of manual workers sharply declined during the first decade of the twentieth century, as Warren's economic growth began to stabilize. Hence the workers joining the labor force in 1900 failed to share in the economic opportunities enjoyed by the three earlier groups.

The preceding analysis of property mobility among Warren's man-

TABLE 6-4

Intragenerational Property Mobility: Property Attained by Skilled Workers

Year	Own No Property (%)	Own One House and Lot (%)	Multiple Property Owners (%)	Rate of Persistence (%)	Number in Group
		1870 Census group*			
1870	59	33	8	—	215
1880	40	34	26	26	56
1890	20	55	25	62	35
1900	22	52	26	66	23
1910	20	47	33	65	15
		1880 Census Group			
1880	63	21	16	—	205
1890	50	40	10	39	79
1900	30	42	28	54	43
1910	28	50	22	42	18
		1890 Census Group			
1890	71	21	8	—	191
1900	44	44	12	43	82
1910	38	43	19	57	77
		1900 Census Group			
1900	73	24	3	—	422
1910	60	35	5	49	205

*Members of this group may have joined the labor force before 1870.

ual laborers suggests the following conclusions:

1. Manual workers living in Warren any time during the forty-year industrial period were much more likely to rent housing rather than purchase their own homes. Less than one-half of all the manual workers residing in the community between 1870 and 1910 reported property holdings. In addition, as late as 1910 the United States Bureau of the Census reported that 48 percent of Warren's 2,670 homes were not owned by the persons who inhabited them.[12]

2. All groups of manual workers who remained in the community for any length of time enjoyed significant property mobility. More than one-half of the semiskilled and skilled workers who lived in Warren for ten or more years owned their homes. Unskilled workers generally required a longer time to acquire a property stake in the community, but within twenty years approximately one-half of the day laborers owned property. The impressive property mobility of all

manual workers remaining in the borough during the town's era of industrialization attests to the presence of considerable opportunity for blue-collar workers.

3. Semiskilled and skilled workers enjoyed greater upward mobility than unskilled laborers. Mobility rates varied within each group from decade to decade but within twenty years of residency no less than 64 percent of the semiskilled or skilled workers owned property. In addition, skilled workers frequently owned several homes.

4. The increase in property ownership for those able to remain in the community for any length of time indicates a strong relationship between property mobility and rates of persistence. Property ownership for those remaining in Warren always exceeded the rates of one-decade residents. Property mobility of third-decade residents also generally exceeded mobility of those remaining in the community for two decades. Clyde Griffen reports a similar relationship between persistence and property mobility in his analysis of another nineteenth-century city, Poughkeepsie, New York. He concluded:

> Those without property left the city much more frequently [than the propertied class]. Whether possession of real estate was a primary influence on decisions to stay or to move cannot finally be determined. The act of investment may reflect prior intention to settle permanently. What does seem clear is that persistence has a stronger association with ownership of real estate than with any other variable available in quantifiable sources.[13]

5. Native-born American manual workers and French and German immigrants were more likely to purchase homes than any other ethnic group. They also remained in the community longer than the other groups. The Irish, Italians, and Swedes, in contrast, frequently stayed in the propertyless class. The Irish left the community more rapidly than any other group; the Swedes and Italians were later arrivals in the borough and thus could not establish a lengthy period of residence.

6. Workers joining the labor force in 1870 or 1880 generally experienced greater property mobility than later arrivals in the community. Approximately four-fifths of the workers in these two census groups, excepting the unskilled, succeeded in attaining property. Between 36 and 60 percent of all the manual workers joining the work force in 1890 or 1900 remained in the propertyless class.

Continued comparison with Newburyport, Massachusetts, reveals property mobility for unskilled workers in that New England town at a rate similar to that achieved by Warren's unskilled. Stephan

Thernstrom reports that "real estate was strikingly available to working class men who remained in Newburyport for any length of time. From a third to a half of these workmen were able to report some property holdings after a decade of residence in the city; after twenty years the proportion of owners had risen to 63 percent in one group and 78 percent in another."[14] Unskilled workers in Warren experienced greater occupational mobility than the laborers in Newburyport, but the rates of property mobility followed similar patterns in both nineteenth-century communities. However, one must recall that Newburyport concluded its economic expansion and population growth by the time of Thernstrom's study—1850-1880. Sufficient housing perhaps existed by 1850 to meet the needs of a fairly stable population. Conversely, Warren's population grew rapidly between 1870 and 1910, creating a continuous shortage of residential housing. In addition, rental housing remained available at fairly reasonable rates. In 1906 the *Warren Evening Times* reported:

> Most of our finer houses are occupied by their owners and those which rent for $30 a month can be counted on one hand, but for $20 finely appointed houses on good streets can be had. For $12 to $15 a month comfortable houses in good neighborhoods are available. There are no tenement houses as families however poor can usually get houses.[15]

In spite of the housing shortage, however, unskilled laborers who remained in Warren for any length of time frequently succeeded in achieving the status of home owners.

7 Wealth and Social Mobility

The analyses of occupational and property mobility in Warren strongly suggest the presence of considerable social mobility for manual workers remaining in the borough for any length of time. However, one final dimension of social mobility requires attention. The size of an individual's estate and his ability to accumulate capital, real or personal, yields much information regarding his social standing in the community. Careful analysis of the wealth accumulated by individuals in the community enables one to determine the extent of economic and social mobility. Regrettably, banking firms in Warren refused to divulge the size of individual accounts deposited between 1870 and 1910. However, the one bank whose existence spans the 1870 to 1910 time period—the Warren Savings Bank—did disclose a simple list of all depositors during that period. Information about the number of savings accounts held by manual workers combined with data on estate holdings reveal much about the economic situation of manual laborers in nineteenth-century Warren.

Saving money became an important function in the lives of Warren's working-class men, and the local community strongly encouraged thrift. Children in school supposedly learned the virtue of saving through a school savings plan organized in 1894. Within two years the deposits of these children exceeded $8,000.[1] Savings, of course, enabled working-class adults to accumulate money to purchase a home. In addition, a worker setting aside a few dollars in a bank acquired status, if only among his peers.[2] An examination of the percentage of savings accounts held by four occupational groups in Warren's largest and most prestigious bank gives some indication of emphasis placed on savings and the worker's ability to accumulate money.

The fragmentary evidence in Table 7-1 suggests that some manual laborers could indeed accumulate enough money to open savings accounts. Seventy-five unskilled laborers lived in Warren in 1870; of this number, eight men (or approximately 10 percent) held savings

TABLE 7-1

Percentage of Workers Holding Savings Accounts in the Warren Savings Bank

Year*	Unskilled (%)	Semiskilled (%)	Skilled (%)	Nonmanual (%)	Total Number of Savings Accounts†
1870	10	34	35	52	233
1880	13	25	27	55	296
1890	21	34	35	69	553
1900	21	40	40	65	968

*Includes all workers residing in Warren in each census year. An examination of those persisting through several decades would obviously yield higher percentages.

†This table reveals only the savings accounts held by Warren workers in one bank and is therefore biased downward. Undoubtedly, workers deposited savings in other banks although probably in much smaller proportions.

accounts in the Warren Savings Bank. Ten years later the proportion of day laborers saving money in the bank increased to 13 percent, and by 1890 one-fifth of Warren's menial laborers maintained savings accounts in the Warren Savings Bank. Considering the low wages of these men, the temporary nature of their occupations, and the high rate of outward migration, the percentage of unskilled laborers with savings is striking. An even larger proportion of semiskilled and skilled workers, of course, held savings accounts; they received higher wages and experienced few periods of unemployment. In 1870, 1890, and 1900 more than one-third of the semiskilled and skilled workers possessed savings in the Warren Savings Bank. Only in 1880 did less than 30 percent of these two groups hold savings accounts; some may have withdrawn money to speculate in the oil fields. In that year, one-fourth of the semiskilled and skilled workers maintained savings accounts. Nonmanual workers, as one might expect, held the largest number of savings accounts in Warren's major bank throughout the late nineteenth century. In both 1870 and 1880 more than one-half of the white-collar workers in Warren held savings accounts, and the number increased to two-thirds in 1890 and 1900. Nonmanual workers in Warren saved money—at least in the Warren Savings Bank—at a significantly higher rate than manual laborers. However, one may infer from the limited evidence available that manual laborers frequently made use of the savings bank.

The analysis of savings accounts held by workers in Warren conceals several important elements of social mobility in the community. Men holding savings accounts may possess anything from one dollar upward in the account. In addition, individuals often held wealth in real estate rather than in personal savings accounts. Finally, an examination of savings accounts held by manual workers tells little about the accumulation of wealth over a period of time. Could manual workers remaining in the community for any length of time accumulate any substantial amount of real or personal wealth? Fortunately, the 1870 manuscript census and borough tax records provide ample data to determine the rate of intragenerational wealth mobility.[3]

An analysis of the ability of manual workers in Warren to accumulate wealth, both real and personal, provides the final test of social mobility in the community. Later in this chapter the concepts of occupational, property, and wealth mobility will be combined to provide final conclusions regarding the degree of social mobility in nineteenth-century Warren.

TABLE 7-2

Intragenerational Estate Mobility, 1870-1910:* Value of Estate Attained by Unskilled Workers

Year	Number in Group	Class One, $0-500 (%)	Class Two, $501-1,000 (%)	Class Three, $1,001-3,000 (%)	Class Four, $3,001-10,000 (%)	Class Five, $10,000 up (%)
			1870 Census Group			
1870	75	81	13	4	2	—
1880	17	59	12	29	—	—
1890	5	60	20	20	—	—
1900	3	67	33	—	—	—
1910	1	100	—	—	—	—
			1880 Census Group			
1880	115	83	11	5	—	—
1890	49	65	24	11	—	—
1900	23	56	17	17	10	—
1910	9	22	33	22	11	11
			1890 Census Group			
1890	75	92	5	3	—	—
1900	27	40	30	30	—	—
1910	14	57	28	15	—	—
			1900 Census Group			
1900	382	82	14	4	—	—
1910	187	51	32	15	2	—

*Includes both real and personal wealth.

Unskilled laborers remaining in Warren for any length of time could acquire an estate but only a few accumulated a sizable amount of wealth. Table 7-2 indicates the extent of wealth attained by unskilled workers persisting in the community. Estate values are organized into five somewhat arbitrary classes for purposes of simplification and clarity. Generally, estates valued at less than $500 usually included certain livestock—horses and dogs—carriages, and money held at interest. According to the assessor's valuation records, few persons in Class One ($0-500) owned real property; an estate which exceeded $500 in value usually included some amount of real estate.

The pattern of estate mobility (Table 7-2) immediately suggests a simple generalization: Fewer than one-fifth of the unskilled laborers joining the work force in any census year began their careers with an estate exceeding $500. Of the seventy-five unskilled laborers living in Warren in 1870, only fourteen men (19 percent) held estates valued in excess of $500. Moreover, only 4 percent held estates in Class Three ($1,001-3,000). One unskilled laborer reported holdings of more than $3,000, but this is largely a statistical artifact—some of the men in the 1870 group undoubtedly worked in the Warren labor force for a number of years before 1870. By 1880 most of the unskilled workers from the 1870 group left Warren. The few who remained achieved only modest estate mobility. Three-fifths of the unskilled laborers in this group remained in Class One ($0-500) in both 1880 and 1890, while two of the three men remaining in 1900 held assets valued at less than $500. Some of the men from the 1870 group, however, did manage to accumulate small estates. Nearly one-third of the laborers remaining in 1880 reached Class Three ($1,001-3,000) and one-fifth did so in 1890. With the exception of the single individual in 1870, none of the unskilled workers from the 1870 group attained Classes Four or Five in any decade.

Unskilled laborers who began their careers in 1880, at the onset of Warren's economic growth, experienced greater estate mobility than any other group of day laborers. Eighty-three percent of the 1880 group began their working careers in the first estate class. Within one decade a fourth of the men still in Warren moved to Class Two and 11 percent attained Class Three status. In 1900 the percentage of the 1880 unskilled workers in Classes Two and Three remained static, but two men (10 percent) attained estates valued between $3,001 and $10,000. By 1910 only nine of the original eighty-three unskilled workers remained in the community and all but two of these men held estates worth more than $500. Three laborers achieved the Class Two and two owned property valued within the limits of Class Three. In addition, one man reached Class Four status, and another held real and personal property valued in excess of $10,000. Most of these latter men, of course, no longer worked at unskilled occupations. Day laborers from the 1880 census group enjoyed greater occupational mobility than any other group; more than 50 percent moved to skilled or nonmanual occupations in both 1900 and 1910 (see Table 4-7). This suggests a strong positive relationship between occupational mobility and estate mobility. Few men who worked all their lives as unskilled laborers ever accumulated any sizable estate, whereas those who experienced considerable occupational mobility also generally enjoyed estate mobility.

Unskilled laborers joining the work force in 1890 and 1900 experienced some estate mobility but not to the extent enjoyed by the 1880 group. Fully 92 percent of the unskilled workers in 1890 owned less than $500 worth of real or personal property at the start of their careers. During the succeeding decade an impressive percentage of these men accumulated wealth; most—nearly two-thirds—left town. By 1900, 30 percent of those remaining moved to the second economic class while another 30 percent reached Class Three. Mobility, however, was not an irreversible upward process, and the patterns of this group reveal the tenuous nature of their property holdings. During the next decade the proportion of laborers in the lowest economic class actually increased from 40 percent in 1900 to 57 percent in 1910. In addition, the proportion of men in Class Three decreased by one-half during the first decade of the twentieth century.

Laborers joining the Warren work force in 1900, as the economy of the borough stabilized, enjoyed less mobility than their earlier counterparts. Nevertheless, nearly one-half of the men from this group still living in Warren in 1910 had advanced beyond the first economic class. Furthermore, twenty-nine men (15 percent) had moved to Class Three, and 2 percent held property valued between $3,000 and $10,000. With the exception of the 1870 laboring group, one may conclude that unskilled workers who remained in Warren for any length of time enjoyed modest economic mobility. Nearly one-half of the day laborers living in the community more than twenty years escaped the lowest, most impoverished class. Few unskilled workers, however, ever attained wealth measured in the most limited terms. Only six men throughout the 1870-1910 period reached the fourth economic class ($3,001-10,000) and only one accumulated wealth which exceeded $10,000.

Semiskilled and skilled workers fared much better than men beginning work as unskilled laborers. Nearly three-fourths of the men joining the labor force as semiskilled or skilled workers eventually escaped the first economic classification. Table 7-3 reveals the rate of intragenerational estate mobility of semiskilled workers living in Warren between 1870 and 1910.

TABLE 7-3

Intragenerational Estate Mobility, 1870-1910: Value of Estate Attained by Semiskilled Workers

Year	Number in Group	Class One, $0-500 (%)	Class Two, $501-1,000 (%)	Class Three, $1,001-3,000 (%)	Class Four, $3,001-10,000 (%)	Class Five, $10,000 up (%)
			1870 Census Group			
1870	67	62	14	12	12	—
1880	19	21	16	36	21	6
1890	17	29	18	29	12	12
1900	9	22	—	22	44	12
1910	1	—	—	100	—	—
			1880 Census Group			
1880	91	91	3	4	2	—
1890	32	44	31	25	—	—
1900	27	33	26	30	11	—
1910	13	15	23	31	31	—
			1890 Census Group			
1890	81	74	17	8	1	—
1900	39	44	33	18	5	—
1910	22	23	32	32	13	—
			1900 Census Group			
1900	147	70	14	12	4	—
1910	71	38	31	21	8	2

In each of the four groups, persistence in the community improved one's chances for estate mobility. Generally, an individual remaining in the community for any length of time accumulated more wealth than a short-term resident. In addition, emigration affected the estate mobility rates of this group of workers in much the same manner as it affected other groups of manual workers. The less successful men usually left the community; hence the rates of upward mobility are greater than they might be if these men had persisted.

Nearly two-thirds of the semiskilled workers living in Warren at the time of the 1870 census owned less than $500 worth of property. Within ten years the proportion of men in the lowest economic class decreased to one in five while one-third reached Class Three and one-fourth advanced to Class Four or Five. During the next decade persistence among this group reached 78 percent (no other group of manual workers ever achieved this rate of stability), again suggesting the positive relationship between persistence and social mobility. The impressive economic mobility enjoyed by this group from 1870 to 1880 obviously increased their propensity to settle. In 1890 one-half of the men still living in the borough from the 1870 group held property in excess of $1,001, and by 1900 the proportion increased to 78 percent. Furthermore, although the numbers are admittedly small, nearly one-fourth of these men achieved Class Four or Five in 1890 and 56 percent did so by 1900.

Workers in the 1880 census group enjoyed similar economic mobility although none achieved Class Five (over $10,000). Only 9 percent of the 1880 semiskilled workers began their careers holding more than $500 worth of property. However, within ten years 56 percent of the remaining men moved up to Class Two or Three. During the next two decades the men in this group continued to progress, and 67 percent moved into the three middle economic classes by 1900 and 85 percent held between $501 and $10,000 worth of property in 1910. Seven of every ten semiskilled workers who joined the labor force in 1900 or 1910 held real or personal property valued at less than $500 at the start of their careers. But within one decade a majority of both census groups still in Warren moved into the three higher classifications. Moreover, 77 percent of the 1880 group reported property worth more than $500 after twenty years of residence in the community.

Clearly, semiskilled workers able to remain in Warren for any length of time enjoyed considerable estate mobility. Only a small minority failed to experience mobility into a higher economic classification. Their jobs provided a modicum of security and a stable, if small, income. Nevertheless, the fact that two-fifths of all men beginning as semiskilled workers could accumulate estates between $1,000 and $10,000 is truly impressive.

Analysis of the estate patterns of the hundreds of skilled craftsmen in Warren between 1870 and 1910 provides the final test of mobility in the borough during its period of industrial growth. As previously indicated, skilled craftsmen were more likely to settle in Warren than were other manual laborers. More than one-half of the skilled workers who remained in the community for ten years continued to reside there in each succeeding decade. The high persistence rate, along with better paying and more stable occupations, contributed to the dramatic estate mobility enjoyed by skilled workers. Many skilled

TABLE 7-4

Intragenerational Estate Mobility, 1870-1910: Value of Estate Attained by Skilled Workers

Year	Number in Group	Class One, $0-500 (%)	Class Two, $501-1,000 (%)	Class Three, $1,001-$3,000 (%)	Class Four, $3,001-10,000 (%)	Class Five, $10,000 up (%)
			1870 Census Group			
1870	215	56	8	17	17	2
1880	56	30	14	37	14	5
1890	35	23	20	37	17	3
1900	23	22	17	43	13	5
1910	15	27	27	27	19	—
			1880 Census Group			
1880	205	82	9	8	1	—
1890	79	38	19	28	6	9
1900	43	21	19	44	9	7
1910	18	18	24	40	18	—
			1890 Census Group			
1890	191	71	17	8	4	—
1900	82	36	24	17	21	2
1910	47	23	21	40	13	3
			1900 Census Group			
1900	422	68	21	9	1	1
1910	205	41	31	22	6	—

workers began their careers with no more wealth than other manual laborers—tools were not considered as part of a man's personal property—but they quickly left the lowest economic classification. Within ten years in the labor force less than 42 percent of any skilled group of workers remained in Class One. Furthermore, nearly 80 percent of all groups reported estates above $500 after twenty years in the community. In addition, skilled workers from the 1870 and 1880 census groups enjoyed somewhat greater economic mobility than craftsmen who came after them. Both the 1870 and 1880 workers lived through the full era of economic growth in Warren which no doubt contributed to their dramatic mobility. Before Warren's industrialization, 56 percent of the skilled workers reported estates valued at less than $500. By 1880 the proportion of craftsmen in the lowest economic classification declined to 30 percent. Ten years later less than one-quarter of the remaining skilled workers continued in the bottom estate group, with most of those experiencing mobility moving into the second or third classification. Between one-half and three-fifths of all skilled craftsmen from the 1870 census group remained in the $501 to $3,000 classes in any succeeding year. The proportion of 1870 craftsmen in the two highest economic classes varied no more than 1 percent during the total 1870 to 1910 period, and approximately one of every five held property valued in excess of $3,000 in any decade.

Skilled workers in the 1880 census group enjoyed even greater mobility than the craftsmen who preceded them. Eighty-two percent of the 1880 census group of craftsmen began their careers in the poverty classification. Warren's economy, however, grew rapidly between 1880 and 1900 and most of these men quickly left the lowest economic group. By 1890 nearly two-thirds of the men who remained in Warren moved up at least one economic class, and 79 percent of those persisting for twenty years experienced some mobility. More significantly, 43 percent of this group still in Warren in 1890 joined the $1,000 and over economic classes and nearly 60 percent reached the same classification in 1900 and 1910. Obviously, the industrialization of Warren provided frequent economic opportunities for both the 1870 and 1880 skilled workers.

Craftsmen joining the Warren labor force in 1890 also enjoyed rapid economic mobility. Between 1890 and 1900 the number of 1890 skilled laborers in the lowest economic class declined by 35 percent. In addition, 40 percent of those remaining in the borough reported estates exceeding $1,000. Ten years later more than one-half of the 1890 group still in the community were included in the top three economic groups. In comparison, only 28 percent of the 1900 group of craftsmen could join the over $1,000 classes after one decade in the community. In addition, 41 percent remained in the lowest economic group in 1910. The somewhat limited mobility of the 1900 group of skilled workers suggests the importance of both the community's economic status and rates of persistence upon economic opportunity. First, workers in all previous groups joined the Warren labor force either before or during the borough's major period of economic growth. The 1900 craftsmen, however, began their careers in Warren just as the rate of growth began to decline, and they experienced fewer economic opportunities than their predecessors. Secondly, the 1900 workers were in the early part of their careers in 1910. Therefore, they did not have the advantage of longevity in the community.

Analysis of intragenerational estate mobility of manual workers in Warren suggests several conclusions:

1. Manual laborers who remained in Warren for any length of time

frequently acquired an estate, but only a tiny minority could accumulate any sizable amount of wealth. Fewer than twenty-five of the several thousand manual workers residing in Warren between 1870 and 1910 ever reported estates exceeding $10,000.

2. Workers who remained in the community for any length of time generally experienced greater upward estate mobility than did short-term residents. Hence the longer a worker resided in the community, the greater were his chances of accumulating wealth. This again suggests a positive relationship between persistence and mobility.

3. Semiskilled and skilled workers in Warren enjoyed far greater economic mobility than unskilled workers. Nevertheless, considering the temporary nature of their jobs and the low wages they received, unskilled workers enjoyed an impressive rate of economic mobility. Stephan Thernstrom, in his study of unskilled laborers in Newburyport, Massachusetts, suggests several clues to the ability of the unskilled to accumulate any money at all. These factors apply to unskilled workers in Warren as well as Newburyport. He concludes, "A study of laborers settled in a particular community deals with a selected minority who tended to be the last to be fired in hard times and the first to be hired when the economy picked up." Both the real estate holdings and savings accounts of Newburyport laborers, according to Thernstrom, "depended upon ruthless underconsumption."[4] There is little evidence to document the level of consumption of Warren's laborers, but they probably saved at the expense of personal consumption.

4. Workers joining the labor force in 1870 or 1880 generally enjoyed greater estate mobility than workers who followed them, but the difference is not as striking as that observed in the previous analyses of both occupational and property mobility. Manual laborers, particularly from the 1890 and 1900 census groups, apparently could accumulate modest estates without experiencing either occupational or property mobility.

This analysis of estate mobility does not suggest greater economic equality or any redistribution of wealth in the community. Before combining the three aspects of social mobility—occupation, property, and wealth—one final dimension of wealth must be examined. An analysis of the distribution of wealth in the borough indicates that only a few people continued to hold the majority of wealth in Warren during its period of growing industrialization.

From 1870 through 1910 Warren experienced the greatest industrial and urban growth in its history. In addition, the number of private business firms increased nearly sixfold during this forty-year span. Oil refineries, manufacturing firms, and financial establishments added to the affluence of the community (see Chapter 2). The new wealth, however, as measured by the assessor's valuation lists of real and personal property, remained concentrated in the hands of a tiny minority.[5] Actually, the town's richest citizens owned a larger share of the borough's wealth in each decade after 1870 than they held prior to industrialization. Table 7-5 reveals the change in the distribution of real and personal wealth from 1870 through 1910.

TABLE 7-5

Distribution of Wealth in Warren, 1870-1910

Level of Wealth	Percentage of Adult Male Population				
	1870	1880	1890	1900	1910
$10,000 or more	6.15	3.52	4.19	2.85	5.39
$3,001-10,000	16.48	6.98	7.85	7.28	14.47
$1,001-3,000	13.32	13.52	18.44	17.88	17.09
$501-1,000	6.00	11.99	12.29	15.62	12.40
$0-500	58.05	63.99	57.23	56.37	50.65

In 1870, five years before the onset of industrialization in Warren, nearly six of every ten adult males in the borough were concentrated in the lowest economic classification.[6] Furthermore, three-fourths of the adult male population held less than $3,000 worth of real and personal property while only 6 percent of the working males held wealth valued at $10,000 or more. During the succeeding decade, which spanned the discovery of oil in Warren, the distribution of real and personal wealth became even more unequal. Fully 64 percent of the adult male population reported estates valued at less than $500. Conversely, the percentage of men possessing over $10,000 in real and personal property declined from approximately 6 percent in 1870 to 3.5 percent in 1880. In addition, the percentage of adult males in the middle economic classifications ($1,001-10,000) declined by almost 10 percent during the decade.

The assessor's valuation of real and personal wealth in Warren continued to increase throughout the next three decades but the distribution of that wealth changed only slightly. In both 1890 and 1900 less than 5 percent of the population held wealth exceeding $10,000, while 56 to 57 percent remained concentrated in the lowest economic classification. A small change also occurred in the middle-class economic groups, as approximately one-fourth of the population held between $1,001 and $10,000 in both 1890 and 1900. By 1910 a small redistribution of the community's wealth occurred, with nearly one-half of the adult male population reporting holdings exceeding $500. In addition, nearly one-third of the 1910 workers reported middle-class holdings of real and personal property valued between $1,001 and $10,000. During this same period rates of persistence for nearly all groups of workers increased significantly (see Chapter 4, Tables 4-1 to 4-3), suggesting a positive relationship between longevity in the community and accumulation of wealth. A greater percentage of workers simply remained in Warren long enough to attain property. However, the great majority of the wealth of the community remained in the hands of a small proportion of the adult population.[7] In each of the five census years the richest 5 percent of the population controlled 65 percent of the real and personal wealth of the community.[8]

The analysis of intragenerational estate mobility indicated that few manual workers ever attained more than $10,000 in real and personal wealth. Moreover, an examination of the wealthiest 5 percent of the population reveals that the greatest share of the borough's new affluence went to those who already possessed wealth.[9] Clearly, manual workers in Warren did not become members of the town's socioeconomic elite through the accumulation of great wealth.

Thus far the career patterns of manual workers in Warren from 1870 through 1910 have been examined in regard to three specific but separate variables: occupation, property, and wealth. This isolation enables one to determine the degree of mobility experienced in each of the important areas by workers in nineteenth-century Warren. However, as previously stated, all three determinants of social position contributed toward the social mobility of a manual laborer. We may now combine these aspects of social stratification in order to reveal the relationship between occupation, property, and estate mobility.

Including all three mobility factors, each manual laborer who lived in Warren from 1870 through 1910 has been isolated to determine his exact starting point on the social ladder. A trace of his career permits a comparison of his initial position with his final occupation, property, and estate holdings. A laborer, for example, might begin his working career in a semiskilled occupation, owning a lot but no house, and he might possess an estate valued at $500. After thirty years in the community he may hold a white-collar occupation, own his own home, and possess an estate valued at $2,500. For most workers, of course, this sort of career spanned only one decade. Others continued working in the community for twenty, thirty, or forty years.

Each of the determinants of social mobility has been divided into several (somewhat arbitrary) steps to illustrate upward or downward social mobility: occupation—unskilled, semiskilled, skilled, and nonmanual; property holdings—no property, ownership of a lot but no house, ownership of a house and lot, and multiple property holdings; estate holdings—$0-500, $501-1,000, $1,001-5,000, $5,001-10,000, and $10,000 and over.

Classification of Warren's three groups of manual laborers into no mobility, limited mobility, intermediate mobility, and high mobility categories enables one to determine the degree of social mobility experienced by typical laborers in the community. The first (no mobility) group includes all workers who failed to advance in two of the three determinants of social mobility—occupational, property, and estate holdings—and who moved up only one step from their starting point in the third group. Workers, of course, who experienced no mobility or downward mobility in all three classifications are included in the no-mobility group. The second (limited mobility) group includes all workers who experienced advances of one step in two classes or who demonstrated mobility of at least two steps in one classification. Workers who advanced at least two steps in two of the three determinants of social mobility, or who advanced one step in all three, were placed in the third (intermediate) group. Finally, some manual workers advanced in all three aspects of mobility employed in this study. These workers constitute the fourth (high mobility) group. Table 7-6, which classifies workers according to length of residence in the community, combines several social processes—geographical, occupational, property, and wealth mobility—to determine the range of social mobility experienced by manual workers in Warren.

Analysis of the mobility of manual workers in Warren according to length of residence immediately reinforces one previously stated generalization: Workers who remained in the community for any length of time made substantial gains over short-term residents. Twenty-year residents from each of the three skill groups enjoyed greater mobility than ten-year residents; thirty-year residents were more successful than men remaining in the community for twenty years.

A full 156 men, 65 percent of the 238 unskilled workers who resided in Warren for a single decade, failed to rise out of the most impoverished segment of the manual laboring class. A few of these

TABLE 7-6

Social Mobility of Manual Workers According to Length of Residence and Considering Original Starting Position

Length of Residence (years)	No Mobility (%)	Limited Mobility (%)	Intermediate Mobility (%)	High Mobility (%)	Number in Sample
		Unskilled Workers			
10	65	20	5	10	238
20	48	38	4	10	29
30	27	37	18	18	11
40	100	—	—	—	1
		Semiskilled Workers			
10	50	35	12	3	95
20	38	23	9	30	44
30	33	24	10	33	21
40	—	—	100	—	1
		Skilled Workers			
10	48	43	4	4	297
20	42	33	18	6	84
30	31	35	15	19	26
40	33	27	20	20	15

men (twenty-seven) managed to accumulate in excess of $500 but remained both propertyless and unskilled. Twenty percent of the ten-year residents beginning work as unskilled laborers succeeded in elevating themselves during this period. Eleven of the ten-year unskilled workers (5 percent) experienced intermediate mobility while only 23 men (10 percent) succeeded in experiencing high mobility.

Day laborers residing in the community for twenty or thirty years improved significantly upon the record of mobility established by the one-decade residents. Fewer than one-half of the workers remaining in the community for twenty years failed to experience some mobility, while only 27 percent of the three-decade residents remained in the no-mobility group. In comparison, one-tenth of the twenty-year men and nearly two-fifths of the thirty-year residents attained white-collar occupations, owned their own homes, or held real and personal property exceeding $1,000 in value. Moreover, approximately 40 percent of the twenty-year residents and 54 percent of the unskilled laborers living in Warren for thirty years experienced either limited or intermediate social mobility.

Workers beginning their careers as semiskilled laborers enjoyed even more dramatic mobility than unskilled workers. One-half of the semiskilled men in the labor force for a single decade succeeded in achieving some mobility, but only 29 percent of the group rose into a skilled or nonmanual position. However, the security and stability of their work enabled one-half of the ten-year semiskilled workers to acquire property and an estate worth $500 or more. Only three men achieved a high degree of mobility after ten years in the labor force. Semiskilled workers able to remain in the community for twenty or thirty years established even more impressive rates of mobility. Fewer than 40 percent of the adult workers from the twenty-year group still held semiskilled occupations after two decades of work. Furthermore, nearly four of every ten semiskilled workers enjoyed either intermediate or high mobility during the twenty-year period. Similarly, 10 percent of the thirty-year residents from this group succeeded in achieving intermediate mobility while another one-third experienced high social mobility.

Finally, skilled workers experienced rates of social mobility similar to that enjoyed by semiskilled workers. Although many skilled craftsmen failed to acquire white-collar occupations, they rapidly attained the other determinants of social mobility: property and wealth. Skilled workers were always in demand in Warren during its era of industrialization. Moreover, the higher wages they received made the accumulation of property and wealth not only possible but probable. Craftsmen, as previously noted, often began their careers with no more wealth than other manual workers. However, they quickly left the lowest economic groups, and one-half of all skilled workers experienced some mobility after only ten years in the community. Eight percent, on the other hand, advanced a minimum of two steps in at least two of the three determinants of mobility or rose at least one step in all three. Approximately one-third of the twenty- and thirty-year residents experienced only limited mobility, but the proportion of intermediate- and high-mobility skilled workers increased dramatically. Nearly one-fourth of all twenty-year skilled workers and one-third of all thirty-year residents experienced intermediate or high mobility. Moreover, only 31 percent of the skilled craftsmen remaining in the borough failed to enjoy any mobility at all. Almost two-fifths of the men in the thirty-year group reported home ownership and estates valued between $501 and $5,000 while another one-fifth owned several homes and held estates exceeding $5,000 in value.

Fifteen men beginning as skilled workers lived in Warren from

1870 through 1910. Five of these men failed to experience occupational, property, or estate mobility. Forty percent, on the other hand, moved up at least two steps in two mobility classifications. Half of these men were upwardly mobile in all three classifications, advancing at least two steps in two or more of the mobility classifications.

Clearly, for the adult male manual worker in nineteenth-century Warren, social mobility, as defined in this analysis, was a distinct possibility. Manual workers from all classifications left the community more often than they stayed, but those remaining for any length of time frequently rose above their original social position. From 50 to 60 percent of all unskilled workers succeeded in achieving significant social mobility after twenty years in the community. An even greater percentage of semiskilled and skilled workers recorded impressive occupational, property, or estate gains. By far the most common form of social advancement for laborers in Warren occurred within the manual laboring universe. Few workers rose from rags to great wealth; however, manual workers frequently attained white-collar occupations, demonstrating the clear possibility that blue-collar workers could, and often did, bridge the gulf separating manual and nonmanual occupations. Furthermore, a majority of manual laborers who remained in Warren for any length of time succeeded in purchasing their own homes and acquiring a modest estate. For workers living in Warren during the borough's era of industrial growth, upward social mobility was enjoyed by many.

8 The Community in 1910

The preceding analysis of the career patterns of the working-class men in nineteenth-century Warren demonstrated the existence of considerable opportunity in the community. Manual laborers who settled in Warren for any length of time frequently attained higher level manual occupations and a substantial number achieved white-collar status. Moreover, those residing in the community longer than a decade usually acquired some property and accumulated a small amount of wealth. Few workers, however, ever attained true riches or were counted among the elite of the community.

The industrialization and urbanization of Warren, which began with the discovery of oil in 1875, introduced a number of changes in the community's social patterns. Warren in 1870 was characterized by a clear but open social structure (see Chapter 2). Immigrants and other newcomers to the community often secured skilled occupations upon entering the work force. Moreover, with the exception of the Irish, a rather smooth assimilation prevailed. Labor was organized into small one- and two-man craft shops or proprietorships with little occupational specialization. The spatial arrangements of the community followed the mixed work and residential traditions characteristic of many preindustrial communities. Immigrants and native-sons, men of wealth and poverty coexisted residentially if not socially. Finally, government, religion, and education occupied important, although limited, roles in the community. By 1910 this community structure had changed significantly. A survey of the Warren social scene late in the community's era of growth will reveal the extent of that change and illustrate its effect on the laboring classes.

Between 1870 and 1910 Warren's population grew nearly sixfold. As the data on persistence illustrated, in- and out-migration contributed to an even greater population turnover.[1] Further analysis of the Warren population suggests that the composition of that population also changed considerably. Table 8-1 reveals the relationship between population growth and ethnicity in Warren during the 1870-1910 period.

TABLE 8-1

Nativity of Adult Male Population by Decade

Birth-place	1870		1880		1890		1900		1910	
	Number	% of Total	Number	% of Total	Number	% of Total	Number	% of Total	Number	% of Total
U.S.A.	397	65	553	65	629	58	1,381	66	2,430	73
Canada	8	1	22	2	33	3	36	2	28	1
England	18	3	29	3	48	4	49	2	31	1
Ireland	46	7	54	6	87	8	107	5	81	2
Scotland	11	2	12	1	10	1	22	1	33	1
Germany	50	8	57	7	83	8	89	4	78	2
Sweden	3	—	24	3	61	6	203	10	321	10
Denmark	15	2	30	3	41	4	81	4	57	2
France	56	9	62	7	71	7	62	3	21	1
Italy	—	—	1	—	1	—	28	1	82	2
Other	5	1	10	1	16	1	33	2	167	5

Before the industrialization of the community, nearly two-thirds of the adult male population of Warren consisted of native-born Americans. During three of the next four decades the ratio of native-sons to immigrants remained relatively stable while the composition of the various immigrant groups changed dramatically.[2] Between 1880 and 1890 the proportion of native-born male workers dropped to 58 percent as a large number of immigrants arrived. Most of these men worked for firms manufacturing barrels, pipelines, and other equipment for the rapidly growing oil industry.

In 1870, three-fourths of the immigrant population consisted of persons of English, Irish, German, and French origin. As industrialization progressed, the proportion of each of these groups declined drastically. By 1890 the combined percentage fell to 64 and the next decade produced a similar decline. In 1900, for the first time in the borough's history, more than one-half of all immigrants came from countries other than the above four. By 1910 immigrants from these four nations were a clear minority, constituting only 21 percent of the combined foreign-born adult male population. Swedes, Italians, and, for a time, Danes replaced the original four groups as a majority. As Table 8-1 illustrates, Swedish immigrants made the most dramatic increases in the late nineteenth century.

In 1870 adult male Swedish immigrants residing in Warren constituted less than 1 percent of the total immigrant population, although more lived scattered throughout the county working mainly in logging. Concurrent with the onset of industrialization, Swedish immigrants migrated to Warren. By 1910 well over one-third of all immigrants in the community originated from Sweden. The major wave of Italian immigration into Warren did not occur until after 1910; however, workers from Italy still constituted 12 percent of all immigrants listed in that census.[3] Equaling the Irish in numbers, the Italians performed an even greater share of the borough's unskilled labor during the first decade of the twentieth century.

In addition to this change in the composition of the population, other demographic changes also paralleled Warren's industrialization. In 1870 artisans or skilled laborers constituted slightly more than one-third of the adult male population of the community. At either end of the occupational continuum unskilled workers and proprietors made up approximately 12 and 4 percent of the work force respectively.[4] Throughout the late nineteenth century major changes occurred in the proportion of each of these groups working in the Warren community. As industrialization progressed, the number of skilled workers needed in the community increased each decade. However, due to both further mechanization and improved productivity, the percentage of skilled workers in the existing population began a gradual decline, dropping to one-quarter of the work force in 1890. Through the next two decades the proportion of skilled workers remained at one-fourth of the existing work force. During the same period the percentage of unskilled workers climbed at a significant rate. By the turn of the century almost one-quarter of the adult male population worked at some type of unskilled labor. Semiskilled workers constituted approximately 10 percent of the work force in each decade of this study. Thus by the close of Warren's period of growth approximately one-third of the work force held jobs in the two lowest skill classifications. The increased size of metal products firms and the establishment of petroleum refineries required large numbers of low-cost operatives who could be trained in a short period of time. In addition, the rapid pace of building construction provided jobs for those without skills.

The proportion of white-collar workers remained relatively stable throughout Warren's era of industrialization at approximately 42 percent of the work force, while the number of proprietors climbed rapidly. By the end of the first decade of the twentieth century 14 percent of the work force owned their own businesses.[5] It appears, therefore, that as industrialization progressed, a considerable number of the borough's citizens had improved opportunities for advancement into the proprietor class. However, the changing occupational structure and the relative decline in the percentage of skilled workers undoubtedly adversely affected the opportunities for upward mobility by blue-collar workers.

By 1910 small craft shops were no longer the dominant feature in Warren's occupational structure. Nearly 1,200 men, approximately one-third of the labor force, worked in the borough's five largest manufacturing firms. Before the industrialization of the community the largest firm employed fewer than 50 men. In 1910 that firm, the Struthers Iron Works, employed more than 500 men with an annual business volume of $800,000. In addition, three firms employed more than 200 men while 50 or more men worked at each of eight other firms. Almost 59 percent of the work force held jobs in the borough's nineteen largest companies producing either manufactured goods, wood products, or refined oil. Most of these businesses were highly specialized, utilizing division of labor practices common in many early twentieth-century industries. The five manufacturing firms, in particular, employed nearly 80 percent of the borough's unskilled and semiskilled laborers. Skilled workers also began working in factories rather than for themselves. By 1910 nearly 41 percent of the 866 skilled workers in Warren held jobs in factories employing 10 or more men.

The impact this increased factory work had on Warren's manual laborers is difficult to discern. Unskilled and semiskilled workers likely received increased job security. As the economy of Warren expanded, workers remained in continual short supply and unemployment for factory workers was virtually nonexistent. "Unattached" laborers, however, continued to be subject to periodic unemployment and layoffs. Weather, for example, remained a constant factor in such occupations as building and logging. Skilled workers, on the other hand, may have viewed increased competition from factory products as a threat, although no public opposition to industrialization emerged during the period.

Concentration of workers in large factories particularly affected those in the cabinet-making and wood-working trades. In 1910 the Warren Chamber of Commerce reported that the four furniture firms in Warren employed more than half of the borough's skilled cabinet makers.[6] Detailed data on other skilled trades are not available, but it is likely that they underwent similar experiences. This transformation in the occupational distribution of Warren's workers raises at least one unanswerable question regarding the mobility experiences of skilled laborers. Did artisans moving from privately owned or operated small shops into larger industrial settings view this as a lateral or a downward move? In his analysis of industrialization in

Philadelphia in the 1830s, Sam Bass Warner, Jr., suggests that artisans suffered both economically and socially:

> During this first era of industrialization, . . . Philadelphia's artisans suffered from two disturbances: A loss of relative standing in their city, and a revolution in the terms and conditions of their work. The first disturbance amongst the artisans took the form of frustrating their rising expectations; the second disturbance took the form of unhinging the craft traditions of the century and setting men to work longer hours, at a faster pace, and in a more socially isolated and economically insecure environment than they had ever labored in before or ever would again.[7]

It is not possible to determine the proportion of artisan-proprietors moving into factory-type production. The Warren city directories usually listed a worker by the type of job he performed but did not list his place of employment. Many of the skilled workers employed in factory-type work no doubt were recent arrivals in the community. Others, formerly unskilled or semiskilled workers, perhaps viewed factory work at a skilled level as a definite occupational improvement. Nevertheless, at least a small proportion of formerly independent artisans undoubtedly left their shops for the factory. Others, particularly the young (as persistence rates illustrate), left the community. Rates of persistence, paradoxically, increased rather than fell as industrialization and concentration of workers increased during each decade of this study.[8] Older workers, perhaps trapped by their age and their inability to adapt to a changing industrial society, persisted in the community despite the increasing competition from factory production.

Yet, if one cannot determine the perceptions of these men it is possible to suggest that the transition to an industrial society required major cultural changes on the part of first generation factory workers. Recently Herbert Gutman posited that

> the American working class was continually altered in its composition by infusions, from within and without the nation, of peasants, farmers, skilled artisans, and casual day laborers who brought into industrial society ways of work and other habits and values not associated with industrial necessities and the industrial ethos. Some shed these older ways to conform to new imperatives. Others fell victim or fled moving from place to place. Some sought to extend and adapt older patterns of work and life to a new society. Others challenged the social system through varieties of collective

associations. But for all—at different historical moments—the transition to industrial society, ... "entailed a severe restructuring of working habits—new disciplines, new incentives, and a new human nature upon which these incentives could bite effectively."[9]

Many workers no longer possessed the freedom of action and independence that existed in preindustrial Warren. Industrialization, and all that it implied, required new work patterns by the first decade of the twentieth century.

The industrial and urban growth of Warren produced major changes in the ethnic and particularly the occupational composition of the labor force. Equally significant were the changes in spatial patterns which occurred during the era. In 1870 Warren's 2,080 residents concentrated in an area approximately seven blocks long and seven blocks wide. Nearly all of the town's population—with the exception of the Irish—and most of its businesses were located within this area. As previously noted, the 1870 residential analysis revealed patterns of mixed work and residence with only an occasional clustering of any ethnic or occupational group. The Irish, the exception to this pattern, lived primarily in the industrial western sector of town. Spatial patterns in 1910 present a marked contrast to this heterogeneous arrangement.

In 1895, the Warren Borough Council divided the town into six (later eight) political wards each containing approximately the same number of persons.[10] The first three wards included most of the commercial establishments of the town while the fourth and sixth wards contained the borough's major industrial firms. The fifth ward, the newest section of town, contained a number of oil wells but otherwise remained almost exclusively residential.[11] An examination of tax records indicated that real estate assessments in each ward followed a particular pattern.[12] Thus houses in any ward of the city had very similar assessments. The first three wards encompassed the older sections of the city and generally contained most of the town's higher priced homes. The third ward along Fourth and Fifth Avenues and the first ward along Market Street included a number of stately homes and were considered the fashionable areas of the community. The second and fifth wards constituted the middle-class areas of the community, made up of frame houses surrounded by large well-kept lawns.[13] Finally, the fourth and sixth wards located along the periphery of the borough included the lower status neighborhoods. Homes in these two wards carried lower average assessments than the other four sections of the town and, particularly in the fourth ward, often had major industrial plants as neighbors.[14] Thus, by using the

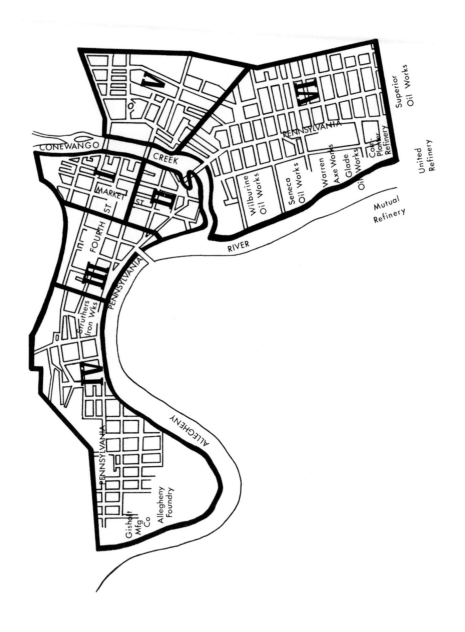

Warren, Pennsylvania—1910 (Political Wards)

Warren ward map, one may construct a useful index of neighborhoods in the borough from 1890 through 1910.

Indexes of dissimilarity were calculated from the occupational and residential information provided by the 1890, 1900, and 1910 Warren city directories. The index measures the degree of clustering of a particular group in some wards in larger proportions than its proportion to the total population of the borough. High indexes, on a scale between 0.0 and 100.0, indicate greater residential segregation. If the index number were 100, for example, the particular group would be segregated entirely within a particular ward or wards.[15]

Indexes of residential clustering by unskilled laborers during the last three decades of this study suggest a shift from the heterogeneous distribution noted earlier. The index values of unskilled workers increased at each decade interval from 26.1 in 1890 to 29.9 in 1900 and 41.0 in 1910. This increased clustering of unskilled workers reflects the greater concentration of industrial firms in the fourth and sixth wards of the town. As industrialization progressed, the size of industrial establishments increased, requiring greater amounts of space. The heavily populated older sections of town (wards one, two, and three) could not accommodate industrial expansion. The fifth ward, confined to the east by steep hills and to the west by the Conewango Creek, provided little room for industrial expansion and consequently remained exclusively residential. The sixth ward, however, ran east of the Conewango Creek for several miles and became a mixed area of residential housing and industrial establishments (primarily oil refineries). The fourth ward, located on a large plain running parallel to the Allegheny River, provided an ideal site for expanding factories. Many of the unskilled workers arriving in Warren after 1895 established residence in these two areas. The proximity to available work and cheap land, particularly in the sixth ward, attracted a number of manual workers. Land developers offered building lots for sale in East Warren (ward six) at $300 each—$5.00 down and $5.00 per month—without interest charges.[16] Thus as the concentration of industrial firms in these two wards increased, the clustering of unskilled workers in the same locations also grew.

An examination of the raw data used to construct the dissimilarity index reveals similar patterns. In 1890, 116 unskilled workers resided in Warren Borough. Nearly one-half (45 percent) lived in the major industrial sector of town, the fourth ward. The second ward, previously classified as a middle-class neighborhood, housed 23 percent of the unskilled and another 23 percent lived in the first ward, one of the better sections of town; fewer than 10 percent resided in the most affluent area of the borough, the third ward.

Between 1890 and 1900, as the population of Warren nearly doubled, the number of unskilled workers quadrupled. At the turn of the century less than one-fourth of Warren's day laborers resided in wards one, two, and three, and by 1910 the proportion had declined to 13 percent. In contrast, the absolute number of unskilled workers living in the fourth ward increased by more than 100 percent, while the proportion living there declined by 20 percent due to the large increase of unskilled workers in the community. The influx of unskilled workers into the sixth ward, however, more than matched the percentage decline in the fourth ward. A total of 56 percent of all the unskilled workers in Warren lived in these two wards at the turn of the century. Ten years later nearly three-fourths of all the unskilled laborers in Warren lived in either of the two industrial sectors of the town with one-half residing in the sixth ward. The industrialization of Warren provided an abundance of jobs for workers lacking specific skills. However, the urbanization which accompanied the industrial growth resulted in a residential pattern that by 1910 all but eliminated the unskilled from the better sections of town.

Semiskilled and skilled workers generally fared better than the unskilled. The greater residential stability of these groups (see Table 4-2) and the security of steady work probably enabled them to purchase or rent higher priced dwellings in the better residential sections of town. Indexes of dissimilarity for semiskilled and skilled workers suggest some mild clustering of these two groups, but it never approached that of the town's unskilled. By 1910 index numbers for semiskilled and skilled workers reached their summit of 24.9 and 18.5 respectively. Like their unskilled counterparts, these men tended to cluster in the less affluent industrial sectors of the community.

The industrialization and urbanization of Warren produced changes in the distribution of the residential population. In 1890—the beginning of the second decade of industrial growth—manual and nonmanual workers frequently lived in the same neighborhoods. By 1910, however, manual workers, particularly the unskilled, concentrated in the poorer sectors of town while white-collar residents dominated the affluent inner sections of the borough.

Analysis of residential patterns in the same political subdivisions by ethnicity yields similar information. In 1870 Warren's major ethnic groups, with the exception of the Irish, were distributed rather evenly in all sections of the borough. Nearly one-half of the Irish workers resided in the fourth ward.[17] By 1900 a trend toward separation along ethnic lines appeared. The newest immigrant groups in the community, the Swedes and Italians, along with the Irish established residences in the fourth and sixth wards. The English clustered somewhat in the fifth and sixth wards. Native-born Americans and the older ethnic groups—Germans, French, and Danes—were disbursed in all six political wards. Table 8-2 displays the changing residential patterns of seven ethnic groups in Warren from 1890 through 1910.

TABLE 8-2

Indexes of Dissimilarity, by Wards, Between Residential Distribution of Native-Born Population and Ethnic Groups, 1890-1900*

Birthplace	1890		1900		1910	
	Index	N	Index	N	Index	N
Germany	18.4	83	4.1	89	7.0	78
France	16.1	71	15.4	62	16.8	21
Denmark	24.6	41	14.1	81	19.6	27
England	15.5	48	15.9	49	20.1	31
Sweden	16.1	61	20.0	203	25.2	321
Ireland	27.9	87	27.9	107	35.0	81
Italy	—	—	51.0	28	56.0	82

*This index differs from the one previously discussed in that native-born workers rather than *all* adult males are used as the referent point.

Warren's indexes were somewhat erratic but reveal patterns of slight, but increasing, separation for the Irish and Swedish residents and marked separation of the Italian residents. In 1890 only the Irish and the Danes exhibited any degree of clustering in the borough's four subdivisions. Nearly half of the Danish residents in 1890 resided in the community's first ward. Occupational rather than ethnic factors, however, likely produced this clustering. As mentioned earlier, four-fifths of the 1890 group of Danish migrants worked at either skilled or white-collar occupations. The nature of their work no doubt meant that many of their jobs were located in Warren's central business district. Consequently, homes in the first ward, within walking distance to work, held greater attraction for these men.

Index values suggest little ethnic separation of four of the older ethnic groups in the community. Only the Swedes, Irish, and Italians clustered to any degree. This pattern continued through the next decade with the index values of these three groups continuing to increase.

Similar patterns emerge from the raw data from which these indexes were constructed. At the end of the nineteenth century, six of every ten Irish-born workers in Warren resided in either the fourth or sixth wards; by 1910 the proportion increased to seven of every ten. In addition, nearly one-half of the Irish immigrants lived in the fourth ward in each of the above decades. Similarly, the Swedes also established residence in both the fourth and sixth wards but the latter subdivision received the largest percentage. In 1900 over one-half of the Swedish population resided in the two poorer sections of the town, with 31 percent living in the sixth ward. One decade later, two-thirds of the Swedes resided in these two wards combined, and 50 percent maintained residence in the sixth ward.[18]

Italian immigrants settled almost exclusively in the poorer sections of town. In 1900, the first year of any significant Italian migration to Warren, 72 percent established residence in the fourth ward. Ten years later the number of Italian-born workers residing in the fourth ward declined to 61 percent but the proportion living in the sixth ward increased from 9 percent in 1900 to 33 percent in 1910. In addition, no Italians lived in the third and fifth wards in either 1900 or 1910 and none lived in the first ward in 1910.[19]

The industrialization of Warren produced numerous changes in the community, as evidenced by the partial exclusion of unskilled workers from the better residential areas. In addition, certain ethnic groups—the Irish, Swedes, and Italians—found it increasingly difficult to establish homes in the town's choice residential locations.[20] Economics, no doubt, played a major role in this separation of occupational and ethnic groups. Homes and land in the better sections of town, whether for rental or purchase, simply required more money than those in the fourth or sixth ward. White-collar workers—largely native-born Americans and the older ethnic groups—could afford to live in the inner sections of town; manual laborers and the newer ethnic groups could not. The result was an increasing residential separation.

Thus far we have viewed the changing Warren social scene through three different aspects: population composition, occupational structure, and residential distribution. The changes in these areas were matched by important changes in the community's political and educational agencies. An examination of the expansion of local government and the politicization of local affairs illustrates both the response of the community leaders to the changing social conditions and the role of the manual workers on these two governing bodies. Chapter 9 discusses the borough government and examines the changing educational system in nineteenth-century Warren.

9 Government and Education

In 1870 the Warren Borough Council and the Warren Board of Education operated informally to fill the needs of the community. Nonpartisan politics characterized election to both bodies, and personal qualities such as friendliness and honesty were the main criteria for election to office. By 1910, however, expanded community needs produced changes in the function and organization of each of these bodies. The following analysis illustrates the nature and response of community leaders to the changing social conditions.

In the 1870s the Warren Borough Council, consisting of nine men (one-third elected annually), and an appointed burgess filled the limited needs of the community. An analysis of the borough budget from 1870 through 1875 reveals that approximately two-thirds of the public expenditures, roughly $4,000 per year, involved the construction or maintenance of public roads and sidewalks. Other important matters included support of the police and fire departments. In addition, the council recognized some responsibility to aid the poor, although its financial contribution in this regard amounted to less than $500 per year.[1]

Council meetings were conducted on an informal basis and held at irregular intervals throughout the year. In fact, not until 1889 did anyone discover that the composition of the council was illegal. In that year the newly appointed borough attorney—in the first year of existence of that appointive office—revealed that the borough bylaws provided for a council of six men; nine men annually had held office from 1870 through 1889. Moreover, the burgess could exercise no power but those of a presiding officer; previously he had acted as a voting member of council.[2] Clearly, these formal restrictions had not concerned earlier members of the town government. Private individuals frequently appeared before the council to air grievances or petition for some desired services (usually sidewalks), adding to the informal atmosphere. Few conflicts arose and most issues were decided by unanimous vote. Candidates for election to the borough council rarely conducted campaigns, and midterm vacancies remained unfilled until the next regular election.[3]

Local political parties, however, followed the pattern occurring throughout the country and became deeply involved in national politics. Local newspapers frequently vilified presidential candidates, and parades, political rallies, and campaign oratory abounded. A delicate party balance existed in Warren during the 1870s and each group campaigned vigorously. Of the eight national and state offices contested in 1872 the largest margin of victory was fifty votes, while presidential candidates Grant and Greeley tied.[4] Partisan politics, however, was generally limited to the campaign and faded following the election.

The Borough of Warren changed significantly between 1870 and 1910 and so did both the function and composition of the borough government. Table 9-1 reveals the occupational backgrounds of the Warren Borough Council during four five-year periods. In the early 1870s, before the industrialization of the community, Warren's councilmen came primarily from two groups. Two-thirds of the men who held office between 1870 and 1875 worked as attorneys, bankers, merchants, and businessmen or were retired gentlemen. Manufacturers and builders held only 13 percent of the council offices while manual workers occupied 21 percent of the council seats. In addition, fewer than one-half (46 percent) of the men holding office lived all their lives in the Commonwealth of Pennsylvania.[5] The council members in Warren during the 1870s were a mixture of entrepreneurs, professional men, and workers. Moreover, little distinction apparently existed between individuals born in Warren and more recent arrivals to the community.[6]

TABLE 9-1

Warren Borough Councilmen by Occupation

Years	Total Number of Offices	Attorneys, Bankers (%)	Merchants, Businessmen (%)	Manufacturers, Builders (%)	Manual Workers (%)	Others (%)
1870-1875	50	29	37	13	21	—
1880-1885	50	17	42	16	20	5
1890-1895	40*	14	44	17	14	11
1900-1905	60†	8	50	20	10	12

*The borough council reduced the number of officers after 1889 in a sliding fashion in an attempt to comply with the borough bylaws mandating only six seats.

†Two councilmen from each of the six political wards held office after 1895.

As the urbanization and industrialization of the community progressed, the composition of the government changed. The merchants
and businessmen and the manufacturers and builders increased their
control of the government in each succeeding decade. In the 1880
period these two groups held a combined 58 percent of the borough
offices. One decade later they occupied 61 percent of the council
seats, and by the early 1900s the proportion increased to 70 percent.
Merchants and businessmen alone controlled one-half of the borough
council seats from 1900 to 1905.[7] In contrast, the attorney-banker
group and the manual workers held fewer positions in each succeeding decade. By 1910 attorneys and bankers occupied only 8 percent of
the borough council seats compared with 29 percent in 1870. During
the same period the representation among manual laborers declined
from 21 percent to 10 percent.[8] However, this does not imply that "big
business" gained control of government in Warren after 1880. Small
businessmen and manufacturers frequently participated in the operation of local government during Warren's industrial era. No more than
30 percent of the councilmen holding office during each decade from
1870 through 1910 held estates exceeding $10,000.[9]

Clearly manual workers in Warren found it increasingly difficult to
obtain status through political activity. The virtual elimination of
laborers from the major ruling body in Warren and the increased
prominence of businessmen in politics may be understood by a brief
survey of the changing function of government in the borough during
the 1870-1910 period.

In 1870 the borough council's role consisted primarily of building
and repairing sidewalks and roads and the supervision of the town's
volunteer fire department and one-man police force. Total government expenditures in 1870 amounted to only $3,600. However,
within one decade the council assumed regulatory as well as super-
visory duties. In 1881 the borough government passed an ordinance
prohibiting the transporting of nitroglycerin—used in oil drilling—
through the town.[10] During the same decade the council, attempting
to prevent fires, prohibited the erection of frame housing on certain
streets within the borough.[11] In addition, ordinances regulating rates
charged by the Warren Street Railway, the water company, and the
natural gas company were enacted during the same decade.[12] For the
first time the town government became involved in what had previously been considered private matters. Businessmen and manufacturers became more politicized partly because the actions of the
borough council began to affect their interests more directly.[13]

Council members, however, also exhibited a strong concern for the welfare of the community. Motivated by a desire to provide services that individuals could no longer supply for themselves, the governmental leaders continued to expand the role of the town council throughout the next two decades. Increased demands for water services, public sanitation, electricity, and public parks resulted in a significant change in the operation of the council. Formal procedures and attention to legal details became much more evident in council activities after 1890. In addition, as the affairs of government became more complex, the borough council began to call upon professionals to assist in managing its affairs. In 1885 the council appointed a full-time health officer to establish and regulate health and sanitation laws; in 1888 a borough engineer was hired, and an attorney was hired in 1889.[14]

By the first decade of the twentieth century the affairs of government influenced the lives of nearly everyone in the community. Council activities included, for instance, the passage of a curfew for those under 16 years of age, establishment of a building code, and a legal suit against the Warren Water Company for supplying impure water to the community.[15] By 1910 borough expenditures exceeded $60,000 annually, including $12,000 interest and principal on a $155,000 debt.[16] The operation of the borough government had become one of the larger "businesses" in the community. The governmental leaders perhaps wished to further their own interests; little evidence exists, however, that these men were motivated solely by specific class interests.[17] Available evidence suggests that the ruling group believed that concern for the public interest would serve their own needs as well. The argument of the borough council in refusing the Warren Street Railway—owned by several prominent men in the community—permission to sell its special three-cent fares only at its office illustrates the council's concern for the public welfare. One councilman, a wealthy banker, stated:

> I am told that their franchise was got through the Council only by promising 3¢ fares to working people morning and evening. It seems to me that by this amendment the street car company can practically annul that condition in the contract for it is manifestly impossible for people who work from seven in the morning to six at night to get to the office to buy their tickets. . . . The whole purpose of the street car company is to be able to collect 5¢ instead of 3¢ from the laborer. . . .[18]

Another councilman added similar comments and concluded, "In my opinion the whole matter resolves itself into one proposition, namely that by this amendment the people's interest . . . would be conveyed into the hands of the street railway company forever."[19] Similar statements appear frequently in the borough council proceedings from 1890 through 1910. This suggests that while the manual worker virtually disappeared from the borough council after 1890 his interests continued to concern the group in power.

The combination of concern for the public welfare and for private interests by the Warren ruling elite suggests a significant difference between large industrial cities and smaller towns in nineteenth-century America.[20] Herbert Gutman, analyzing the "Worker's Search for Power" in *The Gilded Age*, notes:

> The social structure of the large city differed from that of the small industrial town because of the more direct human relationships among the residents of the smaller towns. Although many persons were not personally involved in the industrial process they felt its presence. Life was more difficult and less cosmopolitan in small towns, but it was also less complicated. This life was not romantic . . . yet the non-urban industrial environment had in it a kind of compelling simplicity. There the inhabitants lived and worked together, and a certain sense of community threaded their everyday lives.[21]

The public concerns of the governmental leaders and the high rate of mobility enjoyed by Warren workers contributed to the harmonious relations between the business classes and the laborers. Most of the men belonging to the most impoverished stratum of the working class left the community after a short duration and a permanent proletarian class never developed in nineteenth-century Warren. Furthermore, those remaining frequently climbed several rungs on the social ladder. Consequently, the lack of political power proved to be a small handicap in a community providing widespread opportunities for individual social mobility.[22]

The intensity of local elections increased after 1880 as candidates for borough council conducted vigorous campaigns. The local political parties generally followed the principles and objectives established by the national political leadership. The major issues dividing Warren candidates, however, centered upon efficient government, taxation, increased services (roads, sewage, and sidewalks and, after 1900, the quality of water supplied by the Warren Water Company).[23] Candidates for borough council campaigned on these issues rather than party affiliation, and personalities often decided the outcome of elections. Voting behavior in local elections produced erratic results with neither party gaining significant control in any of the four decades between 1870 and 1910, although the Republican Party recorded a small advantage over the Democrats. Of the 200 borough councilmen elected between 1870 and 1910, 56 percent were Republicans.[24]

Political conflict on state and national levels, in contrast, became virtually nonexistent as Warren voters, following the national pattern, registered solidly Republican majorities from 1884 through 1910. Table 9-2 reveals the voting patterns for three major state and national offices in each presidential election year, 1872-1908. In 1872, as previously noted, neither major political party held any significant numerical advantage. Both the Republican and Democratic candidates for president received the same number of votes in Warren—216—while the Democratic candidates for the United States House of Representatives and the State Assembly won by narrow margins. Democrats also won two of the three offices in both 1876 and 1880. However, by 1884, the slim advantage held by the Democratic Party disappeared and the Republican candidates for all three offices won majorities within the borough. In addition, the Republican margin of victory, with the exception of 1892, increased in each succeeding presidential election year. In both 1896 and 1900 approximately 59 percent of all the votes cast in the borough went to Republican candidates. In 1904 the Republican majority increased to an average of 74 percent, and in 1908 Republicans running for the three major offices received nearly two votes for each Democratic vote. The change in voting patterns in increasingly industrialized Warren mirrored the national pattern and resulted in the Democratic Party's being reduced to a relatively weak majority.

It is tempting, therefore, to conclude that the community's increasing level of affluence contributed to the growing popularity of the Republican Party. However, further analysis of the voting trends in nineteenth-century Warren suggests a different explanation. If a positive relationship exists between one's economic well-being and the popularity of the Republican Party one would expect to find support for the Democratic Party in residential areas inhabited primarily by manual workers. As previously indicated, 85 percent of the adult males residing in Warren's fourth or sixth ward in 1900 and 1910 were blue-collar workers. However, the Republican Party maintained its majority, although in small proportions, in each of these wards from 1896 through 1908 as manual workers living in Warren consistently supported the Republican Party. Only two Democratic candidates— the United States Congressional candidate in 1900 and William Jen-

TABLE 9-2

Warren Major Party Percentages, 1872-1908

Year	Voting Ward*	President (%) Rep.	Dem.	U.S. Congress (%) Rep.	Dem.	State Assembly (%) Rep.	Dem.
1872	—	50.0	50.0	47.3	52.7	47.1	52.9
1876	—	42.7	57.3	53.4	46.6	46.0	54.0
1880	—	49.1	50.9	50.2	49.8	49.8	50.2
1884	—	52.0	48.0	51.8	48.2	56.4	43.6
1888	—	56.3	43.7	54.9	45.1	58.1	41.9
1892	—	51.0	49.0	56.2	43.8	47.2	52.8
1896	Total (All Wards)	57.7	42.3	61.4	38.6	60.4	39.6
	1st Ward	68.1	31.9	71.0	29.0	70.8	29.2
	2nd Ward	68.0	32.0	71.8	21.2	69.8	30.2
	3rd Ward	57.8	42.2	62.3	37.7	61.0	31.0
	4th Ward	51.1	48.9	54.6	45.4	54.3	45.7
	5th Ward	50.1	49.9	53.6	46.4	53.0	47.0
	6th Ward	53.0	47.0	54.7	45.3	52.5	47.5
1900	Total (All Wards)	64.1	35.9	55.4	44.6	60.4	39.6
	1st Ward	72.0	28.0	58.2	41.8	68.5	31.5
	2nd Ward	72.1	27.9	52.8	47.2	62.4	37.6
	3rd Ward	65.1	34.9	51.3	48.7	60.0	40.0
	4th Ward	51.1	48.9	46.3	53.7	50.7	49.3
	5th Ward	69.2	30.8	54.4	45.6	65.4	34.6
	6th Ward	58.8	41.2	51.2	48.8	57.1	42.9
1904	Total (All Wards)	74.0	26.0	70.4	29.6	68.1	31.9
	1st Ward	78.2	21.8	70.7	29.3	78.1	21.9
	2nd Ward	77.7	22.3	72.0	28.0	76.7	23.3
	3rd Ward	72.4	27.6	77.3	22.7	78.1	21.9
	4th Ward	62.5	37.5	57.6	42.4	55.6	44.4
	5th Ward	67.2	32.8	75.3	24.7	66.3	33.7
	6th Ward	77.2	22.8	71.6	28.4	66.6	33.4
1908	Total (All Wards)	63.6	36.4	70.3	29.7	60.3	39.7
	1st Ward	70.7	29.3	75.7	24.3	69.0	31.0
	2nd Ward	68.7	31.3	75.0	25.0	68.7	31.3
	3rd Ward	68.2	31.8	77.3	22.7	60.3	39.7
	4th Ward	49.9	50.1	57.1	42.9	53.2	46.8
	5th Ward	66.0	34.0	70.8	29.2	60.7	39.3
	6th Ward	63.3	36.7	68.2	31.8	58.7	41.3

*Political wards were not organized until 1895.

nings Bryan in 1908—received a majority of fourth ward votes and no
Democrats won election in the sixth ward during this period. Workers
in nineteenth-century Warren obviously did not vote along strictly
economic or occupational lines.[25]

In comparison to other political wards in the borough, however, the
Democratic Party received some sustained support in the sixth and
particularly the fourth ward. Paul Kleppner in his social analysis of
politics in three Midwestern states—Ohio, Wisconsin, and Michigan,
1850-1896—reveals a strong relationship between ethno-religious
backgrounds and voting patterns. Examining both large and small,
urban and rural communities, Kleppner notes:

> Despite the religious heterogenerity of social groups supporting
> each of the major parties, it is possible to abstract an important
> *central tendency*. Those religious groups offering strong support to
> the Republican Party were more pietistic, or evangelical in their
> orientation than those offering similar support to the Democrats.
> Stated in propositional form: The more ritualistic the religious
> orientation of the group the more likely it was to support the
> Democracy; conversely, the more pietistic the group's outlook, the
> more intensely Republican its partisan affiliation.[26]

Studies of voting behavior in the nineteenth century by Kleppner
and others have demonstrated that local Republican Parties appealed
to the evangelical, nativistic, temperate, anti-Catholic elements in the
community. The Democratic Party, conversely, represented the ritualistic immigrant, anti-prohibition groups.[27] Analysis of the ethnic
and religious backgrounds of voters in Warren suggests a similar
relationship. The first, second, third, and fifth wards in Warren voted
overwhelmingly Republican in four national elections from 1896
through 1908. These wards were inhabited almost exclusively by
native-born Americans, Germans, French, and English. Moreover,
most of these residents belonged to the Presbyterian, Baptist, Methodist, Episcopal, and Lutheran (Pittsburgh Synod) churches in Warren.[28] None of these groups adhered to what Kleppner terms the
ritualistic perspective.

The fourth and sixth wards, on the other hand, were inhabited by a
much more heterogeneous—although almost exclusively blue-
collar—group. Nearly one-half of the Irish-Catholics and over 60
percent of the Italian-Catholics resided in the fourth ward after 1895.
Native-born Americans (15 percent), Germans (18 percent), Swedes
(16 percent), and Danes (22 percent) also resided in the fourth ward.[29]
Few of these latter groups belonged to the "ritualistic" religions. The

actual voting patterns of each of these groups, of course, remains unknown. However, when one compares the voting trends in the fourth ward with those in wards one, two, three, and five the evidence suggests that the major Democratic support came from the Irish- and Italian-Catholics. The other ethno-religious groups supplied the slim Republican majority in each election.

Voting patterns in the sixth ward reinforce this conclusion. The proportion of manual workers living in the sixth ward in 1900 through 1910 closely paralleled the proportion residing in the fourth ward. In addition, the fourth and sixth wards contained approximately the same number of native-born American, German, and Danish-born workers. Yet the sixth ward consistently returned a higher percentage of Republican votes. The variables, of course, were the Irish- and Italian-Catholics and the Swedish Protestants. By 1910 one-fourth of the Irish-born workers and one-third of the Italians resided in the sixth ward. In contrast, fully one-half of the Swedes—a much larger group—established residence in the sixth ward.[30] The editor of the *Warren Mail* understood the relationship between religion and the Republic loyalties of Swedish-born workers, declaring:

> This is not the first time the Democratic ringsters have tried, through their emissaries, to corrupt or disaffect this compact body of Republicans in Warren. And to their lasting honor let it be said that the Swedes have stood up manfully and loyally for their convictions through good or ill.
>
> The modern Swede is made of the same reliable material as his ancestors. That race, under Gustavus Adolphus, and the banner of Protestantism . . . has not yet lost its conscientious devotion to principle.[31]

The combination of Swedish Protestantism aligned with the other ethno-religious groups holding the "pietistic" perspective contributed significantly to the Republican majority in the sixth ward. Conversely, the substantial Irish- and Italian-Catholic minorities remained true to the Democratic Party.[32]

The available evidence, therefore, suggests a strong relationship between the political allegiances of workers in Warren and their ethnic and religious backgrounds. Moreover, partisan affiliations cut across both economic and occupational lines. Therein, of course, may lie the manual workers' failure to join the ruling elite and achieve political power in any significant numbers. Workers in Warren simply did not act in concert to achieve common political goals. In addition, the Irish, who frequently achieved political success in other communities, remained numerically too small in Warren to utilize politics as a steppingstone to elite status.[33]

The function and composition of the Warren Board of Education, like the borough council, changed significantly during the community's era of growth. Before industrialization and urbanization, the function of the school committee—similar to the Warren Borough Council—was quite limited. Board members supervised an annual budget ranging between $5,000 in 1870 and $8,100 in 1875. Eight teachers appointed annually instructed approximately 580 students in a single eight-room schoolhouse.[34] The board's major concerns were minimizing expenditures, keeping taxes low, and carefully examining proposed new educational programs and building projects.[35] Taxpayers generally applauded the economics of the board. One letter to the editor of the *Warren Ledger* demanded even greater efforts, exclaiming:

> For a long time back there has been a steadily growing belief that our school system is costing too much, is becoming a serious burden to many taxpayers. . . .
>
> In what particulars can any lessening of expense be carried out, it may be asked. It should be kept in mind that seven-eighths of the school children are destined for industry rather than professional pursuits. Therefore, there is a prevailing sentiment that music, foreign languages, drawing and higher math are not necessary to fit the average public school scholar for the life that is ahead of him or her. . . .[36]

The school board's frugality, however, did not extend to the children of the poor. Families unable to pay school taxes were permitted to present promissory notes to the board rather than lose their homes. Moreover, the school directors, insisting that education was a right as well as a necessity, passed a unanimous declaration providing children of the poor with free books.[37]

The functions of the preindustrial board of education illustrate that body's responsibility toward the taxpayers and also the general sense of common interests that prevailed in the community. The board, elected biannually, was not a representative body in the 1870s. Fourteen men, possessing average estates exceeding $26,000, occupied the fifty-five available seats on the school committee from 1870 through 1879. Table 9-3 displays the changing nature of the educational elite during the period of industrialization in nineteenth-century Warren.

TABLE 9-3

Warren Borough School Directors by Occupation, 1870-1910

Years	Total Number Offices	Attorneys, Bankers (%)	Merchants, Business-men (%)	Manu-facturers, Builders (%)	Manual Workers (%)	Others (%)	Average Estate
1870-1879	60	30	50	20	—	—	$26,163
1880-1889	60	35	42	9	6	8	11,186
1890-1899	84	30	25	14	20	11	15,804
1900-1910	141	20	30	20	20	10	9,436

   In the 1870s the Warren Board of Education—unlike the borough council—consisted exclusively of wealthy white-collar executives and professional men. Merchants and businessmen controlled one-half of the school committee seats while attorneys, bankers, and manufacturers filled the remaining offices. Moreover, the average length of term of office—3.56 years—enabled a small select group of men to dominate educational policy during the decade. One man sat as president of the board during the entire ten-year period. Both manual laborers and immigrants failed to attain a single directorship in the 1870s.

   The composition of the school board changed dramatically during the next three decades. Between 1880 and 1900, the two most progressive decades in the borough's history, the representation of both the merchant-businessman group and the manufacturer-builder group declined. In the 1880s merchants and businessmen controlled 42 percent of the school board offices; during the next decade the proportion declined to 25 percent. Manufacturers and builders held approximately half as many seats (9 percent) in the 1880s as they did in the previous decade. Attorneys and bankers increased their representation slightly to 35 percent in the 1880s but returned to the 30 percent level in the next ten years. The most impressive gains accrued to manual laborers, who controlled 6 percent of the directorships in the 1880s and 20 percent in the 1890s. In addition, the average length of office declined slightly to 2.9 years and the average estate held by school directors decreased to $11,186 in the 1880s although rising somewhat to $15,804 during the next ten years.

   During the first decade of the twentieth century the majority (70 percent) of Warren's school directors continued to come from the three white-collar groups. Manual workers, however, maintained some representation on the board, occupying twenty-eight (or 20 percent) of the 141 available seats from 1900 through 1910. One-fifth of the fifty men holding directorships during this period came from the ranks of the blue-collar workers. Furthermore, the average wealth held by board members declined to under $10,000, as a number of middle-class workers joined the educational elite.

At first glance this increased democratization of the Warren school board may appear somewhat paradoxical, particularly when compared with the changing composition of the Warren Borough Council. However, a survey of the functions of the school committee reveals that the two organizations served different interests and constituencies. The actions of the borough council affected all residents of the community, but enactments regarding zoning, oil drilling, business licenses, and the regulation of utilities directly involved the concerns of the business elite of the community. The functions and responsibilities of the school board also expanded dramatically during the late nineteenth century but remained quite narrow in scope. The school budget grew from $5,055 in 1872 to more than $65,000 in 1910. Bonded indebtedness, which did not exist in 1870, exceeded $150,000 by 1910. Moreover, school enrollment quadrupled and the number of teachers employed by the borough increased elevenfold during the 1870 to 1910 period.[38] However, an examination of the school board minutes reveals that the focus of the committee remained unchanged. Curriculum, employment of teachers, and building construction continued as major concerns of the school committee through 1910. These activities, of course, affected businessmen with school-age children but rarely involved their business interests. Hence their participation on the board of education was not as crucial to them as membership on the borough council.

Laborers, on the other hand, had a greater stake in the policies of the board of education than the activities of the borough council. Residents of the borough viewed education as a means of uplifting all classes in the community. Following a letter attacking the academic department of the high school, the editor of the *Warren Ledger* replied:

Break up your high schools and you take away all chances of advancing from three-fourths of all young men and women who attend them. No wonder the sentiment is not openly expressed against the high schools. They furnish an opportunity to the children of the poorer classes that prompts them to enlarge their sphere of action, to rise in the world. . . . It is the glory of free institutions that they make the chances of success in life as nearly equal as possible. . . .[39]

School attendance and participation by parents at educational activities indicate that residents considered education important. Average daily attendance in school exceeded 90 percent in each year from 1874 through 1910.[40] A "mass meeting" held in 1896 to discuss "moral, mental, and muscular education" attracted more than 1,000 adults.[41] In addition, the town's leading citizens continued to view education as an instrument of social control. Students were frequently warned that "truancy and playing 'hookey' are the stepping stones to vagrancy and vagabondage."[42] The school held the "prime responsibility for inculcating a taste in the child for purity of thought, life and language" and in this respect "the will must be trained and brought under control."[43] A school board resolution adopted in 1901—sponsored by the Warren Women's Christian Temperance Union—honoring Frances E. Willard perhaps best illustrates the perceived role of the schools toward social control. The committee declared:

> Realizing the value and power for good of the example of a noble life, and believing that Miss Willard represents one of the highest and best examples of American woman, the committee on schools suggests that the teachers . . . use a portion of Lincoln's birthday to teach the pupils to emulate the nobleness of character, her untiring industry, her ceaseless efforts to elevate and reclaim fallen humanity.[44]

The school committee frequently responded positively to requests by working-class citizens to expand the curriculum or erect additional buildings. Industrial, commercial, and domestic science programs were added to the course of study to meet the varying interests of the students. A night school opened in 1895 to teach reading to illiterate adults and was later expanded to include commercial and technical courses.[45] New buildings were erected in the fourth and sixth wards in 1901 at the request of the citizens, mostly blue-collar workers, residing in these two subdivisions.[46] The self-interest of blue-collar workers attracted them to join the educational leaders frequently attaining positions of influence on the school board in nineteenth-century Warren.

Education received impressive public and private support in the borough during the era of industrialization. Referendums to increase bonded indebtedness for building construction always passed by large majorities. In addition, individuals often bestowed large financial contributions upon the school board to improve the quality of education. A wealthy oil industrialist completely equipped the school's manual training department and gymnasium; others donated books, pianos, or typewriters. In 1910, eighty-five citizens contributed an average of fifty dollars each toward the construction of a school athletic and recreational park.[47]

School enrollment, however, provides the most reliable index of the high regard for education in nineteenth-century Warren. The first high school commencement in Warren occurred in 1878. From that date through 1910 more than 80 percent of all school-age children residing in Warren actually attended school.[48] Moreover, as previously indicated, average daily attendance exceeded 90 percent in each school term. The financial sacrifices workers made to provide an education for their children attests to their belief in the value of formal training. In 1895, tuition alone ranged between $6.00 and $16.00 per semester per child, depending upon the grade level.[49] The willingness of manual laborers to keep children in school rather than send them to work suggests that workers viewed education as an important element in the success of their offspring.

Graduation, particularly from high school, often enabled one to obtain a white-collar job and occasionally a professional occupation; high school graduates, for example, frequently obtained positions as elementary school teachers. Manual workers living in Warren each decade from 1880 through 1910 constituted approximately 59 percent (the proportion fell to 48 percent in the 1890s) of the adult male population.[50] However, a positive relationship between persistence in the community and successful completion of formal education suggests a higher incidence of high school graduation among children of native-born parents. Hence the built-in bias of this analysis favors finding higher graduation rates for second-generation Americans rather than children of immigrants. In addition, while the exact number of manual laborers with school-age children remains unknown, nothing indicates that they had larger or smaller families than nonmanual workers. Thus one may assume that a reasonably equitable per family distribution of school-age children existed between nonmanual and manual laborers. Table 9-4 illustrates the relationship between parents' ethnicity and occupation and the attainment of a high school diploma.

Approximately one-third of the high school graduates during each decade from 1880 through 1910 came from families of manual laborers. In the 1880s 43 children (35 percent) of blue-collar workers

TABLE 9-4

Percentage of High School Graduates by Parents' Occupational and Ethnic Backgrounds, 1870-1910

Years	Total Number High School Graduates	Foreign-born Parents (%)	Native-born Parents (%)	Manual Parents (%)	Nonmanual Parents (%)
1870-1880*	13	24	76	46	54
1881-1890	122	31	69	35	65
1891-1900	202	29	71	33	67
1901-1910	291	29	71	36	64

*The first high school graduation occurred in 1878.

completed high school. During the next ten years the number increased to 67 (33 percent) and rose to 105 (36 percent) in the first decade of the twentieth century. Hence analysis of high school graduates in nineteenth-century Warren suggests that children of nonmanual workers were twice as likely to earn a high school diploma as children of laboring families. Furthermore, blue-collar workers outnumbered white-collar workers, indicating an even greater disparity of educational attainment between the two groups. Nevertheless, more than one-third of the children of manual laborers succeeded in remaining in school until graduation. This impressive figure, of course, suggests that manual workers frequently possessed the financial ability as well as the desire to provide formal training for their children.

Sons and daughters of foreign-born parents, with the exception of the Irish and Italians, fared better than the offspring of all manual workers. Foreign-born residents, constituting approximately one-third of the population in Warren each decade from 1870 through 1910, succeeded in producing high school graduates almost in direct proportion to their total percentage in the community. Nearly three of every ten high school graduates in each decade from 1880 through 1910 came from families of immigrant parents. Children of German, French, and English immigrants succeeded in graduating from high school most frequently. As previously noted, workers from these three countries experienced greater occupational mobility and established higher persistence rates than other groups of immigrants. Fully one-fourth of the immigrants' children receiving high school diplomas from 1880 through 1910 were offspring of German-born fathers. English and French workers produced the second largest proportion of graduates. Seventeen percent of all children of immigrants completing high school came from these two groups. The Irish, conversely, with approximately the same population as both the German and French workers, produced less than 10 percent of the immigrant group high school graduates.

Two other ethnic groups—the Swedes and the Italians—arrived in Warren in significant numbers after 1890 and experienced contrasting educational opportunities. Ten percent of all children of immigrants graduating from high school after 1890 had Swedish-born fathers. In contrast, Italian-born workers arriving in Warren at the turn of the century failed to produce a single high school graduate during the decade. Of course, the short period of residency of Italian-born workers contributed to this absence of educational success. However, the previously discussed negative treatment (see Chapter 5) and the lack of occupational mobility experienced by Italian-born workers indicates a strong relationship between these factors and the ability to provide a complete education for one's children.

The analysis of the changing social structure in nineteenth-century Warren in Chapters 8 and 9 suggests the following conclusions:

1. The ethnic, native-born composition of the Warren labor force changed little between 1870 and 1910. Foreign-born workers constituted approximately one-third of the labor force in 1870, 1880, and 1900. The proportion rose to 42 percent in 1890 and fell to 27 percent in 1910. The immigrant groups, however, changed considerably during the era. In 1870, the English, Irish, Germans, and French constituted the majority of the town's foreign-born workers. By 1910 immigrants from Sweden outnumbered workers from the four other nations combined and made up nearly 36 percent of the borough's foreign-born population.

2. The occupational structure of the community changed dramatically between 1870 and 1910. Prior to industrialization, Warren was a community of small shops operated primarily by skilled artisans. By 1910, nearly 60 percent of the labor force held jobs in large, highly specialized industrial firms.

3. The division of labor in postindustrial Warren was matched by increasing residential separation. Unskilled workers and certain ethnic groups (the Irish, Swedes, and Italians) were all but eliminated from the more prosperous sections of town. Moreover, industrial, commercial, and residential sectors added to the spatial distribution of the community.

4. The growing public functions of government led to a complex administrative and political structure aided by a small but influential group of professionals. Moreover, the juxtaposition of public and

private interests in the affairs of government contributed to an increased politicization of the community elite. Conversely, manual workers experienced correspondingly less success in gaining access to the borough council during each succeeding decade.

5. The delicate political party balance which existed in preindustrial Warren disappeared by the mid-1880s. The combination of northern European ethnic groups and followers of what Paul Kleppner calls the "pietistic" Christian faiths contributed to an overwhelming Republican partisanship.

6. The community elite continued to exercise strong control over the policies and programs of the board of education, but manual workers succeeded in gaining a voice in the operation of their schools. One-fifth of the school board members during the last two decades of this study came from the ranks of blue-collar workers. Furthermore, while the schools continued to function as an instrument of social control, expanded programs including night school and manual training provided services to most members of the community.[51]

7. Manual laborers and immigrants residing in the borough for any length of time, with the exception of the Irish and the Italians, frequently succeeded in providing their children with formal education. At least one-third of the high school graduates in any decade were children of manual workers. An even greater percentage probably attended school for at least eight years. The impressive educational success of children of blue-collar workers reinforces the previously expressed conclusion that Warren's manual laborers could justifiably view America as a land of opportunity.

10 Concluding Observations: Some Implications

The preceding analysis of social mobility in one nineteenth-century city suggests that dramatic differences existed in the opportunities available to native-born manual laborers, immigrants, and children of immigrants. American-born workers frequently attained higher level occupations, purchased property, and accumulated modest amounts of wealth. Immigrants, however, experienced much more limited mobility although important differences prevailed in the attainments of newcomers of various national backgrounds.

Immigrants of German, French, or English origin frequently secured skilled or nonmanual occupations upon entry into the Warren labor force. Few of these men attained better jobs although those who remained in Warren for a decade or more obtained property and accumulated a small amount of wealth. Irish, Italian, and, to some degree, Swedish immigrants, particularly after 1900, secured only manual (primarily unskilled) occupations upon arrival into the community. Most remained in the low-skill, low-pay universe throughout their careers in Warren. Similarly, Irish, Italian, and Swedish workers experienced greater difficulty attaining either property or wealth than did other major ethnic groups. For most immigrants remaining in Warren for any length of time the initial occupation they secured upon arrival became their lifelong work.

Sons of immigrants enjoyed significantly greater mobility than immigrants starting work in the same skill classifications. In fact, little distinction exists between the mobility rates of all native-born workers and the occupational advances of American-born sons of immigrants. In late nineteenth-century Warren both groups frequently enjoyed impressive social mobility.

Finally, the Warren data reveal a strong positive relationship between persistence in the community and social mobility. The longer an individual remained in the community the greater were his chances for success. Twenty-year residents nearly always recorded higher rates of occupational mobility than ten-year residents. Mobility for thirty-year men exceeded those remaining in the community for twenty years. Similar relationships existed for property and estate mobility. Significantly, rates of persistence for native sons always exceeded those established by immigrants, and white-collar workers remained geographically less mobile than manual workers throughout the study. Hence selective outward migration operated to improve the rates of mobility by removing a disproportionately large number of the least successful workers.

Between 1850 and 1900 the number of American communities of 10,000 or more persons increased nearly sevenfold.[1] The growth of Warren paralleled the industrial and urban growth of hundreds of communities throughout the nation. This suggests that Warren's growth resulted from forces which operated in much the same way in cities throughout the nation. Recent studies of social mobility suggest important similarities between the experiences of workers in Warren and laborers in other nineteenth-century cities. An examination of these findings demonstrates the representativeness of Warren with regard to the problems discussed in this study.[2]

Recently five historians engaged in a collaborative effort to compare data from five eastern cities: Buffalo, Poughkeepsie, and Kingston, all in New York, Philadelphia, Pennsylvania, and Hamilton, Ontario. These cities ranged in size from Philadelphia's population of 565,529 in 1860 to Kingston's 16,640.[3] Each scholar contributed manuscript census data to compare structural similarities and differences in the five cities at the time of the Civil War. Following exacting analysis of the data, the historians concluded that "despite the remarkable variations between cities in terms of their history, their location, their size, and their local flavour, they shared a number of distinct social and demographic characteristics. These shared characteristics," the historians concluded, "make it possible to speak with meaning of a nineteenth century city."[4] Among the shared structural features were occupational structure, occupational ranking, age structure, and property ownership. A brief comparison of some of the findings with the Warren data illustrate how the Warren structure fits the patterns noted in the five cities.

The distribution of occupations in each of the five cities within several broad categories was as follows: manufacturing and laboring, 41 to 49 percent of the labor force; commerce and the professions, 18 to 23 percent; construction and transport, 18 to 29 percent; and miscellaneous occupations, approximately 9 to 13 percent. The Warren data for 1870—the closest to the 1860 period considered in the five-city project—fall within these ranges. In fact, the functional occupational structure of Warren, the smallest of all six cities, matches that of Philadelphia. In both cities 48 percent of the working population engaged in manufacturing and commerce, 11 percent in construction and transport, 20 percent in the professions and commerce, and 13 percent in miscellaneous occupations.

When one considers occupational rank, Warren deviated somewhat from the pattern of the five cities. This is probably explained by the number of small shop owners in Warren in 1870. Between 15 and 20 percent of the labor force in each of the five cities wore white collars to work while the percentage in Warren reached a high of 42. The percentage of workers in skilled occupations in Warren, however, fell within the range of the five cities. In all six cities, between one-third and one-half of all workers held skilled occupations. At the bottom of the occupational structure—unskilled and semiskilled workers— Warren again deviated from the pattern of the five cities. Approximately one-fourth of the Warren labor force held jobs in the two lowest skill classifications. Unskilled and semiskilled categories in the five cities averaged just under one-third of their respective labor force. Thus Warren, the smallest of all the cities, had a somewhat larger representation in the white-collar field and a smaller concentration of workers in the low, blue-collar classifications.

The age distribution of the work force in Warren paralleled that found in the five cities. Except for Hamilton, in all of the other five cities (including Warren) between 35 and 40 percent of the working population was between the ages of eighteen and twenty-nine, between one-fourth and one-third in their thirties, just under 20 percent in their forties, and between 12 and 20 percent over the age of fifty.

The greatest deviation from the structural patterns noted in the five cities and that of Warren was in the area of home ownership. With the exception of Philadelphia, between 24 and 31 percent of the residents in each city owned their own homes. Home ownership in Warren approached 45 percent in 1870, while only 11 percent of the population in Philadelphia in 1860 owned their own homes. The exact reasons for this difference are not clear. They may, however, be tied to the greater proportion of white-collar occupations and small shop owners in the Warren labor force. Many of Warren's workers labored in privately owned small shops in 1870. They often lived behind these shops and owned both the dwelling and the shop. In addition, each of the five cities possessed greater percentages of low-level blue-collar workers than did Warren. It is likely that many of these men were landless proletariat pulling down the rates of home ownership in these cities.

The ethnic composition of the work forces in Philadelphia, Kingston, Poughkeepsie, Buffalo, Hamilton, and Warren varied widely. In Buffalo and Hamilton native-born workers constituted only 20 and 10 percent of the working populations, respectively. In Philadelphia, Poughkeepsie, and Kingston between 45 and 55 percent of the adult males were native-born. Warren's native-born workers constituted nearly two-thirds of the labor force. Yet in each of these cities the distribution of clustering of Irish immigrants and native sons in specific occupational classes was similar.[5] The Irish in all six cities were over-represented in the unskilled occupations and vastly under-represented in white-collar and professional occupations. Native sons, as might be expected, dominated the white-collar occupations and were highly under-represented in the low blue-collar classifications.

Thus a comparison of characteristics in Warren with five other nineteenth-century cities illustrates both the similarity and the uniqueness of the borough's structural pattern. Comparison of the horizontal and vertical mobility patterns of these and other nineteenth-century cities illustrates even greater similarities.

Studies of geographic mobility suggest a highly volatile nineteenth-century population with less than 50 percent of the residents remaining in any community for a full decade. Warren's white-collar workers and native-born residents recorded similar rates of horizontal mobility. Manual laborers and immigrants were even more mobile between 1870 and 1890; the gap in persistence closed after 1890. Clyde Griffen reports a remarkably similar population turnover in another city undergoing industrialization and urbanization— Poughkeepsie, New York—from 1850 to 1880. No more than 45 percent of any group of workers resided in that city for as long as ten years.[6] Persistence of workers in Newburyport, Massachusetts, followed the same pattern; a maximum of 41 percent of the population in that New England city remained longer than a single decade.[7] Persistence rates of immigrants in Poughkeepsie and Newburyport generally paralleled the rates achieved by foreign-born workers in Warren. In addition, during the earlier periods of each study native-born workers exhibited a greater propensity to settle than immigrants; this difference largely disappeared in the final decades.[8] In his study of Newburyport, Thernstrom notes even higher rates of outward migration in five other nineteenth-century cities. For example, "The rate of population turnover in Rochester, New York, for 1849-1859 was even higher . . . and other studies indicate the extreme instability of the manual labor force in such cities as Biddleford, Maine, and Lowell,

Holyoke and Chicopee, Massachusetts."[9]

Peter Knights reveals a similar population turnover in his recent study of *The Plain People of Boston, 1830-1860*. During the three decades of his study, ten-year persistence rates for all residents of Boston, the fifth largest city in America in 1860, ranged between 37 and 46 percent. In addition, persistence rates of native-born residents exceeded those of immigrants in each decade.[10] Persistence rates of Boston residents rose during the latter part of the nineteenth century, yet the outward migration continued at a high rate. Just over a third of the males living in Boston in 1880 left the city by 1890. And nearly 60 percent of Boston's 1910 adult male residents had disappeared from the city by 1920.[11]

High rates of outward migration obviously were not confined to cities of any particular size. Both large and small nineteenth-century cities apparently served as temporary residences where people lived for short periods of time then moved on to other communities. Nor does there appear to be any relationship between geographical location and population stability. In Waltham, Massachusetts, between one-third and one-half of the adult males remained as long as a decade during the second half of the nineteenth century, while rates of outward migration in Omaha, Nebraska, exceeded 68 percent between 1880 and 1900 and 72 percent between 1900 and 1920.[12] In San Antonio, Texas, less than one-half of the adult males residing there in 1870 remained there one decade later. Persistence rates over a thirty-year period, 1870-1900, show a similar outward migration.[13] In addition, native-sons, like those in Warren, demonstrated a greater propensity to remain in San Antonio between 1870 and 1900. During those three decades 49 percent of all native-born white workers sampled remained in San Antonio whereas only one-third of the immigrants did so.[14]

Low persistence rates in Birmingham, Alabama, Atlanta, Georgia, and Cairo, Illinois, also demonstrate the transient nature of the nineteenth-century American population. Over a ten-year period in Birmingham, 1880-1890, only 34 percent of the white workers remained in the city.[15] This pattern is repeated in Atlanta, with less than one-half of the adult male population remaining in the city between 1870 and 1880.[16] Cairo, Illinois, a declining city by the second half of the nineteenth century, exhibited even greater outward migration, with 86 percent of the names appearing in an 1850 sample no longer residing in Cairo one decade later. Between 1860 and 1870 three-fourths of the 1860 sample left the community and 62 percent of the 1870 sample disappeared from Cairo by 1880.[17]

The persistence data from fourteen other cities demonstrate that the high rate of population turnover in Warren reflects the spectacular volatility of the nineteenth-century labor force in most cities, regardless of size or geographic location. Furthermore, the greater persistence rates recorded by native-born workers in Warren appears typical of the migration patterns in Newburyport, Poughkeepsie, Boston, and San Antonio.

Comparison of the relationship between persistence rates and property ownership also reveals striking similarities. In Warren, Newburyport, Poughkeepsie, and Birmingham, those without property left the city much more frequently. In each case more than one-half of those owning property remained in the community longer than a decade.[18] In Omaha, Nebraska, Howard Chudacoff suggests that although the evidence is limited,

> renting . . . [did] breed impermanence. The vast majority of those who moved or emigrated within five years had rented their places of residence. Of those who remained in the city, only one stayed in a rented place for as long as eleven years. . . . In some instances ownership was associated with residential stability. Of those few people who occupied the same place over relatively long periods of time—fourteen to twenty years—most owned their own homes.[19]

It is not clear, of course, whether property ownership created stability or whether the purchase of property reflects one's prior decision to remain in the community. Nevertheless, the correlation between property ownership and persistence in the community noted in Warren, Newburyport, Poughkeepsie, Birmingham, and Omaha suggests that possession of real estate was an important factor in the stability of many nineteenth-century cities.

The occupational mobility enjoyed by manual workers in Warren also reflects mobility rates in other American cities of the age. Comparison of occupational mobility in Warren and Newburyport has received prominent attention in this study (see Chapters 4, 5, and 6) and will not be repeated here. Several other studies—employing somewhat different methodology—also reported the presence of significant occupational opportunity. In Waltham, Massachusetts, slightly more than one-third of the laborers who persisted in that community for five years or more were upwardly mobile.[20] In his analysis of immigrant craft workers in Poughkeepsie, New York, Griffen concludes, "However modest, prolonged and uneven the improvement in condition for the foreign-born and their children after the great influx in the '40s and '50s, it held promise enough to prevent the rejection of the national faith that success came to the industrious."[21]

Other research indicates that occupational mobility also occurred in large industrial cities. In ante-bellum Boston, between one-fourth and one-third of the blue-collar workers remaining for a full decade accomplished at least mild occupational advances.[22] In the same city during a later period, 1890-1940, approximately one-third of all day laborers climbed to nonmanual positions.[23] Unskilled laborers in Norristown, Pennsylvania, also experienced some occupational mobility. Fully 30 percent of all day laborers in that community attained higher level occupations within a single decade, from 1910 to 1920.[24]

Data from two southern and two western cities suggest that these patterns of mobility were not confined to the eastern United States. In Birmingham, "More than one-half of all three groups [1880, 1890, 1900] of unskilled white workingmen sampled who remained in the city for ten years climbed up the occupational ladder. . . . After 20 years, almost one-half of the white skilled and semi-skilled workmen had experienced upward mobility."[25] White workingmen in Atlanta, Georgia, enjoyed similar success. Between 1870 and 1880 more than one-fourth of all native-white manual laborers sampled experienced some upward mobility, and a full 22 percent climbed to white-collar positions. From 1870 to 1896, 52 percent of the sample moved upward, with 48 percent moving from a blue-collar to a white-collar position.[26]

White manual workers in Omaha and San Antonio also enjoyed significant upward mobility, although not as impressive as that of workers in Warren, Birmingham, or Atlanta. In Omaha, 1880-1920, "between 11 and 14 percent of the manual laborers rose to nonmanual positions in five years, about 22.5 percent in fourteen years, and 25 percent or so in twenty years. . . . Conversely, three-fourths of the manual workers accomplished no significant mobility in twenty years."[27] These figures are comparable with those for San Antonio, 1870-1900. In that city approximately one-fourth of all native-born whites and European immigrants climbed the occupational ladder in each decade.[28]

Finally, although he examined the lives of successful industrialists rather than the entire working class, Herbert Gutman provides the most spectacular example of mobility. In Paterson, New Jersey, Gutman reveals:

As a group the developers of the Paterson Locomotive Industry . . . experienced enormous occupational mobility in their lives. In one generation—often in a few years—men jumped class lines and rose rapidly in prestige and status. . . . Almost all started in life as skilled artisans and had risen to become factory foremen or superintendents of large new manufacturing enterprises.[29]

The immigrant sector of the Warren population experienced some occupational mobility but much more limited than that enjoyed by the native sons. This disparity in opportunity also occurred in Newburyport, Boston, and Omaha but not in Atlanta or San Antonio.[30] In Newburyport, Thernstrom reports, "The immigrant workman . . . was markedly less successful than his native counterpart in climbing out of the ranks of the unskilled in the 1850-1880 period. In each of the three groups at each census disproportionately high numbers of the foreign-born remained concentrated at the bottom of the occupational scale."[31] Foreign-born workers in nineteenth-century Boston labored under a similar handicap. In his analysis of "Immigrants and WASPS" in Boston, 1890-1940, Thernstrom concludes, "Not only did the foreign-born start more often at the bottom; they were less often upwardly mobile after their first job, and those who started well were more prone to lose their middle class positions and end up in a manual job."[32]

Immigrants in Omaha also found upward mobility more difficult than their native counterparts. Nearly one-third of the American-born manual workers sampled in 1880 achieved upward mobility and 43.5 percent did so within twenty years. Immigrant workers were noticeably less successful. During the same periods only 13.8 and 17 percent of the foreign-born sample who remained in the city could climb the occupational ladder.[33]

Mobility patterns of immigrants in Atlanta and San Antonio, however, deviate sharply from the pattern noted in Warren, Newburyport, Boston, and Omaha. In both these cities immigrants remaining in the community for any length of time experienced mobility equal to and occasionally exceeding that of their native counterparts.[34] In both cases the presence of black workers—and in San Antonio of Mexican-Americans—who experienced almost no mobility suggests that race influenced one's chances for success much more than ethnicity.

The limited evidence presented here pertaining to a few specific cities does not permit conclusive generalizations. It does, however, suggest that patterns of occupational mobility of native-born and immigrant laborers in nineteenth-century Warren did not differ radically from other predominantly white nineteenth-century cities. One may suggest, at least tentatively, that immigrants frequently experienced less success than their native counterparts. Immigrants residing in cities containing large groups of black workers, however, often enjoyed comparatively greater mobility, their traditional place at the bottom of the occupational ladder being occupied by black or Mexican-American workers.

Comparison of the property ownership achieved by the settled segment of workers in Warren and Newburyport suggests that this form of mobility also occurred in other nineteenth-century communities. Approximately two-thirds of all the skilled and semiskilled workers residing in Warren for two or more decades succeeded in purchasing real property. Unskilled workers generally required a longer time to acquire their own homes, but within twenty years nearly one-half of all the day laborers still in the community owned property. Conditions in Warren, of course, became particularly conducive to working-class prosperity although the rapid growth of the community produced a scarcity of homes throughout the 1880-1910 period. Economic growth in Newburyport, on the other hand, was almost nonexistent after 1850. Nevertheless, laborers who remained in that New England community frequently became property owners. In fact, unskilled laborers in Newburyport recorded even higher percentages of property ownership: Between 63 and 78 percent of all families of unskilled laborers living in Newburyport for twenty years owned their own homes.[35] The impressive success enjoyed by laborers in one dynamic industrial community and one stable industrial city at least suggests that comparable opportunities existed in similar nineteenth-century towns.[36]

Analysis of property ownership in major American cities between 1890 and 1910, however, also reveals that significant differences existed between large and small industrial communities. Nearly one-half of the residents of Warren owned their own homes during this period. Conversely, a great majority of the residents of America's fifty-five largest cities—those with over 100,000 population—rented rather than owned their own homes. Only eleven major American cities reported home ownership exceeding 40 percent of the population in 1890, 1900, or 1910. Furthermore, only one of the nation's fifty-five largest cities exceeded Warren's rate of property ownership during this period.[37] This, of course, suggests that while important similarities existed between Warren and other cities, both large and small, fundamental differences were also present.

Small industrial towns, according to Herbert Gutman, differed from the large urban centers in several important ways:

> Social contact was more direct in the smaller post-Civil War industrial towns and regions. . . . The social distance between the various economic classes that characterized the large city came much more

slowly and hardly paralleled industrial developments. . . .

The small businessmen and shopkeepers, the lawyers and professional people, and the other non-industrial members of the middle class were a small but vital element in these industrial towns. Unlike the urban middle class they had direct and everyday contact with the new industrialism and with the problems and the outlook of workers and employers. . . . While they invariably accepted the concepts of private property and free entrepreneurship, their judgements about the *social* behavior of industrialists often drew upon noneconomic considerations and values. They saw no necessary contradiction between private enterprise and gain on the one hand and decent humane social relations between workers and employers on the other.[38]

The substantial industrial and social transformations produced less class conflict in small communities than in the large urban centers. The sense of community that modified labor-management conflict in all likelihood affected other areas of social change in small industrial centers. What Robert Wiebe termed "the search for order," however, had its effect on Warren and other comparable communities. The depression of 1893 and the Pullman Strike of 1894 generated strong nativistic and anti-labor attitudes in the community. In addition, fear of radical political groups, rapid social changes, and a variety of real and perceived social ills such as prostitution and the "drinking habit," contributed to the anxieties of citizens in Warren.[39] Other small communities no doubt experienced similar problems and attitudinal changes. Wiebe views these events as symptomatic of the breakdown of the "American island community" prior to the emergence of a new system. According to Wiebe:

These were the scattered events that announced a feeling suddenly acute across the land that local America stood at bay, besieged by giant forces abroad and beset by subversion at home. An important qualitative change in outlook had occurred within a few critical years. Emotions that had come and gone in earlier times now stayed to dominate men's thoughts. Once roused, the sense of emergency was self generating. Matters that previously would have been considered separate incidents, or even ignored were seized to fit into the framework of jeopardy, each reinforcing the others as further proof of an imminent danger. By the logic of anxiety, worries became fears, mounting until they had reached a climax in 1896.[40]

Out of this era emerged the "new middle class" of professionals and specialists—doctors, lawyers, business administrators, and others.

Highly organized and exclusive in nature, they replaced the decaying system of nineteenth-century communities with a new system of loyalties.[41] We have noted the growing professionalism of the governmental elite in Warren. In addition, the American Medical Association, National Education Association, American Bar Association, and a number of other similar organizations became prominent in Warren after 1900.[42] Yet the Warren data suggest that the fears of the 1890s failed to generate the crisis atmosphere that permeated America's major industrial centers. Certain immigrant groups—the Italians in Warren—encountered mild hostility, but the town accommodated most foreign-born families in ways that large cities did not. The French, Danes, and Swedes—the largest group of immigrants after 1890—generally received a warm welcome and the local press considered them an asset to the community.[43] In addition, the absence of serious labor conflict and the continued concern of the educational and governmental leaders for the public welfare, along with private interests (see Chapter 9), illustrates the survival of the sense of community in nineteenth-century Warren.

Thus although the pattern of migration and working-class mobility appear similar in large and small industrial cities during the nineteenth century, the admittedly fragmentary Warren data suggest that the size of the community was an important variable in determining the reaction to industrialization and urbanization.

Nevertheless, the dramatic social and economic changes that occurred in Warren from 1870 to 1910 paralleled, in varying degrees, the transformation of hundreds of towns and cities throughout the nation. Important uniformities existed in the mobility and career patterns of workers within each of these communities. In this sense the mobility experiences of workers in Warren reflect nationwide patterns and therefore do enlarge our knowledge of the past.

Appendix: A Note on
Sources and Methodology

There are many ways to study the historical patterns of a city.[1] This analysis of one community's growth in the late nineteenth century centers around several major concepts: community growth, structural continuity and change, social and political organization, and horizontal and vertical mobility. Each constitutes an integral, although not necessarily equal, part of this study. Of primary concern is the extent of social mobility in an expanding community. This concept of mobility, in turn, presents a variety of questions: What constitutes vertical mobility? What factors, economic and social, contribute to the mobility patterns in a particular city? How much mobility actually occurred in the late nineteenth century?

The process of urbanization influenced mobility patterns in American cities. It also affected the structural, social, and political organization of these same cities. The study of mobility therefore not only must examine the experiences of workers in the community but also must present an analysis of the related changes which accompanied urbanization. Stated another way, one cannot explain the mobility patterns in a dynamic, rapidly changing community without some analysis of the community structure and its transformation.[2]

The study of a particular community through the above conceptual framework enables one to more fully understand the complex process of urbanization. What changes occurred in the community during the era? How did the community leaders respond to and thus influence the transformation? Finally, in what ways did the urbanized city differ from the earlier town, and was this change affected by or did it affect mobility opportunities in the community?

The study of social patterns in any city often takes the researcher into previously unexplored sources in search of historical data. As urban historians have recently demonstrated, to find evidence from which to reconstruct the lives of inarticulate men is a difficult but not impossible task. Warren, Pennsylvania, like many other small communities, possessed no reliable or complete written history. Moreover, the written records which do exist seldom portray the lives of working-class individuals. Several sources do exist, however, from which one may trace the careers of the hundreds of manual laborers who lived and worked in Warren between 1870 and 1910. The federal manuscript census of 1870 and 1880 for Warren made it possible to examine the entire population of the community at these two periods of time. The data included on these two censuses—occupation, place of birth, age, property holdings, and other valuable information—enable one to trace the careers of all workers during the 1870-1880 period. Census data after 1880 were unavailable at the time of this writing. To venture beyond the 1880 manuscript, it was necessary to use other sources which provide information similar to that included in the manuscript census.

City directories are the most valuable of the additional informational sources. Use of directories, however, presents several problems. First, their reliability cannot be accepted at face value.[3] City directories in the nineteenth century frequently underenumerated unskilled laborers, itinerants, and female workers.[4] Individuals listed in the Warren city directories of 1890, 1900, and 1910 were checked against those recorded in the tax assessor's valuation lists for the same years. All males over the age of eighteen were to be assessed for tax purposes whether they held taxable property or not.[5] A comparison of assessment and other records revealed that the 1900 and 1910 city directories underenumerated Warren's adult male population by only 4.3 and 5 percent respectively. The 1890 directory missed approximately 6 percent of the adult male population. All males found in either the directories or on the tax rolls were recorded and included in the study.

Use of city directories also presented a far more difficult task. The Warren directories provided five pieces of information on each of the persons listed: name, address, occupation, whether one was a boarder or not, and the name of a spouse living at home. In order to trace individual careers through four decades it was necessary to add three vital pieces of information to the directory data. Place of birth, age, and wealth were included in the manuscript census data but not in the directories.[6]

The ethnic backgrounds of all males included in the 1890, 1900, and 1910 groups were traced by examining seven sources. Immigrant alien dockets, naturalization petitions, naturalization card indexes, and naturalization records usually included an individual's name, age, address, and birthplace. These sources provided the ethnic origin and ages of most of Warren's foreign-born population. In addition, newspapers frequently listed the names and birthplaces of immigrants attending various nationality functions. Church and marriage records also supplied information on the ethnic backgrounds of some of Warren's citizens. By carefully and often painstakingly organizing the ethnic data from these various sources one may determine the origins of nearly all of the community's foreign-born population.

Data on Warren's native-born population were derived from some of the same sources: marriage records and church lists, as well as school, birth, and death records. The church data, of course, also made it possible to record religious affiliation for nearly every member of the community.

Compiling the ages of Warren's adult male population proved much more difficult. For all residents in the community reported in either the 1870 or 1880 censuses who remained in succeeding decades one could simply add ten years to his reported age for each additional decade.[7] However, as the data on persistence demonstrated, that number proved exceptionally small. Data from some of the previously mentioned sources often provided age information; frequently they did not. Hence it was possible to attain the ages of only three-fourths of the occupational universe. Moreover, even those data were extremely suspect due to the wide variety of sources of age information and probably inconsistent methods employed by those responsible for recording age data. An original objective of this study was to determine the function of age in both horizontal and vertical mobility. The transition from manuscript census data to city directories, supplemented by data from various sources, meant that the dimension of age, with some exceptions, had to be sacrificed.

The final piece of information necessary to compile data parallel to those provided by the 1870 manuscript census was the value of real and personal wealth. The 1880 census failed to include this category. A tracing of intragenerational property and wealth mobility was impossible without these data. Supplying this supplementary information proved relatively simple. Tax assessor's valuation books provided data on real and personal wealth, as well as indicating the money held at interest, for each adult male in the community. This information was added to the previously discussed data to compile records on every adult male recorded in the borough at decade intervals from 1870 through 1910.

Completed data cards included the following information for more than 3,600 male residents eighteen years of age or older: place of birth, occupation, place of residence, property holdings, personal wealth and money held at interest, religious affiliation, political ward, marital status, and, wherever possible, age and parents' place of birth.

A third major concern in the use of these sources involved the problem of linking data and individuals from one decade to the next. How is one to know if an individual mentioned at two or more succeeding decade intervals is really the same person? Of course persons with unusual names proved no problem. Several individuals listed in one decade, however, occasionally had the same name. In addition, spelling of a name appearing in two succeeding decades may have been different, for example: Thomas Burke, Thomas Burcke. A system using the following variables facilitated the linkage process: birthplace, religion, initial, age. Data on all individuals were first recorded on IBM cards, then sorted alphabetically. Cards of all verified identical names were then removed from the deck. All similar names were then sorted again based on the four variables in the order of their possibility of linking individuals. Given similar names or similar but not identical spelling of names, two or more individuals were considered the same person if more than two of the variables agreed. In this manner it was possible to link individuals recorded at each decade interval.[8]

In addition to demographic data, this study also relied heavily on local newspapers to trace the major problems and events in the community. Warren in the late nineteenth century possessed a number of newspapers, and two of them proved particularly useful. The *Warren Mail* and the *Warren Ledger* remained in continuous existence for nearly the whole period of this study. Both papers contained obvious editorial bias, but the competition between them enabled one to construct reliable information about the attitudes and issues concerning the community. Every issue of the *Ledger* and the *Mail* was systematically examined, at five-year intervals, throughout the 1870-1910 period. Other newspapers published at the time also underwent examination. In addition, the *Mail* and the *Ledger* were sampled at other periods, particularly during any significant historical event. In all cases events described in one source were checked against other sources to insure accuracy. The newspapers proved particularly useful in describing the excitement which accompanied the oil boom years, 1875 to 1890. However, as one might expect, the interpretation of events by the local press varied widely. Local newspapers also supplied valuable clues to assist the researcher in constructing a satisfactory occupational classification system. Newspaper descriptions of the work performed by the oil "wildcatters," for example, led to the decision to place this occupation in the semiskilled rather than skilled classification. Moreover, they often provided considerable insight into prevailing concerns and emotions of those who lived and worked in the community.[9]

Finally, borough council minutes and school directors' records were helpful in measuring the extent of opportunity to acquire political power in the nineteenth-century community. These records, along with the local newspapers, provided information about local issues and about the men who served on these prestigious bodies. Moreover, the minutes gave some indication of the nuances of power within the community. Some members of both boards dominated the decision-making process. Others ratified but seldom initiated the actions of either board.

Hundreds of nineteenth-century cities experienced, to one degree or another, the transformation wrought by urbanization and industrialization. The community of Warren, Pennsylvania, similarly underwent its greatest era of industrial expansion and population growth during the late nineteenth century. In 1870, Warren contained just over 2,000 people working primarily in logging camps and sawmills scattered across the county. Those not engaged in the lumber industry worked in various small shops or performed skilled craftwork, supplying products to the community's inhabitants. With the exception of cut timber, few items produced in Warren reached markets outside the county. Organized informally, Warren exemplified small-town life in nineteenth-century America and characterized what Robert Wiebe called the "American Island Community."

As industrialization spread throughout the nation, this community, like so many others, felt its effects. By 1910 Warren had become a thriving little city of 11,080 inhabitants, with eleven hotels, six banks, numerous individual business firms (including nine oil refineries), and service to several metropolitan areas via three major railroads. The challenges and opportunities of urbanization, industrialization, and immigration which faced the large American city also confronted, to a lesser degree, small communities like Warren. This study entails an examination of a single, in some respects unique, community, yet one hopes it has revealed something of importance about the life patterns in other nineteenth-century American cities.

Table Sources

4-10 1870, 1880 Manuscript Census, Warren Borough; 1890, 1900, 1910 City Directories; Tax Assessor's Books, Warren, Pa., 1870, 1880, 1890, 1900, 1910 (Books 1870-1900 located in the attic of the Warren County Court House, 1910 in the Warren County Tax Office, Warren County Court House)

5-1 1870, 1880 Manuscript Census, Warren Borough; 1890, 1900, 1910 City Directories; Immigrant Alien Dockets; Naturalization Records; Birth Records

5-2 1870, 1880 Manuscript Census, Warren Borough; 1890, 1900, 1910 City Directories; Immigrant Alien Dockets; Naturalization Records; Birth Records

5-3 1870, 1880 Manuscript Census, Warren Borough; 1890, 1900, 1910 City Directories; Immigrant Alien Dockets; Naturalization Records; Birth Records

5-4 1870, 1880 Manuscript Census, Warren Borough; 1890, 1900, 1910 City Directories; Immigrant Alien Dockets; Naturalization Records; Birth Records

5-5 1880 Manuscript Census, Warren Borough; 1890, 1900, 1910 City Directories

5-6 1870, 1880 Manuscript Census, Warren Borough; 1890, 1900, 1910 City Directories; Immigrant Alien Dockets; Naturalization Records; Birth Records

6-1 1870, 1880 Manuscript Census, Warren Borough; 1890, 1900, 1990 City Directories; Immigrant Alien Dockets; Naturalization Records; Birth Records; Warren Borough Tax Assessor's Books, 1870-1910

6-2 1870, 1880 Manuscript Census, Warren Borough; 1890, 1900, 1910 City Directories; Immigrant Alien Dockets; Naturalization Records; Birth Records; Warren Borough Tax Assessor's Books

6-3 1870, 1880 Manuscript Census, Warren Borough; 1890, 1900, 1910 City Directories; Immigrant Alien Dockets; Naturalization Records; Birth Records; Warren Borough Tax Assessor's Books, 1870-1910

6-4 1870, 1880 Manuscript Census, Warren Borough; 1890, 1900, 1910 City Directories; Immigrant Alien Dockets; Naturalization Records; Birth Records; Warren Borough Tax Assessor's Books, 1870-1910

7-1 Depositors' signatures, Warren Savings Bank, 1870-1900 (located in the basement of the Pennsylvania Bank and Trust Company, Warren, Pa.)

7-2 1870, 1880 Manuscript Census, Warren Borough; 1890, 1900, 1910 City Directories; Tax Assessor's Books, Warren, Pa., 1870, 1880, 1890, 1900, 1910 (Books 1870-1900 located in the attic of the Warren County Court House, 1910 books in the Warren County Tax Office, Warren County Court House)

7-3 1870, 1880 Manuscript Census, Warren Borough; 1890, 1900, 1910 City Directories; Tax Assessor's Books, Warren, Pa., 1870, 1880, 1890, 1910

7-4 1870, 1880 Manuscript Census, Warren Borough; 1890, 1900, 1910 City Directories; Tax Assessor's Books, Warren, Pa., 1870, 1880, 1890, 1900, 1910

7-5   Assessor's Valuation Lists, Warren, Pa., 1870, 1880, 1890, 1900, 1910 (Books 1870-1900 located in the attic of the Warren County Court House, 1910 books in the Warren County Tax Office, Warren County Court House)

7-6   1870, 1880 Manuscript Census, Warren Borough; 1890, 1900, 1910 City Directories; Tax Assessor's Books, Warren, Pa., 1870, 1880, 1890, 1900, 1910

8-1   1870, 1880 Manuscript Census, Warren Borough; 1890, 1900, 1910 City Directories; Immigrant Alien Dockets; Naturalization Records; Birth Records

8-2   1890, 1900, 1910 City Directories; Immigrant Alien Dockets; Naturalization Records; Birth Records; Church Records

9-1   Warren Borough Council Minutes, 1870-1910; 1870 Manuscript Census, Warren, Pa.; 1880 Manuscript Census, Warren, Pa.; 1890, 1900, 1910 City Directories

9-2   *Warren Mail*, 10 November 1872, 11 November 1884, 14 November 1888, 5 November 1896, 15 November 1900, 17 November 1904, 12 November 1908; *Warren Ledger*, 5 November 1880, 11 November 1892; *Weekly News*, 10 November 1876

9-3   Minutes of the Warren Borough Board of Education, 1870-1910; 1870 Manuscript Census, Warren, Pa., 1880 Manuscript Census, Warren, Pa.; 1890, 1900, 1910 City Directories; Assessor's Valuation Lists, 1870-1910

9-4   *Warren Mail*, 1870-1910 (see June issues); 1870 Manuscript Census, Warren Borough; 1880 Manuscript Census, Warren Borough; 1890, 1900 City Directories; Immigrant Alien Dockets; Naturalization Records; Birth Records

Notes

CHAPTER 1

1. Herbert G. Gutman, "The Workers' Search for Power," *The Gilded Age*, ed. H. Wayne Morgan (Syracuse, N.Y., 1963), p. 33.

2. Robert H. Wiebe, *The Search for Order: 1877-1920* (New York, 1967), pp. 3, 4.

3. Ibid., p. 44 ff. In his analysis of community response to the challenges of the 1880s, Wiebe concludes that "the great casualty of America's turmoil late in the century was the island community. Although a majority of Americans would still reside in relatively small, personal centers for several decades more, the society that had been premised upon the community's effective sovereignty, upon its capacity to manage its affairs within its boundaries, no longer functioned." Cf. Michael H. Frisch, *Town into City: Springfield, Massachusetts, and the Meaning of Community, 1840-1880* (Cambridge, Mass., 1972), p. 247. Frisch modifies the position of Wiebe, suggesting that, at least in Springfield, the concept of community did not disappear but underwent fundamental changes. According to Frisch, "The growing public functions of government and the accumulating results of rapid social and physical change were giving to the community a new meaning. . . . Community, in other words, was changing from an informal, direct sensation to a formal perceived abstraction."

4. Stephan Thernstrom, *Poverty and Progress: Social Mobility in a Nineteenth Century City* (Cambridge, Mass., 1964), pp. 205-6.

5. Comparisons of social mobility in various American cities have been approximate at best, because of divergent methodological techniques employed. It seems to me that a sacrifice of some originality in methodological approach is a reasonable price to pay for more reliable comparisons. Thus, in order to facilitate close comparisons with other nineteenth-century cities, this study has adopted methodological techniques used by other researchers, particularly the methodological techniques employed by Thernstrom in his study of Newburyport. The Warren social structure, described in Chapter 2, possessed a number of important similarities with Newburyport. Several significant differences also existed between the two communities. Hence, a careful comparison of the changing social patterns of the two communities seemed most viable.

CHAPTER 2

1. Quenton D. Wolfe, "The Historical Development of Secondary Education in Warren County, Pennsylvania" (Master's thesis, Duke University, 1939), p. 4.

2. S. P. Johnson, "A History of Warren County," *Warren Directory of 1885* (Warren, 1885), p. 5.

3. Arthur J. Reed, "A Study for the Rehabilitation of Warren, Pennsylvania" (Master's thesis, Syracuse University, 1941).

4. S. Kussart, *The Allegheny River* (Pittsburgh, Pa., 1938), p. 99.

5. U.S. Bureau of the Census, *Eighth Census of the United States: 1860. Manufacturers* (Washington, D. C., 1865), 3, p. 531.

6. Holger Elmquist, "An Economic Survey of Warren County, Pennsylvania" (Master's thesis, Rutgers University, 1940), p. 12.

7. *Warren Mail*, 16 June, 1854, p. 3.

8. J. S. Schenk, *History of Warren County, Pennsylvania* (Syracuse, N.Y., 1887), p. 340. In characterizing the lack of community growth during this era, the town biographer Schenk stated: "The decades which followed [1840-1860] were not marked by any extraordinary degree of prosperity. The town kept along on an even tenor . . . slowly increasing in population as a result of being the commercial center of the area. In the destruction of pine forests and in farming, a few of the citizens acquired wealth, but the many . . . barely earned enough to provide shelter and food for their families."

9. Ibid., p. 344.

10. *Warren Mail*, 10 December 1859, p. 3.

11. *The Book of Warren, Pennsylvania* (Titusville, Pa., 1898), p. 7.

12. *Warren Ledger*, 27 January 1876, p. 3.

13. Foreign immigration did not play a large part in the steady influx and outflow of residents in Warren from 1830 through 1870. Of the 1,742 residents living in Warren in 1860 only 417 were foreign-born. New Englanders, New Yorkers, and Pennsylvanians of English and Scotch-Irish origin constituted the main groups until the 1870s. The major wave of immigration hit Warren after 1870 and consisted largely of persons of Swedish, Danish, and Irish origin.

14. *Warren Ledger*, 21 February 1870, p. 3.

15. Ibid., 2 March 1876, p. 3.

16. U.S. Bureau of the Census, *Manuscript Schedule, Ninth Census of the United States: 1870, Warren, Pennsylvania.*

17. Ibid. The figures cited here do not include unmarried sons over 18 years of age living with their parents.

18. Data on this page compiled from Census Bureau, *Manuscript Schedule:*

1870, Warren, Pennsylvania, and from various issues of the *Warren Ledger*, May-October 1870.

19. Due to inadequate information (see Appendix), all nonmanual workers had to be included in a single category. Hence the terms nonmanual and white collar are used interchangeably throughout this study.

20. Census Bureau, *Manuscript Schedule: 1870, Warren, Pennslyvania.*

21. Ibid. See also: Clyde Griffen, "Workers Divided: The Effect of Craft and Ethnic Differences in Poughkeepsie, New York, 1850-1880," *Nineteenth Century Cities: Essays in the New Urban History*, eds. Stephan Thernstrom and Richard Sennett (New Haven, Conn., 1969), esp. pp. 57, 80, 81. Griffen notes a similar difficulty among the Irish in Poughkeepsie but reports that the Irish in that city succeeded in attaining certain skilled positions, particularly brick laying and blacksmithing. He contends however, that "the Irish . . . advanced more slowly into skilled and clerical work than the English and Germans and had more difficulty holding their own in these employments during contractions in the work force."

22. Commonwealth of Pennsylvania, *Annual Report of the Secretary of Internal Affairs* (1881-1882), 10, p. 74.

23. Census Bureau, *Manuscript Schedule: 1870, Warren, Pennsylvania.*

24. Tax Assessor's Valuation Lists, Warren Borough, 1870.

25. Minutes of the Regular Meeting, 1 August 1870, Warren Borough Council, Book 1, p. 313. (Located in the Warren Borough Municipal Office.)

26. The reader may be surprised to note that a larger percentage of French immigrants held estates valued over $500 than United States-born citizens. When the estate value increases, however, the percentage of immigrants in each classification decreases; only native-born citizens controlled the major portion of wealth in 1870. (See Chapters 5 and 6.)

27. Census Bureau, *Manuscript Schedule: 1870*, Warren, Pennsylvania. For a more detailed analysis of wealth distribution, see Chapter 7.

28. Minutes of the Regular Meetings, 1870-1880, Warren Borough Council, Books 1-3. (Located in the Warren Borough Municipal Office.)

29. *Warren Mail,* 24 January 1870, p. 3.

30. Minutes of the Monthly Meeting, June 1872, Warren Ministerial Association. (Included in the minutes of the Methodist Church, 1870-1875, Warren, Pennsylvania.)

31. *Warren Ledger,* 16 December 1875, p. 3.

32. Ibid., 23 December 1875, p. 3.

33. Census Bureau, *Manuscript Schedule: 1870*, Warren, Pennsylvania.

34. Ibid. See also: Griffen, "Workers Divided," p. 58, which reveals a similar attempt to provide education for one's children in nineteenth-century Poughkeepsie, noting "No significant differences between the major nation-

ality groups [including American-born] in the percentage of children reported in the Census as attending school."

35. Minutes of the Regular Meeting, 28 July 1874, Warren School Board of
Directors, Book C, p. 1. (Located in the office of the Warren County Superintendent of Schools.)

36. *Warren Mail*, 8 July 1880, p. 1.

37. Minutes of the Regular Meeting, 8 July 1880, Warren School Board of
Directors, "Superintendent's Report," Book D, p. 240.

38. Stephan Thernstrom, *Poverty and Progress: Social Mobility in a
Nineteenth Century City* (Cambridge, Mass., 1964), Chapter 2. The social
patterns of preindustrial Warren appear rather set but not as rigid as those
described in midcentury Newburyport by Thernstrom. Although a structured
organization existed in Warren as well as Newburyport, the castelike hierarchy never appeared. In addition, religion, still a major factor in Warren, failed
to carry the influence that the puritan denominations did in Newburyport.

39. See various issues of the *Warren Mail* and the *Warren Ledger*,
February-October 1870.

CHAPTER 3

1. Holger Elmquist, "An Economic Survey of Warren County, Pennsylvania" (Master's thesis, Rutgers University, 1940), p. 12.

2. Ibid.

3. *Warren Mail*, 14 July 1860, p. 3; *Crawford Journal*, 4 September 1860, p. 2.
The Drake discovery and subsequent successful oil strikes around Titusville
had little effect on the economy of Warren. Several Warren men struck major
wells producing 10,000 or more barrels per month in lower Warren County,
but since they failed to return to the borough, their discoveries had no
economic impact in Warren.

4. *The Derrick: Handbook of Petroleum* (Oil City, Pa., 1898), 1, p. 203. The
first oil well in the immediate vicinity of Warren appeared two years before
the Beaty discovery, approximately two and a half miles southwest of the
borough. This well, however, produced only five barrels per day.

5. "David Beaty, Warren County Miscellaneous Historical Transcripts,"
(Pennsylvania Historical Survey, Warren, Pa.: Federal Works Agency,
W.P.A., 1937), 2, p. 148.

6. *Titusville Herald*, 21 March 1875, p. 3.

7. *The Derrick*, p. 264.

8. *Warren Ledger*, 23 March 1876, p. 3.

9. *Warren Mail*, 4 April 1876, p. 3.

10. Ibid., 30 May 1876, p. 3.

11. Ibid., 27 June 1876, p. 3.

12. Ibid., 14 August 1876, p. 3.

13. *Warren Ledger*, 4 May 1876, p. 3; 10 May 1876, p. 3.

14. *Warren Mail*, 20 June 1876, p. 3.

15. Ibid., 27 June 1876, p. 3.

16. Ibid., 20 June 1876, p. 3.

17. Ibid., 25 July 1876, p. 3.

18. Ibid., 8 August 1876, p. 3.

19. Ibid., 15 August 1877, p. 3.

20. *Warren Ledger*, 10 January 1878, p. 3.

21. *Warren Mail*, 23 April 1878, p. 3.

22. Ibid., 3 July 1880, p. 3.

23. Ibid., 7 September 1880, p. 3.

24. *Warren Ledger*, 30 October 1885, p. 1. The editor of the *Ledger*, speculating upon the sources of Warren's new wealth, reinforced this conclusion, asking: "But where does the wealth come from? Here is a mystery . . . the result of each year's building and business proves that money is being made. . . . Oil is one resource, and yet the rich oil men *have not stood at the front of this progressive movement. Few have taken up locations here. . . .*" (Newspaper's italics.)

25. *The Derrick*, p. 361.

26. *Warren Mail*, 27 September 1877, p. 3.

27. U.S. Bureau of the Census, *Eleventh Census of the United States: 1890. Mineral Industries in the United States* (Washington, D.C. 1890), p. 447.

28. *Warren Ledger*, 17 July 1885, p. 3.

29. Herbert Eaton, *History of the Petroleum Industry*, Transactions of the Warren Academy of Sciences (Warren, Pa., 1910), 1, p. 101.

30. U.S. Bureau of the Census, *Special Report of Manufacturers: 1905* (Washington, D.C., 1910) Part 2, p. 958.

31. Ibid.

32. Compiled from J. N. Lacy, *Warren County Business and General Directory for 1890* (Warren, Pa., 1890); Parkey and Shawkey, *A Complete Directory of Warren Borough, 1899-1900* (Olean, N.Y.: Olean Evening Herald, 1900); William H. Kirwin, *Kirwin's Warren Borough and Warren County Directory, 1910* (Warren, Pa.: William H. Kirwin Directory Co., 1910).

33. The fragmentary evidence does not fully explain the decrease in the proportion of commercial trade firms but suggests several possible reasons. A small community such as Warren has little need for large commercial trade establishments employing more than one or two men. In addition, as the number of small one- or two-man retail shops increased during the period,

many of the needs of the residents were probably met by this type of establishment.

34.   *Warren Ledger*, 2 January 1880, p. 3.

35.   *Warren Evening Mirror*, Special Edition, May 1896, Part 6, p. 1.

36.   Compiled from Warren City Directories, 1890, 1900, 1910.

37.   Kirwin, *Kirwin's Warren Borough 1910*, pp. 62-67.

38.   The size of these deposits remains unknown as only one of the banks still in existence today would permit even partial examination of its files.

39.   Stephan Thernstrom, *Poverty and Progress: Social Mobility in a Nineteenth Century City* (Cambridge, Mass., 1964), pp. 130, 131. Thernstrom suggests that savings banks in nineteenth-century America contributed to the mobility of upper classes and to the security of the laborer. He concludes: "The savings bank, therefore, may have facilitated capital accumulation and continuing mobility for depositors from higher levels, but to the laborer it offered security. It encouraged mobility into the strata of workmen possessed of a 'stake in society,' only rarely mobility into the entrepreneural class."

40.   *Warren Mail*, 1 December 1910, p. 5.

41.   *Warren Evening Mirror*, Special Edition, May 1896, Part 6, p. 4.

42.   *Warren Ledger*, 21 November 1894, p. 3.

43.   Ibid., 21 May 1890, p. 1.

44.   *Warren Weekly Times*, 16 November 1904, p. 7.

45.   U.S. Bureau of the Census, *Thirteenth Census of the United States: 1910. Population* (Washington D.C., 1910), p. 593; *Manuscript Schedule, Tenth Census of the United States; 1880, Warren, Pennsylvania*; Warren Borough Tax Assessment Books, 1870, 1910 (1870 books located in the attic of the Warren County Courthouse, 1910 books located in the Warren County tax office).

46.   Chamber of Commerce, *Warren, Pennsylvania: The Gem of the Allegheny* (Warren, Pa., 1913), p. 17.

47.   Charles H. Noyes, *Warren Centennial: An Account of the Celebration at Warren, Pennsylvania* (Warren, Pa.: Warren Library Association, 1897), p. 208.

48.   *Warren Ledger*, 13 June 1890, p. 3.

49.   For a comparison of the effects of industrialization upon a large American city see Sam Bass Warner, Jr., *The Private City: Philadelphia in Three Periods of Its Growth* (Philadelphia, 1968), Chapters 3, 4, and *passim*, esp. pp. 49, 61, 63, 64. Industrialization in Philadelphia, 1830-1860, produced more dramatic and broader changes than in Warren, but the net effect of industrial transformation was similar. "By 1860 the combined effects of Philadelphia's rapid growth—the endless grid streets, the scattering of churches, stations, and factories, the flood of immigrants, the novelty, the sheer size, and the pace of the big city—all its elements of change contributed to the thorough destruc-

tion of informal neighborhood street life which had characterized the small scale community of the eighteenth century town." Small town life in Warren was not destroyed but did undergo significant transformation.

CHAPTER 4

1. The term manual worker or manual laborer is used in this study interchangeably with blue-collar worker and refers to all classifications of men who worked with their hands, i.e., unskilled, semiskilled, and skilled workers. Similarly, the terms nonmanual and white collar are used synonymously.

2. Stephan Thernstrom, *Poverty and Progress: Social Mobility in a Nineteenth Century City* (Cambridge, Mass., 1964), p. 164.

3. Compiled from: Clyde Griffen, "Workers Divided: The Effect of Craft and Ethnic Differences in Poughkeepsie, New York, 1850-1880," *Nineteenth Century Cities: Essays in the New Urban History*, eds. Stephan Thernstrom and Richard Sennett (New Haven, Conn., 1969); Peter R. Knights, *The Plain People of Boston, 1830-1860: A Study in City Growth* (New York, 1971), Chapter 5; Stephan Thernstrom, "Immigrants and WASPs: Ethnic Differences in Occupational Mobility in Boston, 1890-1940," *Nineteenth Century Cities*; Sidney Goldstein, *Patterns of Mobility, 1910-1950: The Norristown Study* (Philadelphia, Pa., 1958), Chapter 9; Paul B. Worthman, "Working Class Mobility in Birmingham, Alabama, 1880-1914," *Anonymous Americans*, ed. Tamara K. Hareven (Englewood Cliffs, N.J., 1971), pp. 191-97; Richard J. Hopkins, "Occupational and Geographic Mobility in Atlanta, 1870-1896," *Journal of Southern History*, 34 (1968), pp. 200-13. The latter two studies examined mobility patterns of both black and white manual workers. In both instances, upward mobility of white workers was dramatically higher than for black laborers.

4. Compiled from: U.S. Bureau of the Census, *Manuscript Schedule, Ninth Census of the United States: 1870, Warren, Pennsylvania; Manuscript Schedule, Tenth Census of the United States: 1880, Warren, Pennsylvania*; 1890, 1900, 1910 City Directories, Warren, Pennsylvania.

5. Ibid.

6. Ibid.

7. The occupational divisions used in this study are similar to those employed by Knights in *The Plain People of Boston, 1830-1860*, pp. 149-56. My unskilled, semiskilled, and skilled categories are nearly identical with Knights' classifications I, II, and IV. Some adjustments have been made to comply with local differences and changes in the nature of certain occupations over time. All white-collar workers have been combined into a single division—nonmanual. Both major data sources—manuscript census and city directories—frequently referred to a large number of white-collar workers as "clerk." In some cases, it was possible to determine the exact nature of these clerical duties. In most it was not. The occupational division of "proprietor" presented a similar problem. Several white-collar classification schemes were attempted but abandoned because the inaccuracies of designations seriously distorted any interpretation of occupational mobility of these non-manual workers. Careful crosschecking of designations with other sources, wherever possible, revealed that this lack of specificity in Warren was confined almost entirely to the nonmanual group. For an excellent detailed discussion of the difficulties of establishing an occupational hierarchy from nineteenth-century sources, see Clyde Griffen, "Occupational Mobility in Nineteenth Century America: Problems and Possibilities," *Journal of Social History,* 5 (Spring 1972), pp. 310-30.

8. For a discussion of the differing wage rates of manual and nonmanual workers in the late nineteenth and twentieth centuries, see Robert K. Burn, "The Comparative Economic Position of Manual and White Collar Employees," *Journal of Business,* 27 (October 1954), pp. 257-67.

9. Compiled from: Census Bureau, *Manuscript Schedule: 1870, Warren, Pennsylvania; Manuscript Schedule: 1880, Warren, Pennsylvania;* 1890, 1900, 1910 City Directories, Warren, Pennsylvania.

10. For comparison of persistence rates in other American cities, both large and small, see Howard P. Chudacoff, *Mobile Americans: Residential and Social Mobility in Omaha, 1880-1920* (New York, 1972), p. 41; Hopkins, "Occupational and Geographic Mobility in Atlanta," p. 207; Knights, *The Plain People of Boston, 1830-1860,* p. 63; Griffen, "Workers Divided," pp. 60-62; Merle Curti, *The Making of an American Community* (Stanford, Calif., 1959); Worthman, "Working Class Mobility," p. 182; Thernstrom, *Poverty and Progress,* p. 96. These cities represent the total spectrum of nineteenth-century American communities—large and small, eastern, southern, western, industrialized, and frontier. Yet in all of them the rate of persistence in any decade rarely exceeded 50 percent. (See Chapter 8 of this study for a detailed comparison of persistence in these cities.)

11. Compiled from: Census Bureau, *Manuscript Schedule: 1870, Warren, Pennsylvania; Manuscript Schedule: 1880, Warren, Pennsylvania;* 1890, 1900, 1910 City Directories, Warren, Pennsylvania. Cf. Griffen, "Workers Divided," pp. 56, 57. Griffen reveals similar disparities in the rates of persistence between native-born and foreign-born workers in Poughkeepsie. The Irish and German immigrants, however, recorded higher rates of persistence in that New York city than in Warren. Griffen supplies no reason for this but merely suggests that the Germans and Irish possessed a stronger propensity to settle than other ethnic groups.

12. Census Bureau, *Manuscript Schedule: 1870, Warren, Pennsylvania; Manuscript Schedule: 1880, Warren, Pennsylvania;* 1890, 1900, 1910 City Directories, Warren, Pennsylvania.

13. Compiled from: *Warren Mail,* 1870-1892; "Record of Deaths, Warren County," Books 1 and 2, 1893-1905 (located in the office of the Registrar and

Recorder, Warren County Court House); Department of Health, Commonwealth of Pennsylvania, 1906-1910.

14. Charles H. Noyes, *Warren Centennial: An Account of the Celebration at Warren, Pennsylvania* (Warren, Pa.: Warren Library Association, 1897), p. 207.

15. The shift from the use of the manuscript census to city directories for primary occupational data on the 1890 and 1900 manual workers may conceal some mobility for these groups. Although the various city directories consulted included unskilled workers in their listings, they no doubt omitted many new arrivals to the community. These newcomers possibly appeared in subsequent city directories at higher levels of skill.

16. For another nineteenth-century city with even more impressive upward mobility, see Herbert G. Gutman, "The Reality of the Rags to Riches 'Myth,' " *Nineteenth Century Cities*, p. 113. In discussing the occupational mobility of locomotive manufacturers in Paterson, New Jersey, Gutman concludes: "None came from professional, mercantile, or manufacturing backgrounds. Only one was born in New England, and almost all were British immigrants. These were not 'princes' prepared by training and education to become 'kings' of industry. Instead, they rose from the lower classes and achieved substantial material rewards in their lifetimes. For those of their contemporaries who sought 'proof' about the promise of rags to riches, these men served as model, day-to-day evidence."

17. Thernstrom, *Poverty and Progress*, p. 15.

18. U.S. Bureau of the Census, *Tenth Census of the United States: 1880. Compendium* (Washington, D. C., 1883), 1, p. 456.

19. U.S. Bureau of the Census, *Thirteenth Census of the United States: 1910. Population* (Washington, D. C., 1913), 3, p. 593.

20. Thernstrom, *Poverty and Progress*, p. 95.

21. Ibid., p. 14.

22. Ibid., p. 96.

23. Ibid.

24. Ibid. (Italics mine.)

25. Ibid.

26. Ibid., p. 103.

27. Ibid., p. 112. Thernstrom concedes that skilled workers in Newburyport probably experienced higher mobility rates than the unskilled: "Recent mobility research suggests the likelihood that an investigation of the career patterns of *skilled* families would have revealed substantially greater movement into nonmanual occupations."

28. This is a cumulative figure. Some of the men attaining nonmanual positions no doubt retained them in succeeding decades.

29. Unfortunately, neither the census takers nor the compilers of the various city directories differentiated between office clerks and clerks employed by retail merchants. Probably a significant number of those advancing into nonmanual positions simply became clerks in the many retail stores in Warren.

CHAPTER 5

1. For another highly diverse ethnic community, see Clyde Griffen, "Workers Divided: The Effect of Craft and Ethnic Differences in Poughkeepsie, New York, 1850-1880," *Nineteenth Century Cities: Essays in the New Urban History*, eds. Stephan Thernstrom and Richard Sennett (New Haven, Conn., 1969), p. 57. Griffen, in comparing Poughkeepsie to Newburyport, Massachusetts, contends that "the greater diversity in ethnic composition in Poughkeepsie seems to have been accompanied by a somewhat more hospitable attitude toward the foreign born." Warren followed a similar pattern.

2. Compiled from: U.S. Bureau of the Census, *Manuscript Schedule, Ninth Census of the United States: 1870, Warren, Pennsylvania; Manuscript Schedule, Tenth Census of the United States: 1880; Warren, Pennsylvania;* 1890, 1900, 1910 City Directories, Warren, Pennsylvania.

3. Stephan Thernstrom, "Immigrants and WASPs: Ethnic Differences in Occupational Mobility in Boston, 1890-1940," *Nineteenth Century Cities*, pp. 129-41. Thernstrom reports similar but greater disadvantages for foreign-born workers in securing nonmanual occupations in twentieth-century Boston. He concludes: "Native-born Americans had a distinct advantage in the competition for jobs on the higher rungs of the occupational ladder. . . . Both immigrants and the native-born children of immigrants were far more likely both to begin and to end their careers working with their hands and wearing blue collars."

4. The arrival in Warren in 1900 of a large number of unskilled immigrants did not alone cause the decline in occupational opportunity. When one compares mobility of immigrants and native-born laborers separately, the shrinkage of opportunity shows up in the data for both groups.

5. Stephan Thernstrom, *Poverty and Progress: Social Mobility in a Nineteenth Century City* (Cambridge, Mass., 1964), pp. 100, 101.

6. Ibid., p. 113. In his analysis of American-born sons of immigrants in nineteenth-century Newburyport, Thernstrom reports that "foreign-born workmen and their sons were handicapped in the occupational competition. The sons, however, experienced fewer obstacles to occupational mobility than their fathers; ethnic differences in intergenerational mobility were narrowing somewhat by 1880." This measurement of mobility in Warren, of course, is not strictly intergenerational and limits comparison somewhat. The immigrants' sons in Warren were not necessarily (although many were) directly related to those immigrants listed in Table 6-5. The small number of cases per cell prevented a comparison of a father's occupation with that of his son.

7. *Warren Mail*, 10 June 1871, p. 3.

8. Minutes of the Regular Meeting, 25 May 1874, Warren School Board of Directors, Book C, p. 165. (Located in the office of the County Superintendent of Schools.)

9. J. S. Schenk, *History of Warren County, Pennsylvania* (Syracuse, N.Y., 1887), p. 154.

10. Compiled from: Census Bureau, *Manuscript Schedule: 1870, Warren, Pennsylvania; Manuscript Schedule: 1880, Warren, Pennsylvania;* 1890 Warren City Directory, Warren, Pennsylvania.

11. *Warren Mail*, 22 March 1880, p. 3.

12. Rev. J. W. Smith, "The Evils of Competition," *Warren Mail*, 25 July 1894, p. 31.

13. *Warren Ledger*, 3 August 1894, p. 3.

14. Ibid.; *Warren Mail*, 5 August 1894, p. 3.

15. *Warren Mail*, 8 August 1894, p. 3.

16. It is noteworthy that while immigrants arriving in Warren in 1900 experienced particular difficulties in securing higher level occupations, those who succeeded experienced mobility equal to native-born Americans. This is due largely to the decline of the spectacular mobility enjoyed by earlier American-born workers rather than to an increase in mobility by immigrants.

17. *Weekly Democrat*, 7 June 1900, p. 6.

18. Unfortunately, too little is known about the cultural background of particular immigrants who arrived in America in the late nineteenth century. Those who migrated to small remote communities like Warren may have left small European villages. It is possible that skilled workers coming from traditional backgrounds possessed less motivation than their native-born counterparts to become large entrepreneurs or white-collar workers. Studies of cross-cultural differences of nineteenth-century workers are desperately needed.

19. This speculation is based on limited evidence and should be viewed with caution. Both the local press and the school directors' minutes indicate an implicit and occasionally explicit desire for children of immigrants to become "Americanized." Their definition of this term, however, is not clear.

20. Thernstrom, *Poverty and Progress*, p. 159. Thernstrom reports that in Newburyport, "the pressure to migrate operated selectively to remove the least successful from the community." Hence "members of this group had no capacity to act in concert. . . . Stable organization based on a consciousness of common grievances was obviously impossible."

21. Minutes of the Regular Meeting, 1 April 1889, "Police Regulations," Warren Borough Council, Book 4, p. 134. (Located in the Warren Borough Municipal Office.)

22. *Warren Ledger*, 27 November 1885, p. 3.

23. J. N. Lacy, *Warren County Business and General Directory for 1890* (Warren, Pa., 1890).

24. Thernstrom, *Poverty and Progress*, pp. 162-65. Thernstrom feels that workers in Newburyport—who experienced much less mobility than Warren's manual laborers—"could view America as a land of opportunity despite the fact that the class realities . . . confined most of them to the working classes. . . . These newcomers to the urban life arrived with a low horizon of expectations." Hence "the typical unskilled laborer who settled in Newburyport could feel proud of his achievements and optimistic about the future." Cf. Griffen, "Workers Divided," p. 51. Griffen agrees with Thernstrom's conclusions, claiming that workers "judged their prospects for advancement more by the instances of success in their own trade than by cases of 'rags to riches' in unrelated occupations. . . . Had Newburyport laborers judged their progress by the models of success exemplified in the Horatio Alger novels, they would have despaired. But their frame of reference was the experience of their own kind in their community." Cf. Paul B. Worthman, "Working Class Mobility in Birmingham, Alabama, 1880-1914," *Anonymous Americans*, ed. Tamara K. Hareven (Englewood Cliffs, N.J., 1971), p. 208. Worthman disputes these contentions, warning that "a great deal of caution . . . should be exercised in drawing inferences about the presumed failure of working class consciousness and the absence of class conflict in American cities from these patterns of mobility. High rates of transiency need not inhibit class consciousness, and under some historical conditions may have facilitated its growth. Second, no necessary relationship existed between upward occupational mobility or property acquisition and the way that workingmen viewed the world around them. Some militant, class conscious leaders of the American labor movement were skilled workers who progressed through the ranks and achieved a small amount of wealth and security. . . . Third, the concept of the 'revolution of rising expectations' . . . should serve as a warning that accumulation of small amounts of property and slight upward occupational mobility may not necessarily produce a conservative outlook."

25. Herbert G. Gutman, "The Workers' Search for Power," *The Gilded Age*, ed. H. Wayne Morgan (Syracuse, N.Y., 1963), p. 46, 47. (Italics Gutman's.)

26. Chamber of Commerce, *Warren, Pennsylvania: The Gem of the Allegheny* (Warren, Pa., 1913) p. 17. (Italics theirs.)

CHAPTER 6

1. Compiled from: U.S. Bureau of the Census, *Manuscript Schedule, Ninth Census of the United States: 1870, Warren, Pennsylvania*; U.S. Bureau of the Census, *Thirteenth Census of the United States: 1910. Population* (Washington, D. C., 1913), 1, p. 1364.

2. Tax Assessor's Books, Warren Borough, 1870, 1910. (Books 1870-1900 located in the attic of the Warren County Court House; 1910 books located in the Warren County Tax Office, Warren County Court House.)

3. Compiled from: Census Bureau, *Manuscript Schedule: 1870, Warren, Pennsylvania; Manuscript Schedule, Tenth Census of the United States: 1880, Warren, Pennsylvania;* 1890, 1900 City Directories, Warren, Pennsylvania; Tax Assessor's Books, Warren, Pennsylvania, 1870, 1880, 1890, 1900.

4. Ibid.

5. Ibid.

6. *Warren Ledger,* 21 November 1884, p. 3.

7. Compiled from: Census Bureau, *Manuscript Schedule: 1870, Warren, Pennsylvania; Manuscript Schedule: 1880, Warren, Pennsylvania;* 1890, 1900 City Directories, Warren, Pennsylvania; Tax Assessor's Books, Warren, Pennsylvania, 1870, 1880, 1890, 1900.

8. *Warren Ledger,* 2 June 1890, p. 3.

9. Compiled from: U.S. Bureau of the Census, *Eleventh Census of the United States: 1890. Compendium* (Washington, D. C., 1892), 1, p. 894; U.S. Bureau of the Census, *Twelfth Census of the United States: 1900. Population* (Washington, D. C., 1902), 2, p. 656.

10. The decrease in property holding among Warren's Danish-born probably lies in the increase in Danish population in the community—the Danish population doubled during the 1890-1900 decade—rather than an actual decline in the number of homes owned by Danes in 1900.

11. A more accurate pattern of property ownership, particularly among the native-born, could be attained by grouping residents according to households, thus allowing for the young adult male worker living with his parents. Regrettably, the city directories failed to list offspring. Thus a young adult worker appears as the head of his own family. However, a number of workers listed in the Warren city directories possess the same surnames and addresses as other workers. Hence one may assume that many of these were working sons living with their parents.

12. Census Bureau, *Thirteenth Census: 1910. Population,* p. 1364.

13. Clyde Griffen, "Workers Divided: The Effect of Craft and Ethnic Differences in Poughkeepsie, New York, 1850-1880," *Nineteenth Century Cities: Essays in the New Urban History,* eds. Stephan Thernstrom and Richard Sennett (New Haven, Conn., 1969), p. 59.

14. Stephan Thernstrom, *Poverty and Progress: Social Mobility in a Nineteenth Century City* (Cambridge, Mass., 1964), p. 117.

15. *Warren Evening Times,* Supplement, October 1906, p. 29.

CHAPTER 7

1. Minutes of the Regular Meeting, 26 June 1896, Warren School Board of Directors, Book E, p. 90. (Located in the office of the County Superintendent of Schools.)

2. For a further analysis of the concept of "capitalist status" for workmen possessing savings accounts, see Stephan Thernstrom, *Poverty and Progress: Social Mobility in a Nineteenth Century City* (Cambridge, Mass., 1964), pp. 126-30. Thernstrom examines the contention of the Massachusetts savings institutions that "The instant a workman set aside a few dollars in a bank he qualified for membership in the capitalist class." He concludes: "The typical laborer who settled in Newburyport during this period did indeed patronize the savings banks. Manual workers did sometimes accumulate savings of a thousand dollars or more. If the Newburyport case is at all representative . . . the critics of the Massachusetts savings institutions were mistaken in their skepticism about the extent of working class saving."

3. As a part of the 1870 census, every person was asked to estimate how much real and personal property he owned. The question was dropped from the 1880 schedules; therefore, reliance was placed upon the tax assessor's valuation lists for each succeeding decade. Fortunately, the Warren assessor's valuation lists included both real and personal property and a most valuable item, "Money held at interest." The assessor's figures are probably biased somewhat downward since individuals paid taxes on their reported real and personal property. However, since most property reported by manual laborers was in real estate, the estate figures provide a reasonably accurate index of the economic status of workers in nineteenth-century Warren.

4. Stephan Thernstrom, *Poverty and Progress*, p. 136.

5. The tax assessor's valuation lists probably underestimate the value of estates, particularly of the very wealthy. Fortunately, this does not pose a serious problem in Warren, for very few men possessed great wealth. Assessments, however, do reveal at least the minimum taxable wealth possessed by all adult males in the city.

6. The reader is reminded that the analysis of the distribution of wealth includes all adult males residing in the community during any given census year. Were we to consider only long-term residents of the community, the distribution would no doubt change somewhat. The data on all adult males, however, provide a reasonable estimate of the concentration of wealth.

7. Edward Pessan, "The Egalitarian Myth and the American Society Reality: Wealth, Mobility, and Equality in the 'Era of the Common Man,' " *The American Historical Review*, 77, No. 4 (October 1971), pp. 1021, 1025. Pessan reveals similar inequities in the distribution of wealth in several other American cities, both large and small. In Boston, 1848, 81 percent of the population resided in the lowest—under $4,000—economic group. In Brooklyn, 1841, nearly two-thirds of the population held less than $100 worth of noncorporate property per family. Cf. Stuart Blumin, "Mobility and Change in Ante-Bellum Philadelphia," *Nineteenth Century Cities: Essays in the New Urban History*, eds. Stephan Thernstrom and Richard Sennett (New Haven, Conn., 1969), pp. 204-5. Blumin notes even more spectacular inequities in Philadelphia in 1860: "The wealthiest 10 per cent [in Philadelphia] owned 89 percent of the sample's wealth. The wealthiest one per cent owned one-half!" Cf. Michael

Katz, "Social Structure in Hamilton, Ontario," *Nineteenth Century Cities*, for a discussion of unequal wealth distribution in that small Canadian town.

8.   Tax Assessor's Valuation Lists, Warren Borough, 1870, 1880, 1890, 1900, 1910. (Books 1870-1900 located in the attic of the Warren County Court House; 1910 books located in the Warren County Tax Office, Warren County Court House.)

9.   Ibid.

CHAPTER 8

1.   Data on the yearly in- and out-migration of residents were not available. The work of Peter Knights and Stephan Thernstrom, "Men in Motion," *Journal of Interdisciplinary History* (Autumn 1970), however, reinforces the speculation that the in-migration was much greater than the sum of the out-migrants plus the in-migration, adjusted for births and deaths, for each decade. In Boston, for example, between 1880 and 1890, Thernstrom and Knights found that nearly 800,000 in-migrants produced a net population increase of only 65,179. It is also likely that the in-migration in Warren was several times that suggested by the available data.

2.   During this same period of time, the native-born proportion of the total population remained even more stable ranging from a low of 77 percent in 1880 to 81 percent in both 1900 and 1910. The difference in the percent of native-born adult males and the percent of all native-born residents resulted from the large number of single immigrant men who lived in Warren for brief periods of time. These industrial transients constituted a significant portion of the immigrant population throughout the era of industrialization.

3.   U.S. Bureau of Census, *Thirteenth Census of the United States: 1910. Population* (Washington, D.C., 1913), 3, p. 593.

4.   U.S. Bureau of the Census, *Manuscript Schedule, Ninth Census of the United States: 1870, Warren, Pennsylvania.*

5.   Compiled from: Census Bureau, *Manuscript Schedule: 1870, Warren, Pennsylvania; Manuscript Schedule, Tenth Census of the United States: 1880, Warren, Pennsylvania;* 1890, 1900, 1910 City Directories, Warren, Pennsylvania.

6.   Chamber of Commerce, Warren, Pennsylvania: *The Gem of the Allegheny* (Warren, Pa., 1913).

7.   Sam Bass Warner, Jr., *The Private City: Philadelphia in Three Periods of Its Growth* (Philadelphia, 1968), p. 65.

8.   Clyde Griffen, "Workers Divided: The Effect of Craft and Ethnic Differences in Poughkeepsie, New York, 1850-1880," *Nineteenth Century Cities: Essays in the New Urban History*, eds. Stephan Thernstrom and Richard Sennett (New Haven, 1969), p. 73. Griffen notes a similar increase in persistence among coopers in Poughkeepsie in the face of declining opportunities.

In that city, "the rate of persistence among coopers without property rose from 37 per cent between 1860 and 1870 to 44 per cent between 1870 and 1880, the first decade in which the trade showed a decline in total number of workers."

9.   Herbert G. Gutman, "Work, Culture and Society in Industrializing America, 1815-1919," *The American Historical Review*, June 1973, p. 541. Gutman quotes E. P. Thompson in this paragraph.

10.   Minutes of the Regular Meeting, 7 October 1895, Warren Borough Council, Book 5, p. 169. (Located in the Warren Borough Municipal Office.) It is a simple matter to project the political ward boundaries backward to establish 1890 wards, since city directories provided addresses for all 1890 workers. The 1870 and 1880 manuscript schedules of the U. S. Census did not include addresses; therefore, specific residences prior to 1890 could not be determined.

11.   D. F. A. Wheelock, "Official Map of Warren, Pennsylvania," 1 January 1912.

12.   Tax Assessor's Books, Warren Borough, 1890, 1900, 1910. Property assessments in the third ward remained higher than in each of the other wards in 1890, 1900, and 1910. Assessments for the other five wards followed a distinct pattern for each of the three above census years. In descending order of value, the tax assessments for each ward were: third ward, first, second, fifth, fourth, and sixth.

13.   *Warren Mail*, 27 April 1890, p. 3.

14.   Stuart Blumin, "Mobility and Change in Ante-Bellum Philadelphia," *Nineteenth Century Cities*, p. 186. Blumin notes a similar relationship between the central city and the concentration of wealth in his study of ante-bellum Philadelphia: "Specifically, there is a direct and very pronounced relationship between high average assessment and centrality. The highest averages are in the heart of the city. . . . Immediately to the west of this square are wards of somewhat lower averages, and immediately north and south of it are wards with averages that are appreciably lower. These averages, in turn, are significantly higher than those on the perimeter of the city."

15.   For comparison of indexes in other cities, see Warner, *The Private City*, pp. 13, 170; Paul B. Worthman, "Working Class Mobility in Birmingham, Alabama, 1880-1914," *Anonymous Americans*, ed. Tamara K. Hareven (Englewood Cliffs, N.J., 1971), p. 201; Leo F. Schnore and Peter Knights, "Residence and Social Structure: Boston in the Ante-Bellum Period," *Nineteenth Century Cities*, p. 253.; Howard P. Chudacoff, "A New Look at Ethnic Neighborhoods," *Journal of American History*, 60 (June 1973), p. 78, and Chudacoff, *Mobile Americans: Residential and Social Mobility in Omaha, 1880-1920* (New York, 1972), pp. 65-67. For a most valuable discussion of the uses of the index, see Karl E. and Alma Taueber, *Negroes in Cities: Residential Segregation and Neighborhood Change* (Chicago, 1965), pp. 195-245.

16.   *The Evening News*, 18 April 1895, p. 6.

17. Compiled from 1890, 1900, 1910 Warren city directories; Record of Births, Book 1, 1893-1901, Book 2, 1901-1905 (located in the Office of the Registrar and Recorder, Warren County Court House); Naturalization Card Index, 1830-1906, Naturalization Petition and Record, 1906-1911; Immigrant Alien Docket, Volumes 3-5 (all located in the Office of the Prothonotary of the Court of Common Pleas, Warren County Court House).

18. Ibid.

19. Ibid.

20. The index values discussed on these pages illustrate the degree of clustering by various ethnic groups in the community. However, they do not imply the creation of ethnic ghettos. Workers of all nationalities moved in and out of Warren with great frequency and were not in any sense "locked in." Moreover, workers clustering in particular wards lived among men of other ethnic backgrounds and were not isolated as implied by the modern usage of the term ghetto.

CHAPTER 9

1. Minutes of the Regular Meetings, 1870-1875, Warren Borough Council, Books 1 and 2. (Located in the Warren Borough Municipal Office.)

2. Minutes of the Regular Meeting, 7 October 1889, Warren Borough Council, Book 4, p. 182.

3. Compiled from an examination of the *Warren Ledger* and *Warren Mail*, 1870-1875. During this period not one local candidate placed an advertisement in either newspaper seeking support. The newspapers usually confined their endorsements to "Vote Straight Republican" or "Vote Straight Democrat."

4. *Warren Mail*, 14 November 1872, p. 3.

5. Some of the Pennsylvania-born borough council officers may have been born in other locations throughout the state. The manuscript census lists only the state as the place of birth.

6. Robert A. Dahl, *Who Governs? Democracy and Power in an American City* (New Haven, Conn., 1961). See especially the first three chapters. Dahl discusses three major cycles of ruling elite in New Haven—the patricians, the entrepreneurs, and the ex-plebes. Little distinction is noted in Warren between an old ruling aristocracy—the patricians—and the new businessmen. Moreover, the rise to power of the ex-plebes fails to occur in Warren prior to World War I.

7. Michael H. Frisch, "The Community Elite and the Emergence of Urban Politics: Springfield, Massachusetts, 1840-1880," *Nineteenth Century Cities: Essays in the New Urban History*, eds. Stephan Thernstrom and Richard Sennett (New Haven, Conn., 1964), p. 284. Frisch reveals a similar rise in the political power of businessmen, merchants, and manufacturers in

Springfield. By 1870 these groups accounted for three-fourths of the seats on that city's Board of Aldermen, an increase of 27 percent.

8.   U.S. Bureau of the Census, *Manuscript Schedule, Ninth Census of the United States: 1870, Warren, Pennsylvania*; 1910 Warren City Directory. In absolute terms, attorneys and bankers declined more severely in influence on the Warren Borough Council than the manual laborer group. However, in proportional representation manual workers suffered greater losses. Between 1870 and 1910 the number of attorneys and bankers living in Warren increased by less than 75 percent while the total number of laborers rose by nearly sixfold.

9.   Compiled from: Census Bureau, *Manuscript Schedule: 1870, Warren, Pennsylvania.; Manuscript Schedule, Tenth Census of the United States: 1880, Warren, Pennsylvania*; 1890, 1900, 1910 City Directories, Warren, Pennsylvania; Assessor's Valuation Lists, 1870-1910, Warren, Pennsylvania; Borough Council Minutes, 1870-1910, Warren, Pennsylvania.

10.   Minutes of the Regular Meeting, 7 March 1881, Warren Borough Council, Book 3.

11.   Ibid., 7 April 1884.

12.   Compiled from: Borough Council Minutes, Book 4, 4 April 1889, p. 139: 17 April 1889, p. 143.; 14 October 1889, p. 185.

13.   Frisch, "The Community Elite," pp. 285-86. Frisch reports that similar self-interests motivated the business elite in Springfield but also notes a concern for the public welfare "To picture the elite as suddenly acting out of purely particularistic motives would be to forget their earlier combination of public and private roles, and the sense of leadership that was so important to them. As the city grew, the public meaning of government increased just as significantly as did the implications of its action for private property."

14.   Borough Council Minutes, Book 3-A, 20 April 1885, p. 12.; Book 4, 4 February 1888, p. 3.; 7 October 1889, p. 182.

15.   Compiled from Borough Council Minutes, Books 7, 9, 10, and 11, 7 May 1900, p. 168.; 17 April 1907, p. 212.; 21 December 1906 through 30 May 1911.

16.   Borough Council Minutes, Book 2, 2 May 1910, p. 17.

17.   Frisch, "The Community Elite," pp. 286-87. In his study of the ruling elite in Springfield, Frisch notes a conscious attempt to articulate the differences between public and private interests. He concludes: "The taking on of each new municipal responsibility . . . involved a conscious rethinking of what public needs were, a redefinition of what the government obligation was and should be, and a reevaluation of how private interests were related to public needs." An examination of both the borough council minutes and the various newspapers reveals no such effort in Warren.

18.   Minutes of the Regular Meeting, 5 February 1900, Warren Borough Council, Book 7, p. 137.

19.   Ibid.

20. Joel A. Tarr, *A Study in Boss Politics: William Lorimer of Chicago* (Urbana, Ill., 1971), p. 29. In his analysis of boss and machine politics in Chicago, Tarr notes that machine politicians in that Midwestern city "viewed government and party as a means to satisfy their own and their constituents' material ends rather than for any abstract governmental purpose or cultural goal." For a similar assessment of big-city machine politics, see Zane L. Miller, *Boss Cox's Cincinnati: Urban Politics in the Progressive Era* (New York, 1968), esp. Chapter 10.

21. Herbert G. Gutman, "The Worker's Search for Power," *The Gilded Age*, ed. H. Wayne Morgan (Syracuse, N.Y., 1970), p. 35.

22. Stephan Thernstrom, *Poverty and Progress: Social Mobility in a Nineteenth Century City* (Cambridge, Mass., 1964), p. 186. In his study of workers in Newburyport, Massachusetts, Thernstrom observes that "so long as the ordinary man had a realistic hope of 'getting property at some time,' he would remain within the orbit of consensus politics." Cf. Frisch, "The Community Elite," p. 287. Frisch reinforces this conclusion, exploring the relationship between economic growth and political conflict. He notes: "As long as growth was steady and shared, the conflict did not manifest itself. Confidence in the city's growth and in the momentum of progress overrode occasional objections that the 'public interest' was merely a convenient mask behind which private power could plunder."

23. Compiled from the *Warren Mail*, 1870-1910 and the *Warren Ledger*, 1870-1910.

24. Ibid.

25. Paul J. Kleppner, *The Cross of Culture: A Social Analysis of Midwestern Politics, 1850-1900* (New York, 1970), pp. 28, 33, 34. Kleppner, in his intensive study of voting patterns in three Midwestern states, reinforces the conclusion that little relationship exists between class and political partisanship. Kleppner concludes, "When the relevant data are ordered and systematically examined, it is apparent that no *factual* basis exists for any claim that there was a casual relationship between class and party among rural voters." (Italics his.) Furthermore, Kleppner says, "Neither . . . was there a common voting pattern that could be attributed to shared occupational group values. . . . Whether in urban areas, among rural voters, or by occupational groups, class factors do not help materially to explain the configuration of the midwestern vote."

26. Ibid., p. 71. For a valuable estimate of party strength organized by ethnocultural groups in three Midwestern states, 1850-1900, see p. 70.

27. For further discussion of the image projected by the Democrat and Republican parties see: Kleppner, *The Cross of Culture*, esp. Chapters 2 and 3; Robert D. Marcus, *Grand Old Party: Political Structure in the Gilded Age, 1880-1896* (New York, 1971), p. 9.; Thernstrom, *Poverty and Progress*, p. 182.; and Tarr, *Boss Politics*, p. 21.

28. Compiled from: First Presbyterian Church, Warren, Pennsylvania,

Membership Rolls, 1870-1897, Directory of Members, 1898, 1907; Saint Joseph's Catholic Church, Warren, Pennsylvania, Baptismal Records, 1864-1885, 1885-1912; Methodist Church, Warren, Pennsylvania, Membership Lists, 1866-1880, 1880-1891, 1891-1910; Episcopal Church, Warren, Pennsylvania, Record of Communicants of the Episcopal Church, 1864-1880, 1881-1900, 1900-1910; First Evangelical Lutheran Church, Warren, Pennsylvania, Book C, 1868-1881, Book D, 1882-1890, Book E, 1891-1901, Book F, 1901-1912; Swedish Baptist Church, Warren, Pennsylvania, Universal Church Record, Book 1, 1891-1900, Book 2, 1901-1911. (All records located in the offices of the respective churches.)

29. Compiled from: Church Records; 1900 and 1910 City Directories; Record of Births, Book 1, 1893-1901, Book 2, 1901-1905 (located in the Office of the Registrar and Recorder, Warren County Court House); Naturalization Card Index, 1830-1906; Naturalization Petition and Record, 1906-1911; Immigrant Alien Docket, Vols. 3-5. (All located in the Office of the Prothonotary of the Court of Common Pleas, Warren County Court House.)

30. Ibid.

31. *Warren Mail*, 13 November 1897, p. 3.

32. Kleppner, *The Cross of Culture*, p. 76. Kleppner observes similar loyalty to the Democratic Party on the part of all Midwestern Catholics. He concludes: "Regardless of ethnic background, midwestern Catholic voters were very strong Democrats. This voting pattern was neither accidental nor due to priestly dictation. It was deeply imbedded in the desire of Catholics to preserve their value system and the social norms these values prescribed."

33. Thernstrom, *Poverty and Progress*, p. 184. The Irish in Newburyport, for example, achieved much greater success in gaining political control. Thernstrom notes: "By the turn of the century the descendents of Newburyport's laborers had captured the local Democratic organization." The Irish in Newburyport, however, constituted a larger percentage of the population than in Warren. For a community with an even larger percentage of Irish-born residents, see Dahl, *Who Governs*, Chapter 4, esp. pp. 36-44.

34. Minutes of the Regular Meetings, 1872-1875, Warren School Board of Directors, Book C, pp. 128, 146, 174, 204 (located in the Office of the Warren County Superintendent of Schools); *Warren Ledger*, 1874 School Report, 10 December 1874.

35. Minutes of the Regular Meetings, 4 November 1873, Warren School Board of Directors, Book C, p. 157, 1 June 1876, p. 217. In 1873 one teacher requesting an increase in her $40.00 monthly salary was dismissed. Three years later six of the eight teachers employed by the board made a similar request. All were dismissed.

36. *Warren Ledger*, 20 February 1880.

37. Minutes of the Regular Meeting, 30 December 1878, Warren School Board of Directors, Book C, p. 270.

38.   Minutes of the Regular Meetings, 1870-1910, Warren School Board of Directors.

39.   *Warren Ledger*, 5 March 1880, p. 3. The rhetoric of this editorial was, of course, not unique to Warren. Michael Katz, *Class, Bureaucracy and Schools* (New York, 1971), p. 42, asserts that nineteenth-century urban educational promoters frequently argued that "the public schools would foster the economic prosperity of the community by attracting settlers, increasing land values, and providing properly trained recruits for higher branches of industrial and commercial employment. At the same time, the influence of the high school would radiate to the community as a whole, diffusing culture among the people. . . . Moreover, high schools were expected by their advocates to gather children of all social classes and thereby promote social harmony and justice. . . . It [the high school] provided an education that would foster social mobility and insure individual prosperity in a time of bewildering economic flux."

40.   Annual Report of the Superintendent, 1874-1910 (included in the Warren School Board Minutes), Warren, Pennsylvania.

41.   *Warren News*, 27 March 1896, p. 2.

42.   *Warren Democrat*, 27 March 1896, p. 3.

43.   *Warren Mail*, 26 March 1896, p. 3.

44.   Minutes of the Regular Meeting, 4 February 1901, Warren School Board of Directors, Book F, p. 238.

45.   Robert H. Wiebe, *The Search for Order: 1877-1920* (New York, 1967), p. 119. Wiebe suggests that curriculum reform and the expansion of programs were widespread. Moreover, "Most of the campaigns centered upon the high schools, demanding that they broaden their goals and enlarge their services. With a rush after 1900, that is exactly what they did. Renovating their curriculum to suit a modern industrial society, the high schools acquired a rationale and life of their own in the next twenty years. From 1890 to 1910, both teachers and students increased more than fourfold, then more than doubled again in another decade." Cf. Robert H. Wiebe, "The Social Functions of Public Education," *American Quarterly*, 21 (Summer 1969), pp. 157-58. Wiebe asserts that much of the educational reform after 1900 resulted from the collapse of the self-contained nineteenth-century community. Within this new impersonal society, "the school assumed a radically different role. . . . It became in many instances the only familiar local agency the families in an area could find, the one public institution that might personally connect them with a wider world. . . . Along with interpreter and guide—the most important of the new roles—went additional mediating functions as well. . . . These many activities, by imitating deep local traditions, gave to some rootless folk the comfortable illusion of an operating community, a myth the neighborly, informal rhetoric of school publicity helped to perpetuate."

46.   Compiled from: School Board Minutes, 1895, 1896, 1901, Warren School Board of Directors.

47. Minutes of the Regular Meetings, Warren School Board of Directors, 29 October 1896, Book E, p. 114; 13 September 1902, Book G, p. 183; 6 June 1910, Book I, p. 418.

48. Annual Report of the Superintendent of Schools, 1874-1910, (included in the Warren school board minutes), Warren, Pennsylvania.

49. Letter from the school board clerk to all parents, 1895, (located in the school board minutes, Book E), Warren, Pennsylvania.

50. Slightly lower rates of persistence for blue-collar workers suggest a closer ratio of long-term manual and nonmanual residents.

51. Many of the changes in school board policies and operation of the school may be viewed in the light of the expanding bureaucracy of urban schools discussed by Katz in *Class, Bureaucracy and Schools*, particularly pp. 56-73. This study is not the proper forum for an intensive examination of school bureaucracy, but many of the forms noted by Katz—centralization of control and supervision, differentiation of function, qualification for office, and uniformity—became increasingly prominent in the Warren school system.

CHAPTER 10

1. U.S. Bureau of the Census, *Historical Statistics of the United States: Colonial Times to 1957* (Washington, D. C., 1960), p. 14.

2. Although this chapter attempts to illustrate ways in which mobility patterns in Warren reflected social patterns in other American cities, its primary justification does not lie in its representativeness. Joan W. Scott, "The Glassworkers of Carmaux, 1850-1900," *Nineteenth Century Cities: Essays in the New Urban History*, eds. Stephan Thernstrom and Richard Sennett (New Haven, Conn., 1969), p. 48, illustrates other valuable justifications for such case studies. Scott claims: "I don't think it is necessary to justify a case study by pointing to its representativeness. It seems to me that such studies are valuable for the insights they offer into particular historical processes, for the information they offer indirectly about a society or a period time, and for the questions they raise about similar cases."

3. The data discussed on the following pages were compiled from Theodore Hershberg et al., "Occupation and Ethnicity in Five Nineteenth Century Cities: A Collaborative Inquiry," originally presented at the annual meeting of the Organization of American Historians, Chicago, 1973. Members of the panel were Lawrence Glasco, Michael B. Katz, Stuart Blumin, Theodore Hershberg, and Clyde Griffen. Professor Lawrence Glasco generously supplied copies of the papers. These papers have since been published in *Historical Methods Newsletter* (June 1974).

4. Theodore Hershberg et al., "Occupation and Ethnicity. See p. 1 of Michael Katz's paper, "Similarities."

5. The use of different statistical methods and occupational groupings in the "five cities project" prevents an exact comparison with the Warren data. These differences do not, however, prevent the more general comparisons undertaken here. I have, for example, used the "commerce and professional class" designation of the five cities project as synonymous with white-collar workers.

6. Clyde Griffen, "Workers Divided: The Effect of Craft and Ethnic Differences in Poughkeepsie, New York, 1850-1880," *Nineteenth Century Cities*, pp. 56, 57.

7. Stephan Thernstrom, *Poverty and Progress: Social Mobility in a Nineteenth Century City* (Cambridge, Mass., 1964), p. 96.

8. Ibid., p. 103.; Griffen, "Workers Divided," p. 57.

9. Thernstrom, *Poverty and Progress*, p. 199.

10. Peter R. Knights, *The Plain People of Boston, 1830-1860: A Study in City Growth* (New York, 1971), p. 63.

11. Stephan Thernstrom, *The Other Bostonians: Poverty and Progress in American Metropolis, 1880-1970* (Cambridge, Mass., 1973), p. 222.

12. Howard P. Chudacoff, *Mobile Americans: Residential and Social Mobility in Omaha, 1880-1920* (New York, 1972), p. 41; Howard M. Gitelman, *Workingmen of Waltham: Mobility in American Urban Industrial Development, 1850-1890* (Baltimore, 1974), p. 45.

13. Alwyn Barr, "Occupational and Geographic Mobility in San Antonio, 1870-1900," *Social Science Quarterly*, 51 (1970), pp. 401, 403.

14. Ibid.

15. Paul B. Worthman, "Working Class Mobility in Birmingham, Alabama, 1880-1914," *Anonymous Americans*, ed. Tamara K. Hareven (Englewood Cliffs, N.J., 1971), p. 183.

16. Richard J. Hopkins, "Occupational and Geographical Mobility in Atlanta, 1870-1896," *Journal of Southern History*, 34 (1968), p. 207.

17. Herman R. Lantz and Ernest K. Alix, "Occupational Mobility in a Nineteenth Century Mississippi Valley River Community," *Social Science Quarterly*, 51 (1970), p. 407.

18. Thernstrom, *Poverty and Progress*, p. 118.; Griffen, "Workers Divided," p. 57.; Worthman, "Working Class Mobility in Alabama," p. 186.

19. Chudacoff, *Mobile Americans*, p. 59.

20. Gitelman, *Workingmen of Waltham*, p. 70.

21. Griffen, "Workers Divided," p. 92.

22. Knights, *Plain People of Boston*, pp. 98, 99.

23. Stephan Thernstrom, "Immigrants and WASPs: Ethnic Differences in Occupational Mobility in Boston, 1890-1940," *Nineteenth Century Cities*, p. 129.

24. Sidney Goldstein, *Patterns of Mobility, 1910-1950: The Norristown*

Study (Philadelphia, 1958), pp. 169, 175. Skilled workers in Norristown recorded less occupational mobility than their counterparts in Warren. However, on the whole, skilled workers in both communities recorded greater stability than any other group of manual workers. This suggests that the jump from manual worker to white-collar worker was quite difficult in both communities.

25. Worthman, "Working Class Mobility in Alabama," p. 193.

26. Hopkins, "Occupational and Geographic Mobility in Atlanta," p. 205. In both Atlanta and Birmingham the presence of large black populations—who experienced almost no occupational mobility in Atlanta and limited mobility in Birmingham—provided a pool of unskilled labor which likely enabled the white population to rise more easily.

27. Chudacoff, *Mobile Americans*, p. 101.

28. Barr, "Occupational and Geographic Mobility in San Antonio," p. 399.

29. Herbert G. Gutman, "The Reality of the Rags-to-Riches 'Myth': The Case of the Paterson, New Jersey, Locomotive, Iron, and Machinery Manufacturers, 1830-1860," *Nineteenth Century Cities*, p. 113.

30. None of the other studies cited in earlier parts of this chapter compared the occupational mobility of immigrants and American-born workers in their respective studies.

31. Thernstrom, *Poverty and Progress*, pp. 99, 101.

32. Thernstrom, "Immigrants and WASPs," p. 141. The rate of downward mobility for immigrants in Warren was significantly less than that recorded in Boston, 1890-1940.

33. Chudacoff, *Mobile Americans*, p. 103.

34. Hopkins, "Occupational and Geographic Mobility in Atlanta," p. 205; Barr, "Occupational and Geographic Mobility in San Antonio," p. 399; Worthman, "Working Class Mobility in Alabama." Worthman did not supply mobility data for immigrants in Birmingham; however, one suspects that they are comparable to those of Atlanta and San Antonio.

35. Thernstrom, *Poverty and Progress*, p. 119. See Table 7. Manual laborers in Newburyport recorded significantly higher rates of property ownership than their counterparts in Warren. This is largely because Thernstrom reported property ownership among laboring families while the Warren study includes all manual laborers. Some of the latter, no doubt, were sons of laborers living with their parents. Thus the rate of property ownership in Warren appears somewhat smaller.

36. Ibid., pp. 202, 205. For a comparison of occupational mobility in Newburyport and Norristown, Pennsylvania, and six major twentieth-century industrial cities, see Thernstrom, *Poverty and Progress*, p. 202, Table 15. Thernstrom suggests that property mobility in large cities did not differ radically from that recorded in Warren and Newburyport. He notes: "In the big city slums . . . it is quite possible that a somewhat smaller proportion of laboring families became savings bank depositors and home owners. Nevertheless, it is doubtful that the difference was as dramatic as might be thought. The workmen of large cities too climbed the occupational ladder in time, and left the slums for better nieghborhoods; an exhaustive analysis of building permits issued in three of Boston's 'streetcar suburbs' in the last quarter of the nineteenth century supplies some valuable hints on the gradual operation oi this process in one major city. Nineteenth century Boston indeed had its proletariat, but on the whole the composition of this group was constantly changing."

37. U.S. Bureau of the Census, *Thirteenth Census of the United States: 1910. Population* (Washington, D.C., 1913), 1, pp. 1313, 1314.

38. Herbert G. Gutman, "The Workers' Search for Power," *The Gilded Age*, ed. H. Wayne Morgan (Syracuse, N.Y., 1970), pp. 34, 38. (Italics Gutman's.)

39. Minutes of the Regular Meeting, 20 April 1903, Warren Borough Council Book 8, p. 203. (Located in the Warren Borough Municipal Office.) Prostitution first came to the attention of the borough council for official action in 1903 but evidently had been a problem for some time. The president of the borough council noted, "Houses of ill-fame existing in the Borough . . . are becoming quite notorious and numerous complaints are being made. . . . The police should suppress the houses which are now run openly in the Borough." *Warren Mail*, 7 July 1887, p. 3.; *Warren Ledger*, 13 April 1888, p. 3; June 20, 1890, p. 3. The problem of prohibition had been temporarily resolved between 1887 and 1890 when the judge of Warren County refused to grant liquor licenses during this period of time. In 1891 the court-imposed prohibition was rescinded mainly on economic grounds. The editor of the *Warren Ledger* claimed, "Prohibition has driven thousands of dollars away from here. But we live and flourish because we must. This is a central point of a large oil field and large amounts of money come from the earth. . . . There is a large amount of it going to other places. We could be much better off with a proper amount of legitimate drinking places."

40. Robert H. Wiebe, *The Search for Order, 1877-1920* (New York, 1967), p. 45.

41. Ibid. See Chapter 5, passim, especially p. 129.

42. Parkey and Shawkey, *A Complete Directory of Warren Borough, 1899-1900* (Olean, N.Y.: *Olean Evening Herald*, 1900); William H. Kirwin, *Kirwin's Warren Borough and Warren County Directory, 1910* (Warren, Pa.: William H. Kirwin Directory Co., 1910).

43. *Warren Mail*, 13 April 1903, p. 3.

APPENDIX

1. For a number of conceptual approaches to the study of urban history, see Eric E. Lampard, "American Historians and the Study of Urbanization,"

American Historical Review, 67 (1961), pp. 49-61.; Eric E. Lampard, "The Dimensions of Urban History," *Pacific Historical Review*, 39 (August 1970), pp. 261-78.; Roy Lubove, "The Urbanization Process," *American Institute of Planners Journal*, 33 (January 1967), pp. 33-39.; Robert K. Dykstra, *The Cattle Towns* (New York, 1970), pp. 379-81. Lampard has persuasively argued for an ecological approach encompassing four major concepts: population, environment, technology, and social organization. Roy Lubove suggests an emphasis on the process of city building, focusing upon the city as an artifact, to analyze social and technological change over time. Robert Dykstra argues that, particularly in the context of local history, one should treat "the 'social process'—defined as the interaction of impersonal factors and human factors—as a commanding theme." In this sense, Dykstra emphasizes decision-making, leadership, and politics as major concepts one must analyze to understand changing social organization in America.

2. The reverse of this position is, I believe, also true. Community studies which deal with urban growth without delving into questions of mobility present an incomplete picture of the urbanization process. We need to know how this transformation affected individuals as well as its effects upon formal institutions and organizations.

3. For a most valuable discussion of the reliability of city directories as a data source, see Peter R. Knights, "City Directories as Aids to Ante-Bellum Urban Studies: A Research Note," *Historical Methods Newsletter*, September 1969.

4. Sam Bass Warner, Jr., *The Private City: Philadelphia in Three Periods of Its Growth* (Philadelphia, 1968), pp. 227-28. Warner compares samples from the 1860 manuscript census and the 1860 Philadelphia city directory. He states that the "Principal differences from the Directory Sample lies in its [the censuses] inclusion of many more female occupations, domestics, housekeepers, seamstresses, tailoresses, and the male and female factory operatives."

5. Warren Borough Council Minutes.

6. Property and wealth information were not included in the 1880 federal manuscript census.

7. Ages of individuals reported on both the 1870 and 1880 census frequently disagree. Some of the disagreement may have been due to the particular date which the census taker recorded this information, just before or after a respondent's birthday. In addition, reported ages frequently ended in zero or five—"age heaping." For an interesting discussion of the problems of age accuracy in the manuscript census, see: Peter R. Knights, "Accuracy of Age Reporting in the Federal Manuscript Census of 1850 and 1860," *Historical Methods Newsletter* (June 1971.)

8. For a more detailed description of a record-linkage system, see: Michael Katz and John Tiller, "Record-Linkage for Everyman: A Semi-Automated Process," *Historical Methods Newsletter* (September 1972). A similar linkage system was employed to link data from different sources.

INDEX